Religion without Violence

"No one should be surprised that Peter Ochs cares about helping us live at peace with one another, but it is an added benefit that in this book Peter helps us see how the practice of Scriptural Reasoning enacts that commitment. As always there is more to what Peter has to say than is immediately obvious, but then one of the abiding characteristics of Peter's work is to help us see how attention to 'thirds' makes possible an understanding of one another otherwise impossible. Peace, it turns out, begins with reading together."

—STANLEY HAUERWAS
Duke Divinity School

"Scriptural Reasoning is now a major practice in interfaith engagement around the world and in many spheres of modern life, and Peter Ochs, its co-founder and leading practitioner and thinker, here gives the most comprehensive and authoritative account of it so far. It is a remarkable achievement by Ochs, showing not only how the practice deals with key issues between religions, but also how it connects with peacebuilding, university disciplines, and some core problems faced by our civilization. This book will speak to diverse readers, whether they are unfamiliar with Scriptural Reasoning, beginning to practice it, or experienced in it."

—DAVID F. FORD
University of Cambridge

"This is the first systematic introduction to the practice and theory of Scriptural Reasoning. Peter Ochs is the person whose energy and vision started Scriptural Reasoning and gave it its theoretical basis as a new form of interreligious dialogue based on group readings of Scripture as opposed to theological discussions of religious doctrines. . . . This is an extremely important and timely book."

—STEVEN KEPNES
Colgate University

"Peter Ochs presents us with the fruits generated by over twenty-five years of active engagement with Scriptural Reasoning. Through a wide range of concrete examples of how this practice works 'on the ground', alongside philosophical and hermeneutical reflection, he provides readers with a deep reservoir of resources for building upon his insights and extending them in new future directions. Ochs puts forth a powerful vision of how scriptural engagement across traditions can contribute to repair in today's world."

—DANIEL H. WEISS
University of Cambridge

Religion without Violence

The Practice and Philosophy of Scriptural Reasoning

PETER OCHS

Foreword by David F. Ford

CASCADE Books • Eugene, Oregon

RELIGION WITHOUT VIOLENCE
The Practice and Philosophy of Scriptural Reasoning

Copyright © 2019 Peter Ochs. All rights reserved. Except for brief quotations in critical publications or reviews, no part of this book may be reproduced in any manner without prior written permission from the publisher. Write: Permissions, Wipf and Stock Publishers, 199 W. 8th Ave., Suite 3, Eugene, OR 97401.

Cascade Books
An Imprint of Wipf and Stock Publishers
199 W. 8th Ave., Suite 3
Eugene, OR 97401

www.wipfandstock.com

PAPERBACK ISBN: 978-1-5326-3893-0
HARDCOVER ISBN: 978-1-5326-3894-7
EBOOK ISBN: 978-1-5326-3895-4

Cataloguing-in-Publication data:

Names: Ochs, Peter, author.

Title: Religion without violence : the practice and philosophy of scriptural reasoning / Peter Ochs.

Description: Eugene, OR: Cascade Books, 2019 | Includes bibliographical references and index.

Identifiers: ISBN 978-1-5326-3893-0 (paperback) | ISBN 978-1-5326-3894-7 (hardcover) | ISBN 978-1-5326-3895-4 (ebook)

Subjects: LCSH: Bible—Criticism, interpretation, etc., Jewish, Christian, and Islamic. | Bible—Theology. | Judaism—Relations—Christianity and Islam.

Classification: BS1186 .O45 2019 (paperback) | CALL NUMBER (ebook)

Manufactured in the U.S.A.   11/14/19

For Juliana and Elizabeth

Contents

Foreword by David F. Ford | ix
Acknowledgements | xv

CHAPTER 1
Introduction | 1

CHAPTER 2
How SR Reads and Interprets Scripture: A Scriptural Pragmatism | 24

CHAPTER 3
Pragmatic Reasoning in SR: A Technical Chapter
on SR's Semiotic Roots and Hermeneutic Consequences | 53

CHAPTER 4
Teaching SR: Classroom Narratives | 84

CHAPTER 5
What Is (Really) Going on in the SR Classroom?
SR as Training in "Knowing Enough" | 112

CHAPTER 6
Hearth-To-Hearth Interreligious Peace Building | 150

Bibliography | 205
Index of Ancient Documents | 213
Index of Subjects | 215
Index of Authors | 223

Foreword
by David F. Ford

SCRIPTURAL REASONING IS AN extraordinarily important practice. It has far-reaching implications, not only for each of the religious traditions that takes part in it, and for their engagements with each other, but also for the educational and academic study of religions, for peacebuilding in religion-related divisions and conflicts, and for how the multi-religious and multi-secular modern world can understand itself and address some of its most profound problems. Peter Ochs is co-founder of Scriptural Reasoning, and its leading practitioner and thinker, and this is his major book on the subject. The book distills what he has learned through over twenty-five years of doing and teaching Scriptural Reasoning, as it has spread around the world and into many spheres of life. But, beyond that, Ochs now takes his thinking further, and also challenges readers to read, think, relate, and act in new ways. I have been longing for many years to see this book appear, and it has been worth the wait.

Why is Scriptural Reasoning so significant? As I reflect on this book, and also on my own involvement with Ochs in Scriptural Reasoning since it began, what strikes me most is the way it has combined various dimensions of meaning and practice.

Scriptural Reasoning has enabled the exploration of multiple depths.

There are the depths of my own Christian Scriptures that have opened up as I have engaged in intensive study and conversation with Jews, Muslims, and scholars who may not identify with any tradition—and, later, also with Buddhists, Confucians, Daoists and Hindus, as I have travelled to China and India and taken part in developments of Scriptural Reasoning there.

At the same time, the depths of the Scriptures of those other traditions have opened up in joint reading—and in ways that, in my experience, have not happened through individual study.

There has also been a depth of understanding and engagement with our shared world and with the problems and challenges that we face. Many of these issues cannot be satisfactorily addressed by one religion alone, and some appreciation of the deep meaning that others draw upon is vital to worthwhile conversation and collaboration.

There is also depth of disagreement. As Ochs makes clear, Scriptural Reasoning is not about arriving at consensus (though that may happen on some issues); rather it can do something essential to a pluralist world, which is to improve the quality of our disagreements.

Then there is the depth of relationship that Scriptural Reasoning can enable, and the warmth that can come from what Ochs imaginatively describes as "hearth to hearth" engagement. Some of my closest friendships, within and beyond my own tradition, have been formed through year after year of Scriptural Reasoning. I often think that, if we are to have a healthily plural world, it needs to have such a pluralism of multiple depths that are in conversation with each other and, if possible, also in collaboration.

The ever-widening breadth of Scriptural Reasoning has also been striking. Three obvious aspects of this have been its extension beyond the Abrahamic faiths, especially in China and India; its spread beyond academic and educational contexts into local congregations of various religions, and into hospitals, prisons, business settings, leadership programs, civil society engagements, and a number of situations of division and conflict; and its simultaneous geographical spread, not only in China and India but also notably in North America, the United Kingdom, continental Europe, Egypt, Pakistan, Oman, Israel, South Africa, Australia, Nigeria, and Kenya. Through my involvement with the Rose Castle Foundation, which is based in the UK, hosts the www.scripturalreasoning.org website, and acts as a hub for Scriptural Reasoning, I see something of the growing international interest in the practice, and colleagues in other countries report similar interest.

There is also the long-term character of Scriptural Reasoning. Many interfaith practices and relationships lack staying power. One advantage of gathering around Scriptures is that they are inexhaustibly rich and gripping, and can sustain year after year of joint study, just as each has already sustained centuries of study and discussion in its own tradition. Ochs's own long-term involvement is matched by others who began the practice with him, and by many more who have been taking part consistently over the years. The result is an ongoing, expanding community of readers who have the potential of moving beyond what Ochs calls Formational SR into other forms of the practice that he describes, and through these into long-term relationships, "partnerships of difference" (Nicholas Adams), that can develop beyond study and conversation around texts into collaborations, and even into what one might call covenantal commitments.

Besides the depth, breadth, and length, what about the height? By this I mean the relationship to God, or the transcendent, or however a particular faith relates to ultimate reality. My own conviction is that Scriptural Reasoning is at its best when it is done "for God's sake," or whatever the analogy of this might be in nontheistic traditions. I have been repeatedly amazed by the insights into prayer, worship, and the reality of God that have been inspired (sometimes through disagreement) by intensive conversation around texts with those who pray, worship, and identify God or the transcendent differently than myself.

At least two more points need to be made about the significance of Scriptural Reasoning, both of which are evident in what Ochs writes.

The first is its relevance to Western civilization's modes of thinking, especially some of its dominant ways of knowing and reasoning. These are particularly evident in the modern university and its disciplines, but also in international relations, secular attitudes to religion, and a religion's self-understanding today. Ochs has a remarkable range of reference across several disciplines both in the humanities and sciences, showing how Scriptural Reasoning relates to them both positively and critically, and also has some fascinating thoughts on international relations and the ways religion has been understood, internally and externally, in recent centuries.

The second is the capacity of Scriptural Reasoning to spring surprises. The practice itself is surprising in the people, texts, and contexts it brings together. I have often thought during a session that perhaps never before in history have these particular passages been discussed together by members of the traditions whose Scriptures are being studied. Laughter is often one result of juxtaposing texts, topics, languages, and people, leading to all sorts of humorous misunderstandings or mistranslations, unusual angles, and acknowledgments of sheer oddness or mismatch. Ochs also shows how fruitful novelty can be generated in understanding, imagination, and practice, with far-reaching implications not only for interfaith engagement but also for other spheres, ranging from how academic disciplines relate to each other and the wider society, to the ways conflicts of many sorts can be analyzed, diagnosed, and healed.

This is the first book to combine engagement with all those features of Scriptural Reasoning, and it also adds yet another element, the relationship with Textual Reasoning. Ochs was one of the co-founders of Textual Reasoning too, and it was by sitting in on the extraordinarily lively, learned, and argumentative meetings of that group in the early 1990s that I and others were attracted into co-founding Scriptural Reasoning. Ochs in this book gives the first account of how to integrate, in educational and other contexts, what has been learned from both practices, one focused mainly on how a Scripture is read within its own tradition, the other on reading Scriptures of more than one religion side by side with members of those traditions.

From within Christianity, I have found that one of the most helpful ways of understanding both Textual Reasoning and Scriptural Reasoning is by analogy with the Second Vatican Council of the Roman Catholic Church (Vatican II, 1962–65), which was one of the most important religious events of the twentieth century. The parallel was originally suggested by George Lindbeck, who was a Lutheran observer at Vatican II. He identified a threefold dynamic of *ressourcement, aggiornamento,* and *conversazione. Ressourcement* is the return to sources, centered on rereading classic texts in relation to the present. *Aggiornamento* is engaging with modernity, and discerning, critically and constructively, how to respond to its challenges. *Conversazione* is the practice of conversation across differences, both internal to one's own community and across those with other communities. The wisdom of these three dynamics, and their analogous relevance to any religious or other community that is rooted in the past and wants a healthy future, has in my experience been generally acknowledged among Scriptural Reasoners, and Scriptural Reasoning has been found to be a fruitful way of bringing the three together.

I conclude with some words for readers of this book. It is a book in which, as the saying goes, mice can paddle and elephants can swim. No readers need feel it is not for them, but I hope it might be helpful to make some suggestions about how it might be approached by a range of readers.

The most basic thing to grasp is that Scriptural Reasoning is, first and foremost, a practice. As Ochs says, practice has been primary, and the apprenticeship of taking part in it has been the best way to understand it; then has come reflection and theory, which in turn have influenced practice, leading into further reflection, and so on. Even readers who have never practiced Scriptural Reasoning will probably have analogous experience of reading and discussing rich texts with others. This will be sufficient to appreciate a good deal of what Ochs writes and to follow its implications.

Yet it is undoubtedly an advantage to be able to read this book after having practiced Scriptural Reasoning, especially in the apprenticeship that Ochs calls "Formational Scriptural Reasoning."

For practitioners who are new to Scriptural Reasoning, this book can give basic guidelines and concepts, encourage involvement in Formational Scriptural Reasoning, help in avoiding many pitfalls, and open up a horizon of its significance and potential.

For those who are more experienced, Ochs can enrich their reflection, challenge them in relevant—and sometimes very demanding—ways (whether they are ordinary members of religious communities, academics, teachers of Scriptural Reasoning, or peacebuilders), and help them navigate the complexities and depths that open up.

Yet none of the three groups—outsiders to Scriptural Reasoning, beginners, or experienced practitioners—need to feel discouraged if they fail to understand what Ochs sometimes calls the more "technical" elements in this book, such as the theory of pragmatism or the passages expressed in logical symbols. These require quite a rare level of what might be seen as post-doctoral sophistication, and open up exciting pathways for the testing, refinement, extension, and generalizing of Scriptural Reasoning, but they are not essential to the main message of the book for many readers. To put it simply, readers should be willing to skip some difficult sections. But it will always be worthwhile to go back later (even a long time later) to wrestle with them.

Beyond all the above, the main guidance that I would give on how to approach this book is twofold.

First, recognize it as the most important distillation to date of knowledge and wisdom relating to Scriptural Reasoning, how to teach it, and what its implications are for both religion-related conflict and modern Western ways of knowing and reasoning. If you identify with a religious tradition, this book might enable wiser faith and wiser engagement with other faiths and the contemporary world. If you do not identify with a religious tradition, this book can enable wiser understanding of religion and faith, and perhaps also stimulate conversation and collaboration with religious people for the sake of the common good of our world.

Second, treat it a little like the scriptural texts it discusses. That will mean reading it not only individually but also in groups, ideally with Scriptural Reasoners from diverse religious traditions; exploring diverse interpretations for different contexts; helping to create around it a body of commentary that makes connections, both critical and constructive, with other rich texts and discourses; and being open to its passionate summons to wiser practices of reading, discussion, repair, compassion, and peacebuilding.

Acknowledgements

IN SOME WAYS, I have been writing this book since we founded the practice of Scriptural Reasoning in 1992. During these twenty-seven years, dozens of people have contributed to what Scriptural Reasoning is and to how I understand it. I cannot acknowledge all of them here by name, but I hope they appreciate my deep gratitude for their contributions to this unconventional and challenging but deeply hopeful work. I name just a few. David Ford and, of blessed memory, Daniel Hardy first practiced Scriptural Reasoning with me each summer on the shores of a lake in Salisbury, Connecticut. Basit Koshul later joined the founders as we became a Christian-Jewish-Muslim Society for Scriptural Reasoning. A few years before Scriptural Reasoning, a few us founded a related practice of Textual Reasoning, among them Robert Gibbs, Steven Kepnes, and Laurie Zoloth. I am also grateful to Randi Rashkover and a circle of colleagues and students who helped review, critique, and improve the last stages of writing this book.[1]

My gratitude extends to all the students and colleagues who joined the work of Scriptural Reasoning and Textual Reasoning, initially in the UK and USA and, over the years, in many regions of the globe. We share the deepest hope that this work may be a source of peace.

---

1. My deep thanks to Rumee Ahmed, Jacob Goodson, and Mark James, each of whom read through the entire manuscript and offered helpful comment.

CHAPTER 1

Introduction

THIS IS A BOOK about how to teach and learn the practice and theory of Scriptural Reasoning (SR). As we first developed it in 1992, SR names a method for studying Scriptures across the borders of any tradition. Our prototype was a study of Abrahamic Scriptures: the Tanakh, the New Testament, and the Qur'an studied side by side, so that students, adherents, and observers of any one scriptural canon would feel welcomed to read and comment on verses of the other canons as well.[1] One of our goals was to find better methods for teaching religions by way of the study of Scripture and for teaching Scripture in a way that was enriched by both academic and traditional forms of commentary. Another goal was to find methods for peaceful encounter across religious traditions. After about five years of experimentation, we settled on a single method, which we now label "formational SR study." This method is practiced both as an end in itself and as a means of entering into a broader program of interreligious work. We often hear the term "Scriptural Reasoning" applied to this broader program. In this book, I will use the term in both senses. "Formational SR" will refer to the original practice, which remains a prototype and the single most effective exercise for introducing folks to the mind-set presupposed by all the other forms and applications of SR.[2]

Before September 11, 2001 and more dramatically after it, SR practitioners began to receive requests to apply their craft to matters of interreligious cooperation. As a result, many folks now hear of SR only as a peacebuilding practice or as a means of interreligious fellowship; far fewer know that,

1. More recently we extended SR to Asian scriptural traditions as well.

2. My thanks to Paola Pinzon Hernandez for assistance and editorial help on chapters 1 to 6.

from its inception, SR included a more technical practice of academic study and of textual and even logical analysis. The purpose of this chapter is to introduce SR as an effective response to interreligious conflict as well as a practice of study and teaching, both inside and outside the classroom.

SR did not develop top-down from some initial theory to a set of practical applications. It developed bottom-up from practice to theory to practice, through a series of trials and errors, and through the dynamic interrelations among each stage and feature of SR. While introducing the primary stages and features of SR, I hope this chapter also delivers some evidence of the interrelations that animate them.

THE PRACTICE OF SR: PRIMARY FEATURES

In the book of Exodus, when Moses tries to deliver the Ten Commandments for the second time, the Israelites respond with the declaration *naaseh v'nishmah!*[3] Literally, their declaration means "We shall do it and understand it," but, it was more likely an idiomatic expression for "We are on the job!" or "Consider it done!" The later rabbinic sages offered a homiletic rereading: "We shall first act and then understand," on the model of the angels who respond to God's commands by declaring, "We shall act first and seek to comprehend only afterward."[4] The Jewish philosopher Emmanuel Levinas added a more contemporary twist: unlike modern thinkers who seek to comprehend things in the mind first before experiencing them in practice, the Israelites recognized that truly life-sustaining wisdoms must be practiced first before their meanings can be understood.[5] We have nurtured SR in the same fashion, seeking to experiment with many forms of practice before discovering the one that best fits our goals and working over many years to refine it. We proceeded through experimentation first and only later through theoretical reflection. From the start, we guessed that we would light upon an approach that would exceed our understanding at that time: we might have to take some flights of imagination and explore new kinds of practice until we stumbled upon a good one. We would have to be patient, devoting significant time to trial-and-error research and testing until we uncovered a practice that approximated our goals. Even then, each of us anticipated a lifetime of learning when and how to refine the practice or to move on to other practices.

---

3. Exod 24:7.
4. *b. Šabb.* 88a.
5. Levinas, "Temptation."

Formational SR. The elements of our original practice are quite simple.[6] In what follows, I will offer a prototype of the entire practice of what we call "formational SR."[7] There is, prototypically, a table with at least three chairs placed around it. On the table are three small sets of verses, one from each of the three Abrahamic canons of Scripture: the Tanakh (the Hebrew Bible), the New Testament, and the Qur'an. Each of the three chairs is reserved for a student of one of these three traditions, Islamic, Christian, and Jewish. The verses appear in translation so that all the participants can read them. To begin their session of Scriptural Reasoning, the participants may read aloud together a selection from any one of the canons. Then they discuss what each of them takes to be the "plain" or self-evident sense of the words in those verses. Whatever the canon of Scripture, none of the three participants acts as authority. Together they discuss the plain sense of the verses as if they could read each verse with equal facility. Then, they gradually turn to a discussion of what seems most challenging or surprising, perhaps contradictory or even ungrammatical within the verses. The discussion continues, with each individual speaking approximately as much as every other. The discussion may naturally turn to one or two issues raised by any or all of the texts, or one or two lines of questioning. If the discussion seems to go in all directions at once, someone in the group may, appropriately, try to steer it back to only one or two primary directions or issues. A single session of Scriptural Reasoning might stop right there. Afterwards, participants get up for brief break and refreshment. A second session may turn to a second set of verses, which are reviewed in the same manner. After a while, the participants may also begin to offer observations that, in various ways, relate the discussion of this next set of verses back to the discussion of the first set. In a third such session, the third set of verses is brought into play in a comparable manner.

We discovered that formational SR works best if there are only five to nine people around the study table. We also discovered that SR takes time. A single session takes about an hour and half, and new participants are unlikely to report any significant learning until they have experienced at least four sessions. This means that one's study of SR should begin with a day or day and a half workshop comprising four or more sessions. The alternative is to participate in a group that meets for one session a week (in which case one's "breakthrough" into an initial sense of SR may take about six or more weeks) or, at a minimum, for one session a month (in which case that

---

6. For a most instructive introduction to SR practice, see Kepnes, *A Handbook*.

7. This is a prototype, not a strict rule; our actual practices take many different forms.

breakthrough may take six months). Participants report that, once having entered into the habit of SR practice, they are able to meet less often and still nurture the habit. Best results come from participating in a small group that meets regularly for at least two or more years.

Fellowships of SR study: When a formational SR group meets regularly, we call it a "fellowship of SR study." The basic goal of The Society for Scriptural Reasoning[tm] (founded in 1994) is to nurture as many SR fellowships of study as possible. Our goal is both qualitative and quantitative. The qualitative goal is to provide environments that nurture habits of interpersonal and relational learning, communicating, and reasoning. The quantitative goal is to foster so many fellowships of SR study that the habit-changes nurtured by SR will have a broader social impact. We understand this process to take years. There is no simple, top-down way to nurture the long-range goals of SR by disseminating theories. The goal is to change habits, and that can be achieved only through a slow process of socialization, just as, for example, modern Western patterns of individuated learning and cognition have been disseminated over several hundreds of years alongside models of traditionalist religious learning that were fostered to counter Western individualism. SR fosters modest changes in both individualist and anti-individualist habits of learning, resulting, we believe, in new or stronger habits of relational learning.

WHAT IS SR? SR AS A CLASSROOM

SR is known and transmitted in the doing. This takes place in an intentionally shaped environment. In the coming chapters, I shall examine the kinds of environment that have successfully nurtured SR. These include table fellowships of small groups studying aloud and in dialogue, and university (or seminary) classes that encourage integrative, dialogic study. To shape such environments requires discernment and resources. The criteria for discernment remain immanent in the practice of SR, which means that the practice itself must inform the way that sponsors of SR seek funding, plans, and materials to reshape existent learning environments into places that nurture SR study and practice. This has indeed been the case at the University of Virginia and Cambridge University, where SR learning environments were shaped by practitioners of SR: imperfectly, I trust, but sufficiently successful that the UVA graduate program in Scripture, Interpretation and Practice (SIP) and the Cambridge University Inter-faith Programme (CIP) have transmitted the practice of SR to a second and now third generation of SR teachers and learners.

My hypothesis, difficult to test, is that our efforts to build these environments are successful to the degree that they are informed by the practice and wisdom of SR. I believe, in other words, that an adequate account of what we call "the practice" of SR must include an account not only of the "face" of SR (peers studying Scripture around a table) but also of the material cultures and the sociopolitical institutions and activities that shape the body behind that face. After twenty-five years, we have gained some skill in shaping that face, but the body shapes us. To what extent can our SR practice influence that body's future? The materials out of which one builds SR environments are "found objects": the remains and the living heritage of preceding Western and Abrahamic and Asian civilizations. That living heritage includes gifts (such as healing wisdoms) but also poisons (such as tendencies to hate difference). We may offer SR as a means of distinguishing gift from poison and of helping heal those sickened by the poison, but we also recognize that, short of some end time, our own efforts will retain and transmit some of the poison. This is no reason for discouragement; it is our worldly condition! But it is reason for some sobriety about the goals of SR and, therefore, of this book.

Before SR, for example, some of us may not have perceived *how* the various scriptural canons could contribute directly to the disciplines of the university. We may previously have thought that there were only two ways: either study some canon through the tools of the modern academic sciences or else be careful to erect impassable borders between the precincts of academic and scriptural study. Now we perceive a third way: if we form environments for interactive study among several canons, then *the modes of reasoning* generated by that study may contribute directly to discussions among the academic disciplines. These modes of reasoning *do not* represent the explicit teachings, doctrines, or beliefs *of* any one scriptural canon or tradition, *or* of "the Abrahamic traditions" more generally. They do not correspond to any single form of reasoning we have encountered in the university or in any of the commentarial traditions. But we are beginning to see how they may gift us with wisdoms about what to pursue and what to avoid in the ways we practice our various academic disciplines. (I shall discuss these wisdoms in detail in chapter 3.)

Before SR, furthermore, we may have perceived only two ways that the academic disciplines could contribute to our work in the religious houses: by broadening what we know about the languages of Scripture and the logics of scriptural interpretation, or by leaving the traditions alone. Now we perceive a third way. Despite its failures to nurture non-individualistic modes of teaching and learning in the humanities, the university has provided us an example of how to work together "on" our scriptural canons (through the modern textual sciences) *and* a relatively free environment for experimenting with co-curricular alternatives to this particular *way* of working together. Stepping outside the university classroom, but within the societal precincts of the university, we reshaped the university's model for working together into a practice of inter-scriptural study. Like the indirect contribution of scriptural canons to the model of Scriptural *Reasoning*, the university model of shared scriptural science made an indirect contribution to what became our inter-Abrahamic model of shared scriptural study.

WHAT IS SR? FELLOWSHIPS ACROSS DIFFERENCE

Fellowships among university or seminary students: Since the founding years of SR, many of us have brought the SR approach to our classrooms or co-curricular projects with undergraduate and graduate students. The results constitute a major topic of this book. For now, I will report only this much: I have found small-group SR study to be a significant resource for teaching and learning in almost all my courses, from Introduction to Judaism, and Introduction to Abrahamic Religions, to a broad range of classes in religious studies, theology, philosophy, and in team-taught classes on comparative traditions or on interdisciplinary approaches to belief, practice, interpretation, and reason. At UVA, to take one example, undergraduate and graduate groups have for years met monthly or bi-weekly to pursue student-led study and discussion of scriptural and commentarial texts. More recently, we have begun to extend that work into the local community, with student/community SR groups and also student/community service groups (integrating, for example, Habitat for Humanity service work with town/gown study groups in "narrative reasoning" as well as SR).

SR fellowships of clergy and religious leaders: While generated by university scholars, one primary goal of SR is promote SR fellowships in local communities. We have found that local religious leaders and clergy are excellent partners in this work and that they often value spending several months or more studying with one another before introducing the method to their congregants. Some clergy are initially more comfortable with a less challenging form of formational SR that we have dubbed "parallel Textual Reading" (we welcome suggestions for a better name!). As I note in later chapters, this is our Scripture-specific version of the most customary practice in interfaith: inter-congregational dialogue, where members of each congregation introduce and explain aspects of their religious practices to members of the other congregation(s). In our version, members of each tradition introduce and explain their practices of reading Scripture. Local clergy councils often opt to start SR this way, turning to formational SR, *per se*, only if and when they see signs that the group seems ready for it. One typical sign is that individual group members feel comfortable reading and interpreting their "own" canons of scripture without turning to "greater experts" for approval. Another sign is that individual members feel that they can try to read the "others'" canons without apology or embarrassment: asking questions—and, finally, proposing answers—about specific words and verses rather than about the others' religion or tradition as a whole. This is when, for example, a participant who used to ask "what do Muslims believe about reward and punishment?" or "how does the Jewish tradition deal with the phrase 'eye for an eye'?" now offers comments like these:

> We read in Surah 6:95, "Those who believe (in the Qur'an), and those who follow the Jewish (Scriptures), and the Christians and the Sabians—any who believe in God and the Last Day and work righteousness—shall have their reward with their Lord." I think this reference to "reward" means that these latter—the non-Qur'anic People of the Book—may enjoy life in the hereafter. But are there different degrees of enjoyment?

Or:

> We read in Leviticus 24, "The one who takes the life of an animal shall make it good, life for life. If a man injures his neighbor, just as he has done, so it shall be done to him: fracture for fracture, eye for eye, tooth for tooth." These verses seem to contradict Exodus 24, "If men struggle with each other and strike a woman with child so that she gives birth prematurely, yet there is no injury, he shall surely be fined as the woman's husband may demand of him, and he shall pay as the judges *decide*. But if there is *any further* injury, then you shall appoint *as a penalty* life for life, eye for eye, tooth for tooth, hand for hand, foot for foot." Since the Exodus passage seems to be speaking of monetary equivalents to the damaged body part, I think the Leviticus passage represents a more literal, and perhaps earlier ruling."

When most participants begin to address the group's study texts like this, then the group as a whole begins to treat SR as a time set apart for a unique kind of study: when, for a short time, each one experiments with reading each scriptural canon as if it were his or her own. The rewards of this experiment are great, but only when a group is ready for the experiment. Otherwise, "parallel TR" works fine.

SR fellowships among members of different congregations. These fellowships tend to follow the patterns we have observed among fellowships of clergy. One difference is that congregational groups may find it difficult to avoid leaning on what they consider the authority of their religious leaders and, sometimes even more so, of the other congregations' religious leaders. Until they are able to overcome that difficulty, congregations tend, purposefully or not, to work within the "parallel TR" style. We have found it helpful, sometimes, for clergy to introduce the various Scriptures to their inter-congregational SR group and then depart, encouraging the congregations to accept the challenge of studying each verse of each Scripture, theirs or the others', as if they were authorized to say something about. Often, a remaining challenge is that congregants feel unequally learned in the scriptural traditions and are either too shy to voice opinions or, if they think themselves learned, too eager to compensate for others' reticence by talking at length about "the true meaning" of a given scriptural passage. As I will discuss at length later, the best solution to such challenges is providing excellent facilitators for each group discussion. Someone experienced in SR and good at subtle yet firm facilitation should be present at each circle of study. Since facility at SR is an acquired habit of practice, rather than the product of good ideas, facilitating SR is a form of gentle coaching: encouraging helpful SR behaviors and gently discouraging unhelpful ones until a group gradually gets the knack of this kind of performance. SR can be a springboard for good ideas, too, but these all follow the practice rather than precede it.

SR fellowship among civic leaders: SR practitioners have not yet sufficiently pursued our original goal of moving from more inwardly directed fellowships of SR study to outwardly directed fellowships that would nurture SR study in response to local societal needs. One early vision was to nurture long-term fellowships among civic leaders from a variety of religious backgrounds (limited, of course, to individuals who believe they would enjoy hours of Scripture study). The fellowship should, first and foremost, be enjoyable for its own sake.[8] We envisioned that, after a year or more of enjoyable SR study, a group of civic leaders would share a sense of fellowship deep enough to prepare them to respond in publicly significant ways to certain types of local social crises. Given the participants' experience in civic leadership, we might expect them already to have raised issues of public significance as fodder for their scriptural study: preparing them, all the more so, to respond to certain crises in publicly useful ways. Since there will not be space in this book to revisit the general topic of SR and civic leadership, I will devote extra attention to it now, reporting on our experience of SR and civic leadership in Cape Town, South Africa.

---

8. SR study fails when a notable portion of its participants value it for instrumental reasons only. Ironically, SR study appears to serve secondary ends only when performed first for its own sake.

An illustrative narrative: SR in Cape Town. In 2002, Vanessa Ochs and I went to Cape Town, South Africa to try to nurture a Scriptural Reasoning fellowship among leaders of three mutually distrustful Abrahamic orthodoxies in the city: Orthodox Jewish rabbis, Dutch Reformed ministers, and Shiite imams (at the time these were from Iran). We chose Cape Town because Anglican SR scholars from Cambridge University had previously visited there and initiated some discussion of SR. A prime contact was the delightful John De Gruchy, who served as host for much of our visit, along with faculty from the Department of Religious Studies at Cape Town University. Because of consulting work I had done with *Time*, the magazine also arranged for their African correspondent to follow us around when we were organizing the SR group. Bruce Feiler's book on the children of Abraham was a cover article in *Time* that year so the topic was hot. The new regional *Time* correspondent was there to see if something newsworthy happened.[9]

In Cape Town, there were fairly good relations between the Anglican clerics and just about everybody else, but there were great tensions between the Muslim and Jewish communities; only a few years previously there were some bombings close to synagogues. The official point of contention was news about Israel-Palestine, but there were local sources of uneasiness as well. We found it important to locate and work with clerics and university teachers from the Dutch Reformed community, because their orthodoxy was more comparable to those of the Muslim and Jewish communities. It would have been no challenge to integrate our host Anglicans to this or any kind of dialogue!

We soon attended religious services at several Orthodox synagogues in Cape Town, met the rabbis and received from some of them a modestly favorable interest in our project. It took longer to locate and develop some relations with Dutch Reformed colleagues, but there our efforts proved successful as well. The Muslim clerics, with whom we established contact via intermediaries, were initially suspicious of the endeavor, but we had some back-and-forth communication. Vague plans were set to host a closed-door meeting of some of these religious leaders. The Holocaust Museum in Cape Town offered to host this meeting, but the imams said they would not enter a Jewish space of that kind. Plans were initiated to hold the meeting elsewhere, but the day after our tentative new plan was set, the world news reported some clashes between Israelis and Palestinians in the West Bank. The imams sent us notice that because of Israel's behavior they would not meet with us. For two weeks, we were unable to restart any successful communications with leaders of the Muslim communities. Then I decided to offer a

---

9. Feiler, *Abraham*.

public lecture at the university on the failures of Western secularism. With the help of our hosts, we invited members of various religious communities to attend, with particular attention to those orthodox groups. I gave the lecture, was told that several young emissaries of the imams were present in the fairly large audience, and received a letter two days later indicating that the imams would be happy to attend a meeting, even if it were held at the Holocaust Museum.

About a week later, we held a meeting and it was remarkable. The museum secured a beautiful board room for the event and provided appropriate food for a luncheon. Three religious leaders each from the Muslim, Jewish, and Dutch Reformed religious communities were present, as were several of our Anglican hosts, and the often-present *Time* reporter. After some formal niceties and food, we launched directly into formational SR study of biblical and Qur'anic texts about the time that "Sarah laughed" when she learned that God would enable her to bear a son. For an hour we read the brief selections in their primary languages then in our shared English, discussing our understandings of the plain sense. Participants gradually offered personal interpretations, alongside reports on traditional readings. During the second hour, we (facilitators) asked, "Well, why then did Sarah laugh? What is it to laugh?" Responses came immediately, all around the table, with personal interjections as well as reports on the midrash, hadith, tafsir, and more recent Reformed accounts. We asked a few more questions to extend the discussion. And then the highlight of the session came. I repeated the question, "So *why* did Sarah laugh?" and one of the rabbis picked up the allusion that "laughter" could imply sexual arousal; the imams laughed and added comments, followed by the Dutch Reformed ministers. The mood was fully open, and so it went on through a full three hours of study: a breaking of tension, expressions of surprise that the three traditions shared such interrelated accounts of Abraham and Sarah, expressions of joy and of love of the study of Scripture for its own sake. The discussants began to exchange more technical insights and queries about uses of speech in the texts, idioms, about differences and similarities among a variety of claims from the traditional commentaries. As both Vanessa and I saw it, the group had a natural sense for SR: that the goal wasn't about sharing beliefs or concepts, but of engaging in the joy of study, wherever it might lead. We surmised that the SR study came easily to these participants because they were accustomed to somewhat comparable forms of scriptural study within their own traditions. Even so, we were surprised at the ease with which they allowed themselves to extend the play of text study across canonical borders.

I recall clearly that all of us were energized and moved by the event . . . except for the *Time* reporter. When I returned to the US and called the *Time* editor to see what they might be writing he said, "I am very sorry that you had to be burdened with all this." "What?" I asked. "After all that time," he said, "the correspondent for southern Africa said there was nothing to report. Nothing happened." "Nothing?!" I asked. "In spite of how difficult it was to gather the folks, despite all the previous suspicions and mutual distrust? Even though this simple practice of study seems to cut through all that tension and open the possibility of sustained dialogue across such borders?" "Yes," he answered, "I'm afraid that many of our reporters still identify news-worthiness with bombs and blood."

Before we left Cape Town, this group of religious leaders agreed to meet again on a regular basis, hopefully adding some numbers. During the following year, we learned through e-mail correspondence that the new Cape Town SR fellowship met approximately every two to three months, and the process continued for about two additional years.[10]

Cape Town represented for us a prime example of where, when, and why we would want to nurture SR fellowships among civic leaders. We might imagine that the three-year group fulfilled some of our goals, opening pathways of dialogue among significant religious leaders in a conflict-prone region. To approach our more ambitious goals, such a group would need to be maintained for more years and facilitated by individuals devoted both to study for its own sake and (more subtly) to the longer-range goals of working for civic peace. We assume such work requires occasional intervention, as well, from SR scholars and leaders. We are now working earnestly to nurture civic SR groups in many locations, to introduce networks of communication among leaders of such groups, and to formulate and enact procedures that local and regional groups might follow to move from study to civic action and back to study again. One of my own priorities in the next several years is to work with colleagues and graduate students to make "SR and civic action" a primary rather than secondary dimension of university and seminary education (see chapter 6).[11]

---

10. One of the longer lasting, not-strictly-academic SR fellowships has been the Poughkeepsie/Vassar SR group, founded in 2008–2009. Led by Rabbi Paul Golomb of Vassar Temple in Poughkeepsie, New York, the group examines scriptural issues for their own sake but also introduces local community issues as fodder for text discussion.

11. For many years, I led *A Thousand Cities*, a project to nurture an SR group in as many cities/towns as possible in the USA. That project morphed into *The Scriptural Reasoning Network* (https://www.srnetwork.org/) co-directed by Kevin Seidel (Eastern Mennonite University) and Jacob Goodson (Southwestern College), who also edits the *Journal of Scriptural Reasoning*. SR leaders have also experimented with a broader range of SR fellowships. Supported by government funding, for example, the *Three Faiths Forum* in the United Kingdom initiated a project of nurturing SR fellowships in London prisons, to see if Christian-Muslim SR study might reduce tensions among groups of

WHAT IS SR? A RESOURCE FOR PEACEBUILDING

Religion and Violence Today. To their practitioners, religions may be sources of peace, but contemporary public opinion voices a different view: that religions tend toward violence as much or even more than they tend toward peace.[12] Beyond opinion polls, recent studies suggest that religion is indeed a significant factor in armed conflict around the world. A 2014 PEW research report indicated that "the share of countries with a high or very high level of social hostilities involving religion reached a six-year peak in 2012. A third (33 percent) of the 198 countries and territories included in the study had high religious hostilities in 2012, up from 29 percent in 2011 and 20 percent as of mid-2007. Religious hostilities increased in every major region of the world except the Americas."[13] "Global Peace" as measured by the Global Peace Index (GPI) has been steadily deteriorating over the last seven years, with 111 countries deteriorating and fifty-one improving.[14] Conflict has been driven by a broad range of factors,[15] but interreligious animosity and violence has played a significant role.[16] *Economics and Peace.org* reports, for example, that of thirty-five significant armed conflicts reported in 2013, the top two causal factors were matters of identity (twenty-one conflicts) and matters of religion (twenty-one conflicts).[17]

---

newly religious prisoners. The Forum also tested SR-like study in secondary schools throughout the UK to see if such study might reduce tensions among different varieties of Muslim, Christian, and other ethnic groups. After moving to Israel, one Three Faiths project-leader, Miriam Feldmann Kaye, has successfully instituted related forms of study among Jewish, Christian, and Muslim students in several Israeli nursing schools. For related work, see Kaye, *Jewish Theology*.

12. Public opinion is more suspicious of religions other than one's own; for example, a recent Canadian poll indicated that 44 percent of Canadians identified Islam negatively, 12 percent identify Judaism negatively: http://angusreid.org/faith-in-canada/.

13. http://www.pewforum.org/2014/01/14/religious-hostilities-reach-six-year-high/.

14. One main reason for the global decline in peace has been increased terrorist activity, driven by high profile Islamic terrorist organizations such as the Islamic State, Boko Haram, and al-Qaeda.

15. Thirty of the thirty-five armed conflicts fought last year had more than one cause.

16. Surveying the state of thirty-five armed conflicts from 2013, religious elements did not play a role in fourteen, or 40 percent. Religion did not stand as a single cause in any conflict, but 14 percent included religion and the establishment of an Islamic state as driving causes. Religion was one of three or more reasons for 67 percent of the conflicts where religion featured as a factor to the conflict.

17. http://economicsandpeace.org/wp-content/uploads/2011/09/Peace-and-Religion-Report.pdf. According to the report:

The share of countries with a high or very high level of social hostilities involving

What can be done to reduce religion's contribution to violence around the world? Here, public opinion has little to offer, and the diplomatic corps in both Europe and North America has had almost nothing to offer for the past century. Far less helpful, diplomats have tended to define religion exclusively as a problem and almost never as a resource for peacebuilding. Edward Luttwak traces this problem "to a certain enlightenment overreaction against the constraints imposed by premodern Christendom."[18] For Hoover and Johnston, the problem is that secularization theory almost always included prejudice as well as science.[19] Antireligious secular*ism*, by contrast, is more than an academic theory. It is a normative disposition found frequently among the Westernized intelligentsia, including many foreign affairs professionals. It assumes not only that modernization will have certain functionally subversive effects on religion, but also that secularity is the *correct* direction of history. Religion is thought to be a regressive and irrational

---

religion reached a six-year peak in 2012, according to a new study by the Pew Research Center. A third (33%) of the 198 countries and territories included in the study had high religious hostilities in 2012, up from 29% in 2011 and 20% as of mid-2007. Religious hostilities increased in every major region of the world except the Americas. The sharpest increase was in the Middle East and North Africa, which still is feeling the effects of the 2010–11 political uprisings known as the Arab Spring. There also was a significant increase in religious hostilities in the Asia-Pacific region, where China edged into the "high" category for the first time. The share of countries with a high or very high level of government restrictions on religion stayed roughly the same in the latest year studied.... The study finds that restrictions on religion are high or very high in 43% of countries, also a six-year high.... Pakistan had the highest level of social hostilities involving religion, and Egypt had the highest level of government restrictions on religion.... During the latest year studied, there also was an increase in the level of harassment or intimidation of particular religious groups.... Muslims and Jews experienced six-year highs in the number of countries in which they were harassed by national, provincial or local governments, or by individuals or groups in society. As in previous years, Christians and Muslims—who together make up more than half of the global population—were harassed in the largest number of countries (110 and 109, respectively).

18. He argues, "Astonishingly persistent, enlightenment prejudice has remained amply manifest in the contemporary professional analysis of foreign affairs. Policy-makers, diplomats, journalists, and scholars who are ready to over-interpret economic causality, who are apt to dissect social differentiations most finally . . . are still in the habit of disregarding the role of religion, religious institutions, and religious motivations in explaining politics and conflict.... One is therefore confronted with a learned repugnance to contend intellectually with all that is religion or belongs to it." (Luttwak, "The Missing Dimension," 8–19.).

19. This prejudice has been animated by both secularization *theory* and an antireligious secular*ism*. Secularization theory holds that, as modernization advances, religion recedes.

force that individuals should simply avoid: and if people do cling to it, the state should render it a private matter cordoned off from public life.[20]

Paradigms are, however, beginning to change. Over the past two decades, secularization theory has come under increasing criticism. Catching up slowly with public opinion, academics have begun to write about the gap between persistent secularization theory and the global evidence that religion in fact never went away. Even scholars in politics and foreign affairs are beginning to take note. For example, author and *New York Times* columnist David Brooks declares himself to be a "recovering secularist":

> Like a lot of people these days, I'm a recovering secularist. Until September 11 I accepted the notion that is a world became richer and better educated, it becomes less religious. . . . It's now clear that the secularization theory is untrue. . . . We are living through one of the great periods of scientific progress in the creation of wealth. At the same time, we're in the midst of a religious boom. . . . Islam is surging. Orthodox Judaism is growing among young people, and Israel has gotten more religious as it has become more affluent. The growth of Christianity surpasses that of all other faiths.[21]

Brooks recommends a "six-step program" to "kick the secularist habit," which includes accepting the fact that the secularism of many Western intellectuals is the exception rather than the norm around the globe today and resisting "the impulse to find a materialistic explanation for everything."[22] Beyond his tongue-in-cheek quality, Brooks' critique of current foreign affairs policy is urgent and disturbing:

> Our foreign-policy elites are at least two decades behind. They go for months ignoring the force of religion; then, when confronted with something inescapably religious, such as the Iranian revolution and the Taliban, they begin talking of religious zealotry and fanaticism, which suddenly explains everything. After a few days of shaking their heads over the fanatics, they revert to their usual secular analyses. We do not have, and sorely need, a mode of analysis that attempts to merge the spiritual and the material.[23]

---

20. Hoover and Johnston, eds., "Religion," 1–2.
21. Brooks, "Kicking the Secularist Habit."
22. Brooks, "Kicking the Secularist Habit."
23. Brooks, "Kicking the Secularist Habit."

Interreligious Peacebuilding. About a decade and a half after its emergence in the late 1990s, a new genre of research, "interreligious peacebuilding," is beginning to bear fruits in the way it influences foreign policy analysts as well as an expanding cohort of sympathetic scholars and students. Pioneers in this genre, such as Douglas Johnston, Scott Appleby, Marc Gopin, John Paul Lederach, and Daniel Philpott, work across several fields and disciplines that were previously siloed: foreign affairs and politics, mediation and peace studies, religious studies and sometimes also anthropology, theology, and sociology and history. Appleby's *The Ambivalence of the Sacred* has served as a breakthrough text for these researchers, introducing what I take to be five leading arguments of a new paradigm in the study of religion and foreign affairs:

(1) That religion is a unique and ubiquitous dimension of human experience, belief, and practice, displaying features that are irreducible to features of any other aspect of human experience, belief, and practice.

Public discussion and debate would be improved if we identify religion, in general terms, as "a human response to a reality perceived as sacred. . . . Religion embraces a creed, a code of conduct, and a confessional community. The creed defines a standard of beliefs and values concerning the ultimate origin, meaning, and purpose of life it develops from . . . and finds official expression in doctrines and dogmas."[24] In these terms, a "religious community" is one that teaches its members a particular way to respond to the sacred. Such responses are recorded in the community's memory, in its Scriptures and authoritative teachings, and the transmission of this memory from generation to generation constitutes a "living tradition." This tradition authorizes, "argues for," what it means to be socialized as a member of this community. This tradition is "living" because authority is not a static good but an *activity* of argumentation through which each generation restates, reaffirms, and remembers what it means to be a member of this community.

In these terms, peacebuilders can recognize what we call "religion" in the way that a religious community, through all its complexity and pluralism, reauthorizes each generation to articulate what it means to respond to the sacred. Different agencies, including religious groups, can also join forces in projects of religious peacebuilding. By way of illustration, both Powers and Roht-Arriaza cite the peacebuilding practices of the Acholi in northern Uganda. "The Acholi Religious Leaders Peace Initiative in northern Uganda [was] started in 1997 by Anglican, Roman Catholic, Muslim, and Orthodox leaders . . . , [growing] out of their humanitarian aid programs in the camps for the displaced. They used their influence to play a key

---

24. Appleby, *Ambivalence*, 27.

role in facilitating the peace process between the Ugandan government and the Lord's resistance Army... They also formed local and later district-level peace committees to educate their own people about peace building."[25]

(2) *That each religion and religious group displays some unique features of religious experience, belief, and practice, irreducible to features displayed in other religions or religious groups. The study of religion and religious groups is a study of complexity.*

Religious actors recognize that tradition is pluriform and cumulative, developed in and for concrete and changing situations. Religious traditions are inherently dynamic, comprised of what John Henry Cardinal Newman called "leading ideas," which interact with "a multitude of opinions" and introduce themselves into the "framework and details of social life." This storehouse of religiously approved options is available to religious leaders whenever new circumstances call for change in religious practice. History shows that religious communities, in their self-understanding and in their orientations to the world, change constantly.[26]

(3) *That the unique features of religions and religious groups tend to be displayed in ways that are specific to certain regions of the world at certain times in relation to certain conditions of social and natural environments. At the same time, the experiences, beliefs, and practices of any religious group also tend to display features that may be observed globally in any groups that espouse a particular religious tradition or sub-tradition.*

Appleby warns against trying to capture the meaning or character of a religion or religious group by identifying it with some intellectual construct or ideal type. Such constructs ignore the great variety of "personalities, behaviors and degrees of religious observance" that characterize most members of even the more militant religious movements.[27]

(4) *That, contrary to some stereotypes, traditional religions tend to present their elemental beliefs in ambiguous terms and their behavior rules in terms that are "polyvalent" (in terms that carry many types and levels of meaning).*

This argument is of particular importance in SR, because scriptural study across deep religious difference depends, more than anything else,

---

25. Powers, "Religion and Peacebuilding."
Roht-Arriaza explains that, on a local level, "the Acholi carry out a ceremony called *matu oput*, or drinking the bitter herbs, which involves a recognition of a wrong and reconciliation with the victim's family. A separate ceremony, involving stepping on an egg, is used to cleanse those who have been away from home and allow them to return." Roht-Arriaza, "Human Rights." See Hovil and Quinn, *Working Paper*.

26. Appleby, *Ambivalence*, 32–33.
27. Appleby, *Ambivalence*, 32–33.

on the polyvalence of scriptural words and verses. No matter how much this claim may surprise or challenge contemporary readers, SR scholars are accustomed to seeing the most strictly observant religious teachers read words of Scripture as disclosing a surprisingly broad range of meanings, each appropriate to a different context of reading. Classical and medieval scriptural commentaries offer comparable evidence: the jurist or homilist tends to read a given verse of Scripture as speaking in its unique way to some particular moment of reading in service to some particular community of readers. In Appleby's words, "The ambiguity and internal pluralism of religious traditions invite situational reasoning and pragmatic leadership."[28]

(5) That religions are sources of both peace and violence.

An emergent movement of interreligious peacebuilders recognizes both sides of this argument: that "While . . . there are great untapped resources for peacemaking and conflict resolution in the world's religions, there is also a vast reservoir of texts and traditions ready and waiting to be used to justify the most barbaric acts by modern standards of human rights."[29]

In sum, a previous century's secularization theory no longer speaks to the realities on the ground. It contradicts contemporary field observations about the way politics actually interacts with religion and religious groups throughout the world. The clearer empirical evidence, today, is that the vast majority of human beings across the globe engages in what we in the West would call "religious" activities. The same lesson applies to programs of peacebuilding: religious beliefs and practices should be numbered among the useful resources for resolving religion-related conflict *as well as* among the likely sources of such conflict.

SR and peacebuilding: Reiterating claims by scholars associated with Appleby's work, SR scholars add that religious actors are more prevalent in human populations than conventional analysts suppose, and this includes populations in Western societies. By "religious actors," I mean individuals who in a time of crisis, tension, or uncertainty, may turn to religious practices and beliefs. By "religious practices and beliefs," I mean practices and beliefs that actors, if asked about the matter, would identify as having been drawn from what most readers of this book would identify as a "religion," including not only what we often call "world religions" and any of their denominations, but also what we might label as a "strange" religion, a "sect" or "cult."

---

28. Appleby, *Ambivalence*, 32–33.

29. Gopin, "Religion and International Relations," cited in Dubois, "Religion and Peacebuilding," 257.

The hearth of religion, or what is most valued in a religious group's beliefs and practices: SR recognizes unique features of religions that may correspond to what Appleby calls the sacred, but only as named and characterized within each religious community according to its own language tradition. I like to name these unique features *hearths*, defined loosely as those dimensions of life that members of a religion turn to in times of crisis, tension, or uncertainty in the hope of drawing nearer to the source of their deepest values and identities. Scriptural Reasoning acquires its name from a conspicuous practice in Abrahamic traditions of turning to scriptural texts as a primary means of accessing the hearth of a given religious community. This turning may be enacted through reciting verses, chanting them, studying them, proclaiming what they say, imitating the words or the actions of characters displayed therein, believing what they say, or performing what they command.

When I refer to the "hearth" of a religion, I am not making any claim about what religion or a religion really is or what really are its elemental features. I am, instead, offering a pragmatic or operational claim. Observing some visible behavior I consider religious, for example, I construct a portrait of what might be going on in the world to generate such behavior. On the basis of that portrait, I try to predict what might happen next under certain conditions. If my prediction fails, then I try a new portrait, and so on. If the prediction seems close to what I see next, I treat the portrait as if it were useful in guiding my interactions with the activity/actors in question: useful, but subject to continual adjustment, correction, and refinement. I call the process pragmatic or operational, because, no matter how successful, the portrait has meaning only as an instrument for anticipating behavior, never as the source of an empirical claim about what is out there in the world. In these terms, I have found the portrait of a "hearth" useful for guiding my expectations about certain religious behaviors.

When first adopting this approach, I thought of "hearth" as a central, heated place where family members might gather, first thing, on a cold morning: keeping warm around it, preparing food, and feeling sufficiently comfortable and at ease to share intimate thoughts one with the other. At times I also associated hearth with a bear's den, where mother and cubs share each other's warmth and intimacy. I would imagine that, were an intruder to enter the den, the mother's gentle mood would turn in a heartbeat to a defensive and potentially offensive posture: fearing the intruder and acting to remove the object of fear. I imagined that a human family's morning hearth would operate, analogously, as a refuge where intruders were not expected and where, if they came in, the family's relaxed conversation would be replaced immediately by guarded, defensive postures or, if needed, aggressive postures. I imagined that, in times of daily stress, members of a religious group might turn to certain dimensions of their religion as a hearth-like source of strength and guidance. I imagined that, in infrequent times of serious social distress, a religious group might turn collectively to hearth-like social/religious institutions and practices, where group teachers and leaders might invoke traditions of deep values and wisdom as sources of comfort and guidance in the face of shared threats.

Over the past eight years, I have found this portrait of hearth quite useful for anticipating what may happen in SR study sessions, for planning and facilitating SR groups, and for co-designing and testing tools for diagnosing noteworthy features of religion-related conflict. I applied the notion of hearth first to scripturally based religions, imagining that devout members might gather around texts of Scripture as they would gather around a hearth, opening their hearts to one another and to the questions and hopes they would bring to the scriptural verses. I assumed that, within each tradition, such study would be an intimate, insider's affair, shielded from outsiders, whose presence would interrupt a group's sense of shared understanding, warmth, and trust. I imagined that, as they engaged outsiders, group members would adopt cooler forms of speech that veiled their intimate beliefs and confessions. This way, I could also make sense of the counterfactual character of SR gatherings, where members of different groups of this kind agreed to sit one next to the other and to share at least some modest elements of their hearths. I could understand why, when first joining an SR-study, traditional devotees would express coolness, distance, and caution toward one another, as if this was no place to share Scripture's intimacies. And I could appreciate how remarkable it was that the vast majority of these groups stayed together long enough that group members began to experience the SR environment as neither home-like nor alien: not a place for either caution and coolness or tradition-specific openheartedness and deep warmth. Most often, the SR environment became an in-between place where individuals came to display some of the warmth they associated with at-home Scripture study integrated with a new kind of interreligious and inter-hearth engagement.

But what of non-scriptural religions or populations for which Scripture no longer displayed hearth-like qualities? I have found it helpful to look within such groups for analogues to the hearth I attributed to traditional gatherings around Scripture. I look for some dimension of material culture that the group values most of all and that serves as a focus of gatherings where group members share instruction about deep values, beliefs, and sources of guidance. I think, for example, of the privileged place of dugout sailing canoes in traditional Micronesian societies and of revered navigators who chant oral navigational lore to gatherings of sailors. The lore transmits navigational instructions in poetic verse that also delivers political wisdoms and traditional accounts of the gods and the sea spirits. Readers may think of many other examples, from East African cattle-based societies, to devotees of personality cults, to modern Western devotees of the natural world or of theosophy. For each case, I imagine the hearth-centered behavior of those who gather around a group's highly privileged places, actors, and practices. This imagining is not a source of any testable knowledge of "what is really going on" in any group, but it is a resource for generating testable plans for how to anticipate and, where appropriate, respond to group behaviors and intergroup interaction.

SR practice as hearth-to-hearth engagement: I have already noted that religion is a potential source of both peace and violence. Turning toward a religious hearth can open religious practitioners to means of radically changing, refining, reforming, or even transforming or overturning their conventional habits and rules of action and belief. Such change may entail the elimination of tendencies toward hatred or violence, or it may mean upsetting tendencies toward acceptance and tranquility, thereby unleashing unexpected passions of anger or rebellion. The SR account of turning toward such hearths overlaps in many ways with Appleby's account of turning toward the sacred. "Turning" opens capacities to both peace and violence in ways that are somewhat comparable to what Appleby calls the ambiguity of the sacred, opening pathways of many kinds, including peace but also including much else.

The ambiguity or vagueness of religious discourse: The ambiguity of religious belief is among the most powerful reasons that religion is as much a resource for peace as for violence. In the context of SR, the terms I tend to use for ambiguity are *vagueness* and *polyvalence*. Polyvalence is another way of referring to the vagueness of words: that words will appear to have not just one but potentially many meanings. This does not mean that the words are necessarily confusing, only that readers must enter into a more intimate relationship with the words to discover which meaning is active at which time, and in which place and context of reading.

In these terms, the ambiguity of religious discourse is its vagueness, not its generality. The force of Appleby's account is to correct the broad misconception that religions imposed hard and fast doctrines and rules. People tend to confuse the authority of religious doctrines and rules with their generality. Charles Peirce offers more intuitive definitions. He suggests that to speak *generally*—as in "the wagon is *red*"—is to allow listeners to further determine the generality as they see fit (imagining this or that type of red), which implies that a generality retains its force whatever the listener thinks and independently of any relationship to the listener. To speak vaguely, however—as in "*somebody* in this room is smoking"—is *not* to lend such freedom to the listener; it is to claim that both speaker and listener are constrained by the facts of the case, in this case by the character of whoever is smoking. Vague claims thereby engage both speaker and listener in a binding, two-way relationship: something, somewhere is what it is, and we must both work to find out where it is. The expected response to a general claim is therefore either "okay, I get it," or "no, I don't think that is true." But the expected response to a vague claim is to engage this speaker in a long series of questions, which may lead to a long series of conversations that would help both speaker and listener to get closer to the intended object, which is to see it less vaguely.

Readers may find it odd that Peirce associates vagueness with both empirical knowledge and polyvalence. If I say something in order to draw your attention to something out there in the world, why should I encourage your trying out a range of different ways of understanding what I have said? For Peirce, this is because I do not want you to be misled by my words, which may mean something different to you than they do to me. My goal is to utter words that will bring you into some relationship (of seeing, knowing, or engaging) with that thing out there rather than with my words alone. I therefore encourage you to try out different meanings of my words until you come to engage the thing that I hoped you would engage (and, yes, this engagement may include your telling me that the thing really isn't what I thought it was). What, however, if I seek to draw your attention to something that is not literally visible? I may, for example, hope that you will see that Jack loves Jill, or that some business transaction was corrupt, or that God is really in this place, or that this scriptural verse has this meaning. The primary subjects and arguments of this book concern such cases: claims about what is purportedly real or out there but not literally visible. I will argue in the book that such claims share two characteristic marks. On the one hand, such claims call for polyvalent reading just as in empirical claims. On the other hand, the words that deliver such claims are not strictly instrumental as they appear to be in most empirical claims. Drawing on Peirce's work, I will argue that these two marks are integrated only through the community and tradition of discourse that speaker and listener must share if they are to share relationship to the object of such claims. I attribute such a community and tradition to the *hearth* of any religious group. In these terms, a claim about invisible realities is truth functional only with respect to such a hearth and is not truth functional for participants who gather around different hearths. Under conventional conditions, different hearths offer incommensurable contexts for evaluating the meanings and judging the truth or falsity of claims about invisible realities. While it cannot erase that type of incommensurability, SR introduces a third context for engaging claims across the borders of different communities and traditions of discourse. Different from the context for engaging empirical claims and the context for engaging claims about the reality of invisibles, this third context pertains strictly to claims about invisibles introduced across the borders of religious groups and their hearths.

Postponing most comments to the following chapters, I will offer only a few words about the place of vagueness and polyvalence in this third context, of which the prototype is the setting of SR. SR tends to engage participants from very different and often antagonistic text traditions in increasingly binding relations as co-readers. When first entering an SR circle, traditionally religious participants tend to bring with them a presumption of monovalence: that they know the meanings of individual terms and verses in their traditional readings of Scripture and that, therefore, those who offer different meanings have misread their texts. In the early years of SR, I did not realize that this presumption was most often inoperative back home. Around their traditional hearths, the same participants tended to exercise polyvalent readings, challenging one another to double-check their assumptions that a meaning appropriate to a particular setting was also appropriate to another one. I gradually adopted the hypothesis that traditional readers turned to monovalent readings in strange settings, away from the protection of traditional hearths and that they applied this strategy to readings both of their own and of other text traditions. This hypothesis contributed to my initial idea of "hearth" and to a theory about the role of polyvalence in SR: that, in settings like SR, monovalent reading accompanies both cool and hot, or stressful, relations among members of different religious groups and that non-monovalent reading accompanies a warming of cool relations and a cooling off of hot ones. I theorize that such polyvalence does not, however, imply any loosening of devotion to a traditional religion or to the authority of Scripture. To the contrary, it signals intimacy with Scripture and with those who share in reading Scripture: an intimacy that frees traditional readers to experiment, modestly, with Scripture's range of potential meaning so that, when the context of reading calls for decision or action, readers have greater trust that their context-specific decisions and commitments are guided by the most reliable reading.

I theorize that there is a distinct difference between the intimacy achieved around the traditional hearth and the much more modest intimacy achieved in long-term SR groups. The traditional hearth nurtures the greatest intimacy members of a religious group experience with Scripture and with their fellow readers. A successful SR group nurtures something different: a new space unlike the traditional hearth as well as the traditional experience of engagement outside the hearth. The new space of SR nurtures something closer to this: a secure environment in which a few (five to ten) members of different traditions allow one another, within a discrete period of time in a discrete setting, to read scriptural excerpts independently of their implications for decision, commitment, or action. There is no explicit discussion of this independence and no strictly shared assumption about how one's individual reading in SR compares with one's reading at home. I imagine that SR works best when the topic I have just raised is not on the table as part of SR study. Such theorizing may in fact interrupt the modest intimacy of this third space, either by stimulating traditional fears or cooling the modest warmth that participants gradually feel toward one another within the group. I imagine that the group's "modest intimacy" is unique to the SR setting and that it may concern relations among the text traditions themselves as well as among the individuals sitting around the table. Individuals may come to experience various kinds of interpersonal warmth and cross-border adventure and discovery. But, to understand SR more deeply, I think we should also think beyond individual experience and discuss what it may mean for different traditions of language and meaning to interact one with the other: that is, for interaction to take place on the level of system and discourse beyond the nodes of our bodies' neurological and protoplasmic activity.

I think of SR's modest intimacy as taking place most significantly in the interaction among languages and systems of action and belief. I therefore think of polyvalence and vagueness as characteristics of relations between individuals and systems of language and meaning, and I think of such relations as the "third context" and "third space" for giving, receiving, and adjudicating claims about what is real and invisible. In such a third space, typical of SR, meanings are vague and polyvalent because they are entertained independently of the spheres of decision and action that necessarily reduce Scripture's polyvalence to monovalence in order to serve the needs of this-worldly behavior. Such needs arise in spacetime-specific contexts and require spacetime-specific judgments. Such judgments are monovalent, but only for a given spacetime context. Such monovalence cannot extend to a religious group's system of discourse and practice of scriptural reading in general, since the monovalence is not a characteristic of religious authority, but only of the specificity of decision and action in worldly time and space.

CHAPTER 2

How SR Reads and Interprets Scripture
A Scriptural Pragmatism

"Deep calls to deep at the thunder of thy cataracts; all thy waves and thy billows have gone over me" (Ps 42:8).

IN CHAPTER 1, I introduced SR from the outside: its history, some descriptions of how we practice it, an overview of some of its purposes and goals, and a few illustrations of when and where SR has been practiced. To learn how to teach SR, readers will want to examine it from the inside as well. By "the outside," I mean the public display of SR, especially the specific methods we have found most successful: how to sit around the table, for example, or what texts to choose. By "the inside," I mean the cognitive, intuitive, and sapiential knowledge that an experienced practitioner has gained of the overall purpose and spirit of SR. In this sense, SR is no different than any other religious, aesthetic, ritual, or wisdom practice. To practice any of these, one must learn some things by rote (the "alphabet" of the practice, the set of building blocks that is the same for everyone) and some things through the kind of non-identical repetition that makes a practice one's own. The latter element is not optional: there is no non-personal way to enter the inner life of a practice of this kind.

I. INSIDE SR: FROM DEEP TO DEEP

The purpose of this section is to introduce one insider's view of SR: a sample of what we old time scriptural reasoners have slowly learned through our personal engagements in SR. To make sense of what we learned, readers will need to begin fashioning their own, inner accounts of what SR means, revising the accounts to make sense of each new lesson learned about SR or about comparable modes of study and encounter. The inner patterns of reasoning and relationship that we associate with SR are not displayed in some wholly general way, but only by way of the concrete settings of each fellowship of study: of the specific, interpersonal and intertextual relations that formed among a given set of people from a given set of text traditions in a given space and time. The reasonings that emerge within such settings may have many other applications (they are *reasonings*),[1] but *not just any* application: only after the fact may we learn that one reasoning seems to apply to any setting of a certain type X, while another reasoning seems to apply to settings of type Y. These are, in other words, the kinds of reasoning we might otherwise associate with kinds of wisdom or with habits of judgment gained through years of a given type of experience.

The Scriptural Text is the Primary Teacher. While egalitarian in various ways, SR also models the asymmetrical dimension of scriptural study. The asymmetry begins with the authority that SR practitioners lend to what we will call the "plain sense" of scriptural texts. For the Tannaim (the founding generation of rabbinic sages), this is the *peshat*, or the meaning of the text in its intra-scriptural, literary context, which meaning includes the unconditional un-substitutability of the literal, black-on-white letters-and-spaces of the inherited, Masoretic tradition of the written text of Tanakh—the *torah she b'khtav*—every "jot and tittle." As we will discuss below, the *peshat* does not carry performative meaning—which is displayed only through deeper-readings *in situ*—but bears only the range of grammatical implications implied by the order of the letters and the range of intra-textual semantic meanings of these letters within the flow of the biblical text. This means that the plain sense allows the scriptural text to retain its literary coherence without, at the same time, freezing its capacity to address its readers in their specific historical space-time. For Christian readers of SR—and here we generalize a bit for the sake of a simple introduction—"plain sense" tends to refer to the *sensus literalis*: as in Hans Frei's formulation, for example, the consensual sense of the words of Scripture for the evolving and

---

1. In chapter 2, I examine "reasoning" only within the contexts of textual, scriptural, or reparative reasoning. In chapter 3, I address the philosophic question of how to characterize reasoning more generally.

catholic community of the church.² There are occasional tensions between this meaning and the rabbinic one, but these tensions enliven rather than interfere with the flow of SR reasoning. The Christian *sensus literalis* tends to treat more of the text's meaning as determined, up front, but less of the literal letters and spaces as necessarily contributing to that meaning. Muslim scholars of SR tend to read more like the Jews in some ways and more like the Christians in others. Here, the plain sense refers to the *zahir*, or visible sense as opposed to the *batin* or inner, interpreted meaning. While Muslim scholars of SR are less willing than the Jewish scholars to refer to the indeterminacy of scriptural semantics, they also assume that the *ayaat*, or individual verses, of the Qur'an will display their meanings only through their relations to many other verses and to the entire literary context of a *sura* (chapter) as well as its setting in the life of the Prophet. A verse or even a *sura* does not teach by itself, therefore, but by way of the tradition, in light of *hadith* and *sunna* and later commentators.

Despite differences among the three traditions' ways of reading the plain sense, SR scholars tend to agree, overall, that the plain sense has an asymmetrical authority in their study fellowship: it is the immediate sign of God's authoritative presence among them and Scripture's clearest figure for the role of teacher in an SR classroom.

A deep concern of SR is to temper the modern tendency, excited by the Enlightenment, to press individual thinkers to overcome their creatureliness—as if not overcoming it meant remaining childish or boorish or petty or irrational or merely tribal. Scriptural reasoners may suggest that this tendency imposes unreasonable and unworldly choices on individual thinkers, as if they had to choose between two masters: for example, either local custom or universal reason, either personal, familial, and ethnic identity or the identity and goodness of humanity per se. Scriptural reasoners may suggest choosing both, but not in an additive sense, as if "universal concepts" had discrete existence separate from "local habits" and that thinkers had always to wear two identities. Scriptural reasoners tend, instead, to read their earthly identities—somatic, psycho-social, ethnic, tradition-specific—as also signs and conduits of God or the Absolute and to read this Absolute as more universal than "universals." They do not, therefore, refuse Enlightenment aspirations to serve all humanity, to know the world and the good, but they read and adopt these as aspirations to serve God who created humanity, to know the creation, and to behold and serve its goodness. This re-inclusion of Enlightenment into the Abrahamic project generates an

---

2. Frei, "Literal Reading." For related sources, see Lindbeck, *Church*; Jenson, *Canon and Creed*; Soulen, *Divine Names*; Hughes, "Sources Chretiennes."

approach to universality and particularity that readers may find surprising at first but that should enable students of SR to move comfortably back and forth between academic and scripturally based ways of reading and reasoning. Our comments on the plain sense offer a good place to introduce this approach.

Interpretive reading moves from "deep to deep." As the Psalmist says, "Deep calls to deep at the thunder of thy cataracts; all thy waves and thy billows have gone over me" (Ps 42:7): Scripture and reader meet each other at comparable depths. Alongside the psalmist's image of waves crashing, scriptural reasoners may remember that it is crisis and suffering, in particular that of the reading community as a whole, that most often exposes "the watery depths" of both reader and text, reader to text. This is what philosophers might call the "pragmatism" of SR: that it understands reading beyond the plain sense most often to be reading for the sake of repair. The reader may observe something disturbing in the plain sense: something that needs repair in the text, whether a grammatical or semantic conundrum, some apparent contradiction among verses of a text, *or* something that appears morally or religiously offensive in light of what the reader expects of the text. But on what ground will the reader recommend repairs? And how will the reader know if the repair is right or wrong, helpful or not helpful? While recognizing that readers have answered and will continue to answer these questions in a variety of ways, a pragmatic approach is particularly useful in the interreligious setting of SR. We may note five major features of this approach:

(i) The problem in the plain sense should be read as a sign that something needs to be repaired in the relation that joins the text to a community of readers. This does *not* mean either that the text needs to be adjusted to fit the community or the community needs to be adjusted to fit the text. (These are, we might say, plain sense ways of putting things, while the problem *in* the plain sense calls for repairs beyond the plain sense.) It means, instead, that the reader is being called to open up a deeper story about what is now amiss in the community of readers. *Disclosing this story should, in turn, call up a deeper dimension of the story of Scripture.* This deeper story will most likely also be troubling: either because it enables the reader to see even more sharply what is amiss in the reader's world, or because it seems to connect this trouble to troubles in the deeper story of Scripture itself, or, most likely of all, because, in a less clearly either-or way, it opens the reader even more painfully to the "groanings" of the world (to use a Pauline phrase).

(ii) When moving forward from an apparent problem to its hoped-for repair, the reader must distinguish carefully between what we call "Textual Reasoning" and "Scriptural Reasoning." The term *Textual Reasoning* was first

used in the mid-1980s by a group of Jewish text scholars and philosophers to name the patterns of reasoning that emerged in their communal study of classic rabbinic literature.[3] When we formed the SR group, we drew a distinction between two kinds of reasoning out of sacred sources. *We used the term "Textual Reasoning" to refer to tradition-specific ways of reading, interpreting, and reasoning about Scripture by way of a tradition's primordial literatures of scriptural commentary.* This therefore means reasoning about Tanakh by way of rabbinic literatures, Bible or New Testament by way of Patristic literatures, or Qur'an by way of the literatures of hadith and Sunna. We extended the domain of any Textual Reasoning to include medieval, modern, and contemporary commentaries as well, provided the reasoning reached back to its basis in Scripture and in a single tradition of reading Scripture. Our tendency is to mark this term with the name of a given tradition, so that we have Jewish or Christian or Muslim Textual Reasonings.

We used the term *Scriptural Reasoning* to refer to the *simultaneous study and interpretation of texts from all three Scriptures by a community of participants gathered from all three Abrahamic traditions*. In this case, the defining movements of study are from plain sense to deep reading, from one scriptural canon to another and then back again, and from reading to reasoning. While comparing canons is a useful instrument of study, it is not a goal of study. For each SR meeting, the shared goal is to "feast" on a modest set of texts (with an equal portion from each canon); the goal for each individual is to study all the texts with comparable intensity and for their own sake[4]—to understand, to question and inquire, to consider; the goal for group dialogue is to allow the texts to be illumined by all participants' readings and questions; to allow each verse to illumine each other verse within a given canon and across the canons; to allow the flow of verses to call up the readers' deeper recognitions and concerns; to leave time and space for a flow of dialogue to emerge and, through the dialogue, various lines of reasoning—about the meanings and implications of given verses or relations among verses; about the textual, social, ethical, or theological issues that may be raised by the reading.

---

3. See Ochs and Levine, eds., *Textual Reasonings*, 3–7. For founding statements of the methods of TR, see Kepnes, ed., *Why Textual Reasoning: Journal of Textual Reasoning* (New Series) Vol. 1.1, including the essays by Steven Kepnes, "Introducing the Journal"; Robert Gibbs, "Why Textual Reasoning"; Aryeh Cohen, "Why Textual Reasoning"; Randi Rashkover, "The Ground of Textual Reasoning"; Shaul Magid, "The Brokenness (and Sacrality) of the Human Voice"; Jim Fodor, "Textual Reasoning as Social Performance."

4. See Ford, *Christian Wisdom*, 81, 120, 203, 302–3, 349. See also Higton, "For Its Own Sake."

It is important to maintain separate environments for Scriptural Reasoning and for Textual Reasoning. SR fails when the contributing traditions are given either too little or too much consideration. "Too little consideration" occurs when individual participants fail to consult their traditions as resources for preparatory study, when they fail to listen to their hearts and deeper beliefs when reading, or when group facilitators fail to cite traditional—as well as academic—commentaries when preparing and introducing texts selected for group study. "Too much consideration" occurs when individual participants voice traditional commentaries as their defining contributions to group study or when a single tradition is consulted as the authoritative source for understanding its own canon. *Except for initial introductions to the plain sense of each set of texts, individuals or tradition-specific sub-groups must not be permitted to lecture about the scriptural texts,* as if given texts had given meanings and these individuals knew what they were. *A very firm yet subtle distinction sits at the heart of SR: on the one hand, the group honors the sacred bond between members of one tradition and their scriptural canon; on the other hand, no tradition is treated* during the give-and-take of group study *as if it had privileged access to the meanings of each verse within that canon.* These meanings rest with their author, and they are equally pursued by all readers. *In these ways, Textual Reasoning is out of place in the circle of SR study—just as much as Scriptural Reasoning, with its openness to inter-traditional exchange, is out of place within the circle of Textual Reasoning.* Over the years we have learned that an SR session is headed for trouble when it begins to look like three parallel sessions of Textual Reasoning: the Jews teaching the Christians teaching the Muslims teaching the Jews (and so on) about "their own" texts. SR is not show-and-tell among the traditions, nor is it interfaith dialogue. At the same time, SR is also troubled when the individual traditions are poorly embodied in the character and intentionality of individual members. Is there a contradiction, therefore, between SR practice and the religiosity of its members? No, not if these two constituents of SR are bound together in the relational patterns of SR itself.

(iii) *Within the context of SR study, problems in the plain sense are therefore signs that SR is an appropriate place to give voice to troubles among the Abrahamic communities as well as within each community.* This means that SR is a place, at once, where these troubles can be heard and where answers to them can be sought. The "pragmatism" of SR includes an understanding of Scripture as a place of special sorts of sign. *According to what we might call SR's theory of signs (or, technically, its semiotics), problematic words or verses or texts in Scripture are dual signs, at once, of some trouble that has been festering in the reader's world and of some source of repair that is yet to be opened in a world that links this entire company of readers to this entire* set of canons.⁵ This means that, as represented in these problematic words, Scripture is the face of a three-part relation that draws particular places of human suffering into reparative relations with the "One who speaks and the world is" (*amar vayehi*), who is the One who speaks these words, Creator Revealer and Redeemer, who "comes when you but call," who names himself as "I am with you" (*ehyeh imach*) or Emmanuel or friend. SR study is another means, outside the liturgical practices of each community, to call on this Redeemer, especially about troubles that concern all three communities at once or that can be ameliorated by the concerted efforts of all three communities at once.⁶

(*iv*) *Within the context of SR, SR reasoning is a face of this redemptive or reparative presence.* SR reasoning is SR fellowship as collaborative engagement among group members, among the canonical traditions as they are given voice around the table, and among readers and scriptural verses. For some scriptural reasoners, this collaborative engagement *already answers* what most troubles them. They are troubled by inter-Abrahamic and inter-religious enmity and violent conflict, and they are most troubled by their fear that the traditions lack indigenous resources for a reparative response to this strife. SR answers their fear: not because it directly ends strife, but because it demonstrates that the traditions do not lack such resources. *The resources lie in the traditions' founding discourses, or Scripture, which become active sources of repair when engaged in ways comparable to SR*. For such scriptural reasoners, SR's collaborative engagements therefore serve as an eschatological or at least hopeful sign: a glimpse of inter-Abrahamic (or also interreligious) engagement without enmity or violent conflict. The source of hope is the way that engagements like SR introduce a three-part hermeneutical relation among text, readers, and God, which includes three-part relations among texts and readers from different canons.

(*v*) *SR as apprenticeship in reparative reasoning.* But how can such a three-part relation define a *pattern of reasoning*? In SR, such a pattern is not something one sees written on a piece of paper and then reads and obeys it. *Instead, it is a prototypical pattern of activity that one tends to acquire by participating repeatedly in a certain type of three-part relation*. The circular sound of this formula is a sign that *SR is learned by apprenticeship within SR groups, not by any kind of individuated reading*. But this does not mean that "Scriptural Reasoning" is a name *only* for what goes on strictly within an SR fellowship. *An SR fellowship may be the prototypical place to acquire*

---

5. For complementary studies in SR and semiotics, see Ticciati, "Scriptural Reasoning and the Formation of Identity."

6. See Kepnes's extension of SR-like practice to "liturgical reasoning": Kepnes, *Liturgical Reasoning*.

the patterns of Scriptural Reasoning, which patterns may then inform one's reasoning in all sorts of places. An analogy would be that, after learning (or not learning) how to love others in one's family, one may hope (or fail) to love others in many other places.

When, finally, we add the term "reparative" to "Scriptural Reasoning," we refer to an activity that, guided by the pattern of SR, helps move something away from a state of trouble or suffering. In these terms, readers may begin to see *the fellowship of SR study as not only a place for SR activity, but also a prototypical place for learning-and-teaching SR so that SR-like activities may be carried on elsewhere.* To speak of SR study as prototypical suggests that it may raise up an activity that may be transported elsewhere, not only as patterns of reparative text study but also as patterns of some more general practice of repair. We may then conceive of the prototype of reparative SR as a fellowship for studying scriptural texts that some group considers troubled or wounded. In prototypical study, group members uncover troubles or wounds in their own social lives that appear to converse with these troubled texts, deep to deep. They then share in a dialogic practice of reading and interpretation that, according to SR, may open pathways of healing or redeeming both text and reader simultaneously. If SR is transportable, it is because these pathways are not merely experienced in the moment but also *learned* as patterns of reparative reasoning that can be enacted elsewhere. We may suppose that, if these patterns of reasoning are transportable enough to be enacted in other contexts of scripture study, then they might be transportable enough to be enacted in other contexts of living, as well. By learning to reason reparatively in relation to troubled scriptural texts, scriptural readers may also learn to reason reparatively in relation to troubled social contexts of many sorts. They may learn, in other words, something of what the founding Abrahamic communities may have meant by reading Scripture as God's commanding and healing word: that the practice of reading Scripture is an apprenticeship in the practice of helping heal the world.[7]

From one perspective, the movement of reparative study concerns the hermeneutics of text reading: it goes from (1) examining the troubled plain sense of a set of texts to (2) uncovering deeper meanings behind the plain sense to (3) observing the power of such deeper meanings to guide reparative action into the world. *From another perspective, this movement addresses the readers' societal lives*: it goes from (1) recognizing the societal troubles they bring with them to text study, to (2) taking time off to study Scripture as an unexpected source of (3) possible approaches to repairing those troubles as well as a source of hope that the world offers resources for

---

7. Ochs, "Jewish and other Arguments."

attending to such troubles. *From another perspective, the movement of study addresses the SR group's practices of reasoning*: it goes from (1) a practice of fellowship for which troubled texts and troubled societies first appear as independent objects of study, to (2) a dialogic practice of reading that may give rise to a shared practice of reasoning that brings troubled texts and societies into mutually illuminating relation, to (3) patterns of reparative reasoning that appear to be transportable from this fellowship of study to the group members' various, societal homes.

Illustration: David Ford's reparative study of Ephesians

David Ford offered his 2001 essay, "'He Is Our Peace': The Letter to the Ephesians and the Theology of Fulfilment,"[8] as an illustration of the reparative character of SR. Prepared for the inaugural issue of the *Journal of Scriptural Reasoning*, "'He Is Our Peace'" is a reparative reading of texts from *Letters to the Ephesians* that have traditionally been read in a supercessionist manner. Ford's reading fits naturally into the argument of this chapter, because he presented it, explicitly, to complement my account of reparative reasoning in *Peirce, Pragmatism and the Logic of Scripture*. Ford cites Charles Peirce's pragmatic maxim as frame for his reading:

> "[T]he pragmatic meaning of a conception is the sum total of its practical consequences for the long run of experience."[9] How might that maxim relate to the quotation from the *Letter to the Ephesians* in my title? The whole verse is: "For he is our peace, in his flesh he has made both groups into one, and has broken down the dividing wall, that is, the hostility between us" (2.14). The reference is to Jews and Gentiles, and in view of "the long run of experience" over nearly two thousand years it must constitute a major problem for the interpretation of Ephesians today. If pragmatic scriptural reading aims to read "in response to human suffering" and "with a community of readers for the sake of changing the practical and communal conditions of suffering,"[10] then in view of the terrible history of Christian persecution of Jews there is a need for correction of Christian conceptions of Jews. The constructive question is whether there might be a valid and strong reading of Ephesians

---

8. Ford, "He is our Peace."

9. Paraphrasing Peirce, "How to Make Our Ideas Clear" (1878), in Peirce, *Collected*, Vol. 5, Par. 402. Future references to this collection will be to CP, followed by volume and paragraph number (CP 5.402).

10. Ochs, *Peirce, Pragmatism, and the Logic of Scripture*, 313.

that not only resists Christian hostility to Jews but even allows the communities today to be of mutual blessing. How might this tradition not only correct itself but even surpass itself with the aid of a pragmatic reading of Ephesians?

The problem: Illustrating the movement of reparative study we diagramed above, Ford begins his reading by examining the troubled plain sense of a set of texts that accompanies his SR community's recognition of a certain set of societal troubles. He argues that the plain sense of Ephesians offers a realized eschatology from which "it is a short step to a supersessionism which sees no further role in history for the Jewish people outside the church": "a plan for the fullness of time" in which "he [God] has put all things under his [Christ's] feet and has made him the head over all things for the church, which is his body" (1:22–23). For Ford, it is therefore easy to imagine how Ephesians could have contributed to Christian efforts to write Jews out of history, "with all sorts of appalling consequences when Gentiles became dominant in the church and the balance of power between Judaism and Christianity shifted in favor of the latter."

Seeking a means of repair: Ford seeks alternative ways of reading Ephesians that might help repair its problematic legacy. He proposes a pragmatic approach:

> In Ochs's terms, I have identified "something burdensome in the plain sense" of Ephesians.[11] This now stimulates me to suggest what he calls a midrashic, or pragmatic interpretation. As he says, such a reading is to be judged by how well it resolves the given problem "for a given community of interpreters":[12] in my case, for the Society for Scriptural Reasoning at the end of a century marked by the Shoah. What might be the "non-evident meaning"[13] of Ephesians on this matter . . . ? In this case, the problem is not mainly in what Ephesians says explicitly. It lies more in its "pragmatic meaning" in the millennia that followed—though in fact for many Christians the problematic reading has been read as the plain sense and has shaped their "common sense."

Resources for repair: Ford then proposes rereading the plain sense of Ephesians in ways that could resist supersessionist tendencies in the church: "The most obvious resistance comes in the ethics of Ephesians. It is an ethic of non-coercive communication, of speaking the truth in love (4.15), of 'all

---

11. Ochs, *Peirce, Pragmatism, and the Logic of Scripture*, 6.
12. Ochs, *Peirce, Pragmatism, and the Logic of Scripture*, 7.
13. Ochs, *Peirce, Pragmatism, and the Logic of Scripture*, 6.

humility and gentleness, with patience, bearing with one another in love' (4.2). If such speech and action were to characterise relations with those outside as well as inside the community then, whatever the beliefs about Jews in relation to God's *oikonomia*, there would be respect, communication and peace. The root of this resistance within Ephesians is in who Jesus Christ is believed to be." Ford seeks warrant for his rereading, first, in the plain sense of Ephesians, then in the plain sense of the New Testament canon more broadly, then in his estimate of the potential consequences of such rereading for challenging societal habits associated with the older, supersessionist readings. I will offer only a brief summary of his effort. His first step is to show how "Ephesians itself can be read as correcting and redefining the Pauline Christian tradition." Noting that Ephesians is customarily seen as dependent on the *Letter to the Colossians*, he recommends paying more attention to "where the two diverge": for example, where, "Ephesians develops the Colossians themes of the church as the body of Christ and of 'peace through the blood of his [Christ's] cross' into an explicit focus on peace between Jews and Gentiles in the church." Another example is the way Ephesians intensifies "Colossians theme of *pleroma* (the fullness of God dwelling in Christ 1.19, 2.9) . . . in its cosmic scope and its relation to Christian living . . . and to the church, and love in the community (3.14–21)." Citing my account of Peirce, Ford suggests that his reading of *pleroma* illustrates defining features of pragmatic reading. For example, his reading recognizes *pleroma* as an irremediably *vague sign*, which, "by the logic of pragmatism . . . 'reserves for some other sign or experience the function of completing [its] determination.'"[14] From this perspective, earlier supersessionist readings were overly precise, privileged as if they captured, once and for all, the one clear meaning Scripture has intended, rather than displaying meanings appropriate to the faiths of certain previous Christian communities but not necessarily to other Christian communities in the past, present, and future. Complementing a pragmatic approach to SR, Ford challenges presumptions that there is only one natural language meaning or equivalent to *pleroma* and that meaning is determined independently of the faithful community that is reading. He offers his revised meaning not as an eisegesis but as a recovery of the plain sense *for* the reparative context of reading that he identifies and that he now reports to the SR community.[15]

14. "Consequences of Critical Common-Sensism" (1905), CP 5.505.
15. For a reading of Ephesians that takes these verses as its hermeneutical key, see Ford, "Communicating God's Abundance." Readers may appreciate this excerpt:

> "I pray that you may have the power to comprehend, with all the saints, what is the breadth and length and height and depth, and to know the love of Christ that surpasses knowledge, so that you may be filled with all the fullness of God. . . ." (Eph 3:18–20).

II. INSIDE SCRIPTURAL REASONING AND TEXTUAL REASONING

In its broadest meaning, SR includes two sub-practices: study-across-difference within a single scriptural tradition and study across the borders of different scriptural traditions. We publicly associate SR with the latter practice, which we might label "SR per se" or that which is typified in formational SR. But the former, which we label "Textual Reasoning" (or TR), also makes an irreplaceable contribution to the overall practice of SR. My main goal in this section is to introduce some of the primary similarities and differences between TR and SR (*per se*) and, thereby, to invite readers to begin to formulate their own opinions about what is really going on in each of these and in SR as a whole.

The Development of TR and SR: Through the 1990s and early 2000s, we (founding members of the Society for Scriptural Reasoning) applied the name *"Textual Reasoning"* to the kind of scriptural study we performed within the boundaries of any particular religious denomination, and we applied the name *"Scriptural Reasoning"* to our study of several scriptural traditions at the same time. We also used these terms, equivocally, to refer to several variations of each practice.

TR referred prototypically to the circles of strictly Muslim or Jewish or Christian textual study that many of us practiced before we began SR and which we continued to practice while we were also forming circles of SR study. We adopted the label *"textual"* reasoning, because each circle tended to examine Scripture by way of traditional and modern *texts* of commentary

---

God is the most important consideration of all in relation to *pleroma*. This prayer acknowledges that; it denies that Christians or others have an overview of the meaning of *pleroma*; and in Ochs's terms the text is "an ultimately vague sign of the God whose activities correct it and clarify its meaning" (Ochs, *Peirce*, 287). Ochs notes that, "By the logic of pragmatism, a vague sign 'reserves for some other sign or experience the function of completing [its] determination' (5.505)." Therefore, if God is the object of an ultimately vague sign, then whatever defines this sign would also be vague, and only God would complete the determination of the sign of God." The meaning of "fullness" has to take into account the infinite dynamic abundance of a God of love, fulfilling prayers in ways we could never have imagined. But since these dynamics can, as those centuries demonstrate, also go so terribly wrong, it is salutary to try to learn disciplines of reading which encourage facing up to the burdens, failings, errors, sufferings, and remediable or irremediable vaguenesses occasioned by interpretations of scripture. One of the great strengths of Ochs's approach is that it encourages a tradition to find within itself the resources for its own correction and redefinition and also to "believe that, through the mediation of particular community members, communities of scriptural reading may themselves enter into dialogues that strengthen each community's practices of reading by complementing and clarifying them" (Ochs, *Peirce*, 314). The attempt to fulfill this double programme is at the heart of the Society for Scriptural Reasoning.

on the Scripture, rather than studying Scripture by itself alone. We also applied the term TR, secondarily, to our efforts to devote some time to Muslim or Jewish or Christian TR during our week-long SR conferences. Sometimes we would separate into three separate groups to refresh our separate ways of practicing TR. Sometimes we would invite scholars of the other two religions to join a session devoted to a single tradition of TR. Finally, we observed that many interfaith groups favored a method of study we labeled "parallel TR": inviting representatives of one tradition at a time to introduce its Scripture to the other. In this approach, participants listen politely to one another's teachings about Scripture, asking questions without stepping over the borders of someone else's text tradition.

SR referred prototypically to formational SR, our best method for introducing participants to an interpersonal approach to study, where "reasoning" names a group activity rather than the province, alone, of the individual mind. We also applied the term SR, secondarily, to analogous forms of dialogic or relational study or inquiry. For example, some biblical scholars applied the term SR to their new, dialogic and intertextual studies of the Bible; some historians of religion applied the term to their study of "dialogic encounters" between two religions (for example, missionary Catholicism and Chinese Confucianism); and some philosophers applied the term to the way they reason philosophically out of scriptural sources.

TR vs. Traditional Methods of Scriptural Study: Circles of TR differ from traditional circles of religious study. Both recognize that, when examined independently of a tradition of commentaries, a scriptural text (even a word or verse) may signify more than one possible meaning, usually several: that is, the texts may be *polysemic* or *multivalent* ("many-valued"). (Here, I employ the term *meaning* in a very general way, to include "significance," "sense," "reference," *and* "illocution" or "performative significance.") Traditional chains of commentary seek to reduce this broad range of possible meanings to very few, even to only one authorized meaning. Circles of TR—which welcome members of many denominations—try to avoid this kind of reduction, at least until participants have devoted significant time to discussing and debating a broad range of traditional interpretations. Even then, textual reasoners tend to argue that a given text bears a singular meaning only for a given context of interpretation.

It is difficult to nurture dialogue across the borders of different traditions of scriptural commentary. This is because each circle of traditional study tends to generate singular (or monovalent) readings of the scriptural commentaries, leaving little room for lively dialogue with other traditions of scriptural study. Scholars from one tradition might introduce their readings and interpretations to the other scholars, but they are rarely prepared to invite these others to share in their process of study itself. TR introduces difference into traditional patterns of study. Because they share a single canon of scripture, participants in TR are stimulated to seek a common understanding of Scripture. At the same time, because they belong to different sub-traditions of scriptural study, they are also stimulated to defend conflicting understandings. *Unlike traditional circles of study, TR is designed to push its individual participants to pursue contradictory goals and, thereby, to experience either frustration or a desire to change the conditions of study.* The hope of TR is that, in the pursuit of change, many participants will stumble upon the pursuit of dialogue across difference as a new way to conduct ancient rituals of learning. *TR offers an environment where participants may, against their expectations, fall into patterns of simultaneously reasoning freely (individually) and cooperatively (interpersonally) and in ways that affirm each other's different sub-traditions. As we will see, this "fall" is the source of both TR and SR's capacity to introduce something otherwise unachievable within the hermeneutical and epistemological frameworks of the modern university: a mode of reasoning that simultaneously serves the interests of several different scriptural traditions and of the contemporary university.* The individual participant in TR or SR falls into this mode of reasoning the way one might fall asleep or "fall" into a dance step or a musical rhythm. Unlike reasonings that are limited to an individual's neural system, this mode of reasoning belongs, at once, to a circle of reasoners and to the dimensions of their various traditions of belief and knowledge that are active during some session of study. Each participant's reasoning is constrained by the interests, rules, and relationships that characterize such a circle of study, but no more or less than an individual is constrained by the settings and contexts of any other tradition- or discipline-specific project of reasoning.

Distinctive Features of TR as a Mode of Interpreting Scriptural Sources

An initial hermeneutical rule of TR: a scriptural text displays its truth-values only *to* some community of readers or hearers. I do not mean that there is only one such community of readers (!), but that each historically specific community must discern anew what Scripture signifies.

A second hermeneutical rule of TR: I find it most helpful to identify this rule through terms introduced by Judaism's rabbinic sages: The *plain sense of scripture* [in Hebrew, the *peshat*] *displays the will of the Absolute but displays it indeterminately:* in other words, no human readers can discern, once and for all, what truth-values are signified by the words of Scripture.

Scripture displays its determinate meanings only by way of its interpretation and performance within some historically specific community of readers. These interpretive meanings [in Hebrew, the *derash*] have truth-values, but only for that time and place. Scripture must be examined and interpreted again to identify its determinate meaning for any other or subsequent time and place.

Interpretive meanings are usually examined by the academic sciences of reception history, ethnography (identifying cultural contexts of reading), ritual and poetic theory, and pragmatics (sciences of performed meaning, as recommended by Austin, Wittgenstein, Peirce, and others). *They are examined, as well, by all the traditional commentaries* (including legal interpretation, ethics, homiletics, theology).

TR seeks to transform contradictory interpretive tendencies into contrary interpretive tendencies. As a project in both peacemaking and textual understanding within any single Abrahamic religion, TR provides a way to transform conflict into constructive dialogue across difference. TR begins by recognizing non-constructive differences within a single tradition of study. In the 1980s, for example, founders of the Society for Jewish Textual Reasoning observed irresolvable competition among various sub-disciplines of Jewish Studies: text-historical vs. literary vs. philosophic studies, and all the academic studies vs. traditional or synagogue-based study. We labeled this a "competition among logical contradictories," and we designed TR as a way to preserve competitive differences while "transforming contradictories into contraries." By "contradictory," we meant a difference that is irresolvable because it assumes a "zero-sum (either/or) game." If, for example, text-historical and philosophic approaches are contradictory, then to affirm (undertake and fund) one approach is to deny the other one. Our goal was to provide an environment for transforming "either/or" differences of method into differences that often sharpened and deepened an overall inquiry. We concluded that the way to achieve this is *not* to ask each individual scholar to learn many differences (this approach reduces excellence and overemphasizes the study of broad generalities), but to supplement the university's individualized model of scholarship with an additional, teamwork model. While maintaining our individualized research, we would also join circles of TR study, in which members of the various disciplines would study together (often adding traditional rabbinic scholars as well). Before each meeting we would all do preparatory studies in a given set of scriptural texts plus rabbinic and medieval commentaries. Before our meetings, we shared brief essays on these texts, each of us writing from the perspective of our primary discipline. We then devoted our meetings entirely to group study of the scriptural and commentarial texts. We each spoke freely from out of our own intellectual perspectives, but we also listened with interest to all the other perspectives. We allowed heated argument as well as more gentle discussion, as we gradually learned new habits for achieving what previously seemed impossible: circles of study that allowed each individual person and discipline full self-expression while we also formed new bonds of interpersonal and interdisciplinary inquiry.

After a few years of this practice, we observed that, while we each maintained our different disciplines of study, we also practiced our disciplines in a somewhat new way. I began to write Jewish philosophy, for example, in a way that also prompted my readers to do supplementary work in historical and literary studies. I did not try to perform all these studies myself, but I began to consult regularly with scholars of history and literature when I plotted out my philosophic projects. In logical terms, my philosophic discipline differed from their disciplines, but not in contradictory ways.[16]

Characteristics of TR that Re-Appear in SR: During our first decade of work in the Society for Scriptural Reasoning (SSR), we observed that successful participants pursued two goals simultaneously during both TR and SR study: (a) they participated in our sessions for the joy of "study for its own sake," without worrying about the ultimate truth-or-falsity of participants' individual comments; (b) they articulated and tested their own truth-claims about individual words and verses of Scripture, but they did not worry if others interpreted those texts differently. We also observed that successful participants displayed virtues that were at times like and at times unlike the virtues most valued in the university and in traditional circles of study:

- TR and SR participants sought to understand the plain sense of each scriptural text as illumined by all available resources: from scientific studies of history and language to traditional commentaries to new hypotheses raised within the TR or SR study circle. They were prepared to discover that there might be only one convincing meaning of a given text or that the evidence pointed to a range of possible meanings. They were eager, moreover, to examine several dimensions of "meaning," both semantic and performative. They sought to extend their own understandings of the texts and to enjoy hearing the varieties of opinions and insights brought by the study circle.

---

16. They differ as "contraries" (where $\sim (a \vee \sim a)$) or different members of a universe of many members $(a, b, c \ldots n)$, rather than "contradictories" or competing members of a universe that allows only one or the other $(a \vee \sim a)$.

- They valued the results of intense individual thought and of group dialogue.
- They studied with scholarly discipline and with a deep sense of humor: pursuing laughter as well as insight, celebrating the fruits of individual reflection while also acknowledging the finitude of each person's and each tradition's truth claims. They recognized that finitude is not a liability but a mark of all worldly truths. Just as the biblical prophet declares to God *hineni*, "Here I am," so too each verse of Scripture may declare to each reader at a given moment: "Here I am. This is my meaning here and now. This meaning is how I truly show myself to you at this moment. This truth is a mark of my intimate relationship with you here and now. But it is therefore also a reminder that I may, in another moment, appear to show myself differently to you or to another. This is how I retain my intimacy and thus my truth at each moment that I am carefully read."

The primary difference between SR and TR is that, in SR, there is plain sense and interpretive meaning, but no shared "truths." As discussed earlier, SR study focuses on scriptural texts, alone, without the commentarial texts that tend to determine the conditions of truth and falsity within each tradition of religious belief and practice. As in TR, SR study begins with discussion of the plain sense of a scriptural text. Participants then voice problematic or challenging aspects of the plain sense. These challenges stimulate efforts to reread or reinterpret the plain sense and, thereby, to propose interpretive meanings that might respond to what some of the disciplines found problematic in the plain sense. The indeterminacy of the plain sense is one source of the power of SR, enabling participants from one tradition to comment, without offense, on the sacred sources of another tradition. One can contradict (and thus "offend") a determinate meaning, which must be either A or not-A, but one cannot contradict a meaning that is not yet either one or the other. Another source of the power of SR is the freedom of each individual participant to propose ways of determining the meaning of any given text, even if these proposals serve the religious convictions of only that one participant. Unlike the plain sense, which participants tend to share, such proposals display the unique properties of an individual interpretation: one that displays the determinate meaning (a) of the plain sense (b) *for* a single interpreter (c). If another interpreter (d) proposes a different meaning (e), this proposal would not contradict the first one, but simply differ from it.[17]

17. In semiotic terms, the two proposals may be diagrammed as abc and ade: logical contraries but not contradictories. This distinction is central to the success of SR in inviting non-conflictual discussion and disagreement across difference.

According to the theory of SR, contradiction generates conflict across the borders of different traditions; mere difference ("contrariety") provides the occasion for lively but peaceful discussion and debate. This peace comes with one cost: unlike TR study, SR study is not about truth or falsity. For SR, truth or falsity is a characteristic only of determinate claims about the interpretive/performative meaning of Scripture, and such claims are available only within traditional circles of scriptural study or, in a moderated sense, within tradition-specific circles of TR. The Bible identifies a second species of "truth" that *can* apply to SR study. This is truth as *emet*, a Hebrew term derived from the root *amn*, connoting "faithfulness." SR is deeply concerned with this species of truth: the faithfulness that joins each SR reader to the plain sense of Scripture and that, we hope, joins each SR scholar to every other.

Distinctive Features of SR as a Mode of Interpreting Scriptural Sources

An initial hermeneutical rule of SR: SR is not a place where scriptural texts display their indigenous truth-values as they would be displayed, in TR, to a particular community devoted to a particular scriptural canon as rule of life. During a formal session of SR, the rule of SR is to suspend one's customary search for the true meaning of the scriptural texts, whether those of one's own tradition or of another's. The rule of SR is, instead, to search after the really possible meanings of each text and, where appropriate, each verse, each phrase, each set of texts. From a historical perspective, the set of really possible meanings includes all those proposed within the reception history of any text (including traditional, legal, academic commentaries, and so on). From a semantic and logical perspective, this set includes any meaning that is permitted by the letters, words, and grammar of a text. Each SR group sets its own goals and guidelines and displays its own tolerance for how much to include or exclude from the set. Our only general counsel is not to exclude too much (for example, by including only what a given tradition appears to favor or what academic scholarship appears to tolerate) and not to include too much (for example, by setting too low a threshold for what the text might permit). The scriptural texts cannot fully provide guidelines for the practice of SR, since there is no reason to assume these texts were canonized with the expectation that members of other canonical communities would join in the reading, let alone join in for the sake of something like SR. SR is something unimagined by the texts but pursued, nonetheless, within their individual tolerances.

A second hermeneutical rule of SR: Around the table of SR study, Scripture is read for its own sake but also for a set of purposes specific to each SR gathering. While we do not prescribe what these purposes must be, I have over the years observed that SR groups tend to read best when they read for reasons like these: for the joy of reading Scripture; out of a passion to discover everything that may be immanent in the various texts of Scripture; for the sake of friendship with fellow readers; to listen "over the borders" of the scriptural canons (to hear what these related but different canons have to say); to seek ways of repairing today's troubled relations among the scriptural communities; to hear God's word more fully (which may include hearing it speak in unexpected ways). I have also observed that SR groups do not read well when they are overly focused on only one or two of these purposes. If, for example, they read only for "the sake of peace" or only "for friendship," they may fail to read carefully enough to allow Scripture to set its own terms for peace and for friendship; if they read only to expand and explore the limits of what scriptural words and verses may mean, they may fail to hear its performative meanings (or hear when it commands, teaches wisdom, or sets limits rather than only loosening them).

Reading on behalf of the various disciplines of the academy. Various academic sciences of literature and text-historical reading enrich the work of SR as well as TR.[18] They may, however, play a somewhat greater role in TR, where they provide resources for balancing the authoritative voices of sub-traditions of reading, whenever these traditions threaten to de-legitimate other sub-traditions. Within SR, ironically, the academic sciences may at times receive more from the SR study fellowship than they give. For one, one may at times hear a greater variety of interpretive voices around the SR study table than one hears around the table of academic study. In this case, SR study may expand the fields of what count as "data" and what count as "legitimate sources of explanatory hypotheses" for some disciplines of contemporary academic study. For two, members of some SR study groups may, over time, find themselves engaging in patterns of reasoning that they have not previously encountered in their traditions of study or their disciplines of academic inquiry. In this case, the results of SR challenge the academic disciplines to recognize and examine previously overlooked forms of reasoning.

"Deep reasonings" for peace and for repair. Nicholas Adams characterizes Scriptural Reasoning as a source of both "deep reasonings" and

---

18. See Quash, "Heavenly Semantics." Also see Weiss, "Scriptural Reasoning and the Academy."

"reparative reasonings."[19] The reasonings that appear to arise uniquely out of SR study are, I believe, stimulated uniquely by a "deep" dimension of scriptural literature. Since this is a dimension that, in Charles Peirce's terms, is known "only by its fruits,"[20] I am led to speculate that SR study may at times provide occasions for displaying this fruit. Some contributing factors may be the context of crisis that informs some SR study sessions and also the depth of scriptural reading (when it occurs), the reparative movement of study across deep differences among the scriptural canons, and the capacity of some study groups to remain intensely focused over prolonged stretches of time.[21]

More Detailed Illustrations of the Primary Characteristics of SR and TR

What, in sum, are the characteristics of SR practice? Despite their periodic efforts over thirty years, members of the Society for Scriptural Reasoning (SSR) have not succeeded in capturing a reliable written record of what goes on during an SR study session.[22] It appears that, like a sand painting, the singularity of SR belongs to time-and-space-specific oral events and cannot be accurately preserved or reproduced. Because SR is not an event of conventional language use, its singular character cannot be captured within the language conventions we employ when offering reports or even audio and visual recordings of what took place. Why? The theory I share publicly concerns the relationship between conventional discourse and its frames or transcendental conditions. SR invites participants in apparently incommensurable religious language games and conventions to converse together about different, but in varying ways consanguineal, foundational texts. The activity and its settings generate a variable range of emotive as well as cognitive and religious/valuational responses. Early in the process, participants may display seemingly contradictory expressions of, on the one hand, discomfort, anxiety, and detachment—perhaps about the interreligious and intertextual setting—and, on the other hand, muted excitement about

---

19. Adams, "Reparative Reasoning"; and Adams, "Making Deep Reasonings Public." For related essays, see James, "Pairs"; Rashkover, "Adams, Hegel"; and Harris, "Improving the Quality."

20. Peirce claimed that his pragmatism was "only an application of the sole principle of logic which was recommended by Jesus, 'Ye may know them by their fruits'" [Matt 7:16] and it is very intimately allied with the ideas of the gospel": Peirce, "Search for a Method," (1893) CP 5.402n2.

21. On the ethical implications of SR, see Gibbs, "Reading with Others."

22. The best effort is Higton and Muers, *Text in Play*.

the interpersonal setting and of more micro-displays of warmth about the familiar texts of sacred Scripture set immediately before them. I theorize that these apparently contradictory expressions are symptoms of what appears, within the terms of conventional language use, to be SR's impossible goal: to invite speakers of, say, three conflicting language conventions to converse about their deepest thoughts and beliefs. SR's goal would not be impossible, however, if communication were achieved beyond the limits of those language conventions: not through translation (or through the errant presumption that some general or even universal language convention were in the offing), but through the non-conventional communication that SR may foster. To experience this kind of communication, readers would need to experience several sessions of formational SR study. To remain within the bounds of this book, I offer a second-best option: detailed excerpts from a journal issue devoted to an extended session of SR study. To appreciate the features of SR study, however, one must also appreciate the features of TR study. In the college classroom, I offer training and reflection on TR first, SR second, because SR enacts and responds to the dramatic tension that both binds together and separates readers from different traditions of scriptural study and commentary. To conclude this chapter, I therefore offer detailed illustrations of tradition-based practices of study that are comparable to TR.

Healing Words: The Song of Songs and the Path of Love

"Healing Words" is an issue of *The Journal of Scriptural Reasoning* (JSR) that celebrates a 2002 session of SR Study that took place alongside the Annual Meeting of the American Academy of Religion.[23] Before the SR session, participants studied three reflections that were composed for the occasion. During the session, participants briefly discussed the reflections and then turned to intensive around-the-table SR text study of "Song of Songs" and "Path of Love." The JSR issue includes the three framing essays, overviews of the session, and ten response papers composed after the session. Such excerpts would not enable readers to experience the communicative activity of SR, but they should, nonetheless, offer readers indirect evidence about the leading characteristics of that activity.

---

23. Nelkin et al., "Healing."

Illustration #1: Introducing the Overall Shape of the Study Session.

As noted by Guest Editor Dov Nelkin, the JSR issue "considers the potency and problematics of the language of sexuality and desire as a mode of describing, either directly or by way of metaphor, the encounter with God."[24] The issue juxtaposes three essays that take contrasting approaches to the overall theme. Jewish scholar Alon Goshen-Gottstein and Christian theologian Ellen Davis both address the *Song of Songs* as a canonical text. For Goshen-Gottstein, it is a uniquely problematic text because it acquires scriptural status only through glosses offered by its long chain of interpreters. For Ellen Davis, the *Song* is intrinsically canonical, because it offers a source of repairing ruptured relationships displayed in the antecedent scriptural texts. Muslim scholar Omid Safi is forced to take a different approach, because the Qur'anic canon includes neither a version of the *Song of Songs* nor a parallel. He chooses to examine commentarial texts that "incorporate the lush language of love and sexuality in a manner immediately familiar to interpreters of the Song."[25]

Illustration #2: Reading from Affliction to Healing.

General Editor Willie Young observes a parallel between the reparative reading enacted in both the sources and the interpretive practices of SR participants. The three authors show how their communities of scriptural interpretation read the sacred texts as if the texts may suffer affliction and as if caring readers could help them heal: "In each case, the scripture allows itself to be stretched, or even broken, so that the community can find new life within it. . . . Intertextual reading repairs scripture so as to repair and heal communities. As this pattern emerges, we may begin to see how the brokenness of scripture is not a change in God, but rather leads to a change within us."[26] Young illustrates several features of this pattern of reading, which I label "*hermeneutical healing*":

- *Sensitivity to multiple levels of meaning (polysemy)*
- *Respect for the plain sense of a Scriptural text (or its elementary narrative or assertion). The reader returns to the plain sense after each "deeper" level reading.*

---

24. Nelkin, "Editor's Introduction to the Articles."
25. Safi, "On the 'Path of Love' Towards the Divine: A Journey with Muslim Mystics."
26. Young, "The Song of Songs."

- *Claims that, on deeper levels of reading, scriptural texts address specific afflictions within the reading community.*
- *Hopes that such readings also open pathways toward healing these afflictions.*
- *At the same time, Young illustrates how patterns of hermeneutical healing may also introduce instruments of affliction into scriptural commentary. Seeking values that may heal communal affliction, a reader could, knowingly or unknowingly, affirm values that prove to be sources of suffering for others.* On Young's reading, Bernard of Clairvaux's allegorical commentary on of the *Song of Songs* illustrates features of this phenomenon:
- *Multiple levels of meaning; responding to afflictions in the reader's community:* "Bernard's willingness to shift between levels of meaning, identifying his audience with various figures in the Song, resembles Davis's multiple interpretations of the harmony or unity signified by the Song. . . . It can be read in multiple ways that respond to and repair issues and divisions in the community."[27]
- *Readings as potential sources of affliction:* "As Davis suggests . . ., the one thing the Song doesn't represent for Bernard is precisely what it says—human, erotic love. The ongoing polemic in his writings between the "fleshly" and spiritual interpretations must have been quite useful in disciplining a monastic community, but given its association with anti-Jewish polemics, its value in the context of Scriptural Reasoning is dubious. This is one of the points at which I find myself challenged and troubled by his work, in spite of its wondrous beauty."[28]

Young introduces Franz Rosenzweig's reading of *Song of Songs* as a prototype for hermeneutical healing. Rosenzweig shows how the Song "epitomizes an I-Thou relation, rather than an objective, third-person description. Lyricism, as a self-sacrifice to the moment, cannot simply be recorded, but is only manifest from inside the event—in this case, the event of love, in which the speakers emerge from concealment toward one another."[29] For Young, the SR essays illustrate two of the ways in which scriptural commentaries may seek to serve as agents for such love: *by integrating fragments into new wholes, and by uncovering where, in the human heart, God's attributes of love can be retrieved:*

27. Young, "The Song of Songs."
28. Young, "The Song of Songs."
29. Paraphrasing Rosenzweig, *Star*, 194.

- *Integrating fragments into new wholes:* For Davis, "the Song itself is largely composed from fragments from other books in scripture."[30] For Goshen-Gottstein, rabbinic commentaries imitate the Song's integrative performance by collecting disparate fragments from the Song and reintegrating them in ways that display otherwise inevident instructions for healing. This process of hermeneutical healing trains the rabbis' readers to attend to human suffering the way the rabbis' commentaries attend to afflictions in the Scriptural text.

- *Uncovering divine attributes of love:* Safi's reading of "Divine Love" discloses an experiential/conceptual rather than hermeneutical instrument for instruction in divine healing. In Sufi discourse, "God takes on a range of humanizing attributes. . ., including characteristics most often associated with human love. As God takes on these attributes, the beloved is brought more intimately into God's presence. . . . The path of love is iconographic; in that it lets us see through our words to the living God whom they represent."[31]

Illustration #3: Study across Difference, Study that Affirms Difference.

Neither the study session nor the journal issue sought to unify different readings of the same texts, different theologies, different hermeneutical preferences, different ways of understanding affliction and healing. In many ways, SR *was* the co-presence of these differences through discussion and writings, and SR was the performance through which presence-through-difference retained its edge and dynamism. In other words, difference is not a source of affliction for SR; the co-presence of difference is SR's source of joy. In Young's words, "Editing this issue of the *Journal of Scriptural Reasoning* has been a joy, as the issue has borne far greater fruit than any of us could have anticipated at the outset. Confronted with the bounty of love, from the *Song of Songs* and the Sufi *Path of Love*, I feel like John Cusack's playwright character in *Bullets Over Broadway*—with much to say, yet also hearing the words, 'Don't speak! Don't speak!' Rather, I will let love speak for itself, as the authors and respondents think with their scriptures and traditions, and with one another."[32]

30. Davis, "Reading the Song Iconographically," in "Healing."
31. Paraphrased by Young, "The Song of Songs."
32. Young, "The Hope-Fulness of Scriptural Reasoning," in "Healing."

A More Detailed Illustration of the Primary Characteristics of TR

As noted earlier in this chapter, SR emerged historically out of TR, and, to understand SR's practice of inter-canonical study, one should first experience and reflect on prototypical features of TR's tradition-specific study practices. Having previously introduced a series of these features above, (app. 38–41), I conclude with a more detailed illustration, drawn from a single type of TR-like study: classical rabbinic midrash, as illustrated in the fourth-century midrash collection *Sifre Devarim* (*Sifre Deuteronomy*) and as introduced by a single contemporary rabbinic scholar, Steven Fraade. The following account should help readers appreciate the primary directions of TR study, even if the features of classic rabbinic commentary are not identical to the features of other traditions of TR study.

Fraade offers a helpful overview of traditional scriptural commentary:

> Ancient scriptural commentaries—even as they closely scrutinize the particles of the text to which they attend—are always about the text as a *whole*. By this I mean that they not only seek the text to be held in high regard by its interpretive community, but for the interpretive community to regard *itself* in relation to that text as mediated by its commentary. . . . Such a commentary is [therefore] not simply a series of declarative assertions about the meaning of words in the text but an attempt to *effect* a relationship between that text overall and those for whom it is 'scripture', predicated on the assumption not only that the text needs and deserves to be interpreted, but that the community for whom it needs to be interpreted itself needs to be engaged in the activity of interpretation to understand itself and *transform* itself into what it ought to be. Ancient scriptural commentaries are not simply constative conduits of meaning.[33]

In sum, Fraade characterizes ancient scriptural commentaries as (a) *scriptural texts* that engage their (b) *interpreter* (or interpretive community) in (c) a *relationship* mediated by scriptural commentary. Through this relationship, the interpretive community is "transformed into what it ought to be." Drawing on Mikhail Bakhtin's notion of the "dialogic work of literature," Fraade refers to the scriptural commentary's "double-dialogue," as it shuttles

---

33. Fraade, *From Tradition*, 13–14. As sources of his notion of double-dialogue, Fraade cites, among others, McGann, *Social Values*, 19–31; and Fish, *Doing What Comes Naturally*, 57–67; with antecedent sources in John Searle, J. L. Austin, and Mikhail Bakhtin.

back and forth between "the text that it interprets and the society of 'readers' for whom and with whom it interprets."³⁴

By way of illustration, here is an excerpt from *Sifre Deuteronomy*, followed by Fraade's commentary on prototypical features of the Sifre's "double-dialogue." *Sifre* is commenting on Deuteronomy 32:7, from the song Moses delivered before his death:

> Remember the days of old (*olam*)
>
> Consider the years of each and every generation;
>
> Ask your father and he will inform you,
>   Your elders and they will tell you.

"The Sifre divides the verse in order to explicate its parts and does so twice."³⁵ Here are excerpts from the first set:

> [A] "Remember the days of old": [God said to them:] Take heed of what I did to the earliest generations: what I did to the people of the generation of the Flood, and what I did to the people of the generation of the Dispersion [the Tower of Babel], and what I did to the people of Sodom.
>
> [B] "Consider the years of each and every generation": You can find no generation without people like those of the generation of the Flood, and you can find no Generation without people like those of the generation of the Dispersion and like those of Sodom, but each and every individual is judged according to his deeds.
>
> [C] "Ask your father and he will inform you": These are the prophets as it says, "When Elisha beheld it, he cried out [to Elijah], 'Father, father' " (2 Kgs. 2:12).
>
> [D] "Your elders and they will tell you": These are the elders, as it is said, "Gather for Me seventy men of the elders of Israel" (Num. 11:16).

And here are primary features of the *Sifre's* practice of text interpretation, which I have excerpted from Fraade's account and re-labeled within my own vocabulary:

1. *Commentaries are dialogic-and-vague ("doubly dialogic" in Fraade's terms).* For Fraade, "commentary" refers to "a systematic series of explanations or interpretations" (from *Webster's*). The commentary atomizes an extended "base-text" (such as Deut 32:7 in its plain sense)

---

34. Fraade, *From Tradition*, 13–14.
35. Fraade, *From Tradition*, 75.

into successive subunits, attaching interpretive comments to each sub-unit.[36] Clearly distinguishing commentary from each sub-unit of base-text, the *Sifre* returns, "sooner or later," to add new comments on the same sub-unit. Fraade applies the term *dialogue* to this process of reading and return, explaining that he employs the term "somewhat fictively, as we do not simply have in commentary two voices equally present and responsive to one another. Rather I intend the term to denote the dynamic, interrelational ways in which commentary creates and communicates meaning. Such meaning is not simply inherent in the text being interpreted and brought to the surface by the commentary, nor is it simply produced by the commentary and conveyed . . . to its readers, nor is it simply produced by their reading of the commentary. Rather, it is to be found in all three, and especially in the . . . socially situated discursive universe that the commentary progressively constructs by inter-responsively drawing together and engaging the polyphonic world of Scripture with that of its students."[37]

2. *Commentaries that are dialogic-and-vague are interactive and (to varying degrees) relationally binding.* For Fraade, "interactive" commentaries display the mutual influences of both textual and interpretive contexts of signification. Neither text nor interpretation wholly determines meaning; each influences the other. Fraade explains that the plurality of [*Sifre*'s] students advance [the commentary's] unfinished work by filling-out, but never finally, the anonymous narrative voice which is only partially present in the text itself... As [they]... work through the commentary, the commentary works through them.[38] These students are therefore *bound* to Scripture as unending source of new information about itself in relation to them.

3. *Commentaries that are dialogic-and-vague engage Scripture as vague but made definite through the time and relational context of interpretation. Scripture's meaning therefore varies with respect to variations in context.* To say that Scripture's words and verses are vague is to say that their meanings are not disclosed through any binary relation (such as of "sign to object") and that they may be disclosed through triadic relations that identify the specific time, context, or mode of interpretive relation through which specific meanings appear. Even with respect to a given context, relations between text and meaning are not formulaic; the interpretive relation between Scripture and commentator must be

36. Fraade, *From Tradition*, 1–2.
37. Fraade, *From Tradition*, 14.
38. Fraade, *From Tradition*, 19.

renewed on each occasion of interpretation. Examining sub-units C and D of the commentary on Deuteronomy 32:7, Fraade explains that:

> In the *Sifre*, as in other rabbinic collections, the rabbinic sages view themselves as the extension of [the] biblical class of lay elders, especially in their appointment to positions of judicial and administrative responsibility over the larger Jewish community. The commentary's juxtaposition of "prophets" and "elders" may also serve subtly to associate the two. . . . Thus, according to the rabbinic "chain of tradition," Joshua transmitted the Torah to the elders, who passed it on to the prophets, who . . . passed it on to the proto-rabbinic elders of Second Temple times.[39]

According to this reading, the sign "elders" displays its meaning in the context of the prophets' work, then again in the context of the work of the Second Temple elders, then again in the context of the rabbinic sages' commentary, then again, we may assume, in their students' commentary, and so on.

4. *Commentaries that are dialogic-and-vague identify Scripture as multivocal/polysemic.* Multivocal or *polysemic* means "having more than one probable meaning." In a weaker sense, this is a direct implication of the fact that meaning varies with respect to context. In a stronger sense, this means that, even with respect to a given context, one cannot discount the possibility that a text may allow more than one meaning. As a vivid illustration, Fraade lists *Sifre's* thirteen different readings of the initial words of Deuteronomy 32.1. In a more recent essay, he observes "that the most elementary reader of early rabbinic midrash would recognize that on virtually every 'page' of the tannaitic midrashim . . . we find multiple interpretations of single scriptural words or phrases."[40]

5. *Commentaries that are dialogic-and-vague tend to display self-reference.* Acknowledging their status *as* commentary, such commentaries signal that their words are not literal windows to divine intention or to *the* meaning of Scripture. We may thereby draw a distinction between commentaries whose contexts of meaning (or "interpretants")[41] *we analysts* may identify even if the commentators do not and commentaries whose self-reference does this work for us. In the former case, a commentary may appear *clear*, displaying a binary relation between

---

39. Fraade, *From Tradition*, 70.

40. Fraade, "Response," 342. Fraade refers to his "treatment of *Sifre Devarim Ha' azinu*, pis. 306, to Deuteronomy 32:1 (ed. Finkelstein, *Sifre*, 308–35), 123–62.

41. See below, p. 68.

commentary and Scriptural object. In the latter case, a commentary signifies its vagueness and some manner of its context-specificity. Fraade comments that the *Sifre* "portrays the broader class of rabbinic authors *as* among the *objects* of its commentary— as, for example, anti-types of the biblical 'elders'—so that subsequent readers will be bound to re-interpret these objects as they re-read the scriptural base-texts of Sifre's commentary."[42] Sifre's dialogic-and-vague commentaries are ribbed by layers of reflection, including and extending beyond self-reference.

In sum, I have devoted Chapter 2 to reviewing the primary hermeneutical activity that characterizes SR. This is a movement "from deep to deep": moving from challenges or "problems" in the plain sense of each scriptural text to the interpretive and reparative reasonings that draw each SR study group into a fellowship of reasoning across canonical borders. I have devoted most of this chapter to examining the reparative purposes of SR and the different ways that SR is performed in its two sub-projects of Textual Reasoning and of Scriptural Reasoning *per se*. In chapter 3, I turn to more philosophic questions: From the perspectives of academe, what species of reasoning are these? And how did SR come to integrate scriptural study and philosophic-like reasoning?

---

42. Fraade, "Response," 342.

CHAPTER 3

Pragmatic Reasoning in SR
A Technical Chapter on SR's Semiotic Roots and Hermeneutic Consequences

IN SR AT ITS best and most intense, souls encounter one another more from the inside out than the outside in. In other words, the encounter is not merely dialogue among people who sit beside one another. Through dialogue or other means of communication, the encounter is also among deeper—that is, rarely visible—dimensions of human lives. Depending on the vocabulary you use, you might refer to this dimension as "the heart," "the soul," "the source of one's deepest tears, or hopes, or joy, or love"; or following Emmanuel Levinas, you might refer to a place of utter singularity, where the I is face to face with the wholly singular other, a place of response that stretches back to the immemorial past; or perhaps you identify this as the place where one stands as mere creature before the creator God. SR at its best and most intense opens relationship among places of this kind, heart to heart, deep to deep. I am speaking, however, only within the terms of my analysis of the possible consequences of SR when it is pursued by certain kinds of people over extended periods of time. I do not mean that teachers and students of SR should begin their study with any expectations of this kind, or even thinking in these terms, lest their self-consciousness about such claims inhibit any levels of successful SR practice. Even at advanced stages of study, what I am claiming does not describe what individual participants actually think and speak about during their hours of shared study. As I use the term, the *heart* is not an element of anyone's individual consciousness; it makes its appearance only by way of its effects, which means only by way of someone's interpretation of those effects. So why do I bother to share this interpretation with you? Because I would not have continued to work on SR these past twenty-five years if I did not believe that SR had the potential to engage human beings at this depth. And why not? Because I believe the interreligious and inter-ethnic violence of our age is a symptom of the inadequacy of what I will label "positivist" efforts to mend human relations on "the surface" alone.

Positivist efforts to mend human relations are founded on the belief, for example, that matters of the heart or soul are not matters about which we can make publicly verifiable diagnoses of societal maladies and launch publicly verifiable projects of societal repair. Such efforts designate a limited range of phenomena as sources of actionable data: information from which we can launch publicly verifiable diagnoses of societal maladies and, then, plan and execute publicly testable projects of societal repair. Along with issues of nutrition, health, economics, and social-psychological well-being, these societal maladies include international, interreligious, and interethnic violence. Over the past four decades, we have enough evidence that positivist methods of Western diplomacy have failed to diagnose and repair most forms of specifically interreligious violence, along with many related forms of intergroup and interethnic conflict. SR has promise because, against the mainstream models of diplomacy and negotiation in the West, SR calls for stakeholders to bring their heartfelt convictions to the table, along with the concerns of interest to the positivists (food, land, and so on). Here, "heartfelt convictions" refer to elemental beliefs, as displayed in traditional or sacred discourses and literatures. But how can antagonists voice such beliefs to one another across the table? One defining claim of SR is that different identities are not the source of conflict but, in fact, preferred sources for repairing conflict.

SR's potential contribution to peacebuilding complements its contribution to the academic study of Scripture, comparative Scriptures, and comparative religion. In each case, the contribution is hermeneutical: opening deeper levels of study and of relationship through the work of scriptural text interpretation, with heightened attention to the semantic range ("semantics") and performative force ("pragmatics") of scriptural words and verses, to multiple levels of reading, and to the ways these levels provide openings to cooperative dialogue across the borders of canons and identities. In this chapter, I introduce some of the primary patterns of reasoning displayed in these hermeneutical activities: an illustrative sample from out of my own perspective as a Jewish philosopher within the circle of SR scholars. I begin with a lexicon of the analytic terms I use to describe these patterns of reasoning.

Individuality: We speak, write, read as individuals: not in the philosophic sense of some "fully determined," or "utterly unique" beings, but in the everyday sense of speakers, writers, readers of flesh and blood, situated somewhere, burdened and blessed by certain histories and by certain networks of relationship. We might call this, metaphorically, an Aristotelian rule of thumb: yes, there are forms (*eide*) or somewhat generalizable concepts and patterns, but we grasp and share them only as embodied in or across individuals.[1]

Ecology: Individuals do not live or act in isolation but inhabit ecosystems, complex and variously integrated contexts of activity.[2] When highly integrated, these contexts enable individuals to participate in dynamic ecosystems and networks. When minimally integrated, these contexts may appear haphazard and unpredictable, environments where individuals participate in few relationships, exposed to chance encounters, some of them dangerous.

Intelligence: Individuals are characterized by intelligence, which refers to capacities bearing such names as sensation, memory, repetition, perception, conceptualization, negation, and reasoning. I will briefly define each of these terms, not to introduce some philosophic scheme, but to enable author and readers to share a reasonably clear vocabulary for talking about the place of thinking and reasoning in Scriptural Reasoning. Each of the following definitions refers to some elemental capacity of individuals to do something specific. *Sensation*: to influence or be influenced by other individuals, where "to influence" means "potentially effecting changes in." As I define it, sensation does not include awareness, which means that an individual's judgments about such influences are all indirect. *Perception*: to become aware of the influences of other individuals. This means that individuals do not see what influences them as if through a clear window; instead, they perceive what they may have sensed, and their perceptions are tested over time. This does not imply that individuals lack reliable knowledge of influences, but that such knowledge is a matter of probability or degree of reliability, rather than of seeing or not seeing. *Concepts* name and record the effects of sensations, perceptions, and other concepts. *To record a concept* is to do something innovative: to think of a name, image, or mark and consider it a stand-in for these effects. By *stand-in*, I mean a sign of something else, so that, by seeing the consequences of manipulating this sign, one acquires a hypothesis about something else: what might result, for

---

1. More technically put, concepts name sets of sensations or also sets of sets.

2. Ford applies the term relational ecology to characterize networks of relations nurtured by SR: relations among ideas, institutions, and practices as well as people.

example, if one engages this something in a comparable way. *Memory*: to associate a single name or image with a set that one is not now in the act of recording. *Repetition*: to remember a perception or concept and then record it. In this sense, repetition is a non-innovative way of recording perceptions and concepts. *Negation*: to dis-associate a perception or concept from some set that is currently associated with it. *Thinking*: to attempt to influence, or effect a change in, any concept or set of concepts. *Ways of thinking*: records that enable one to remember the effects of some individual's thinking. Such effects are typically recorded as complex sets of concepts, which sets may be identified with ways of thinking.

Individuals and Groups: Individuals may refer to flesh-and-blood individuals or to groups or societies or systems that tend to individuality. As they tend toward individuality, such systems also display collective activities of intelligence, such as sensation, perception, memory, thinking, and reasoning. I realize that readers may consider it odd to refer to *group thinking*. But I consider SR to be a kind of group thinking, so I face the task of explaining this notion without alienating most readers. If your habit is to apply the notion of thinking/reasoning only to flesh-and-blood individuals, then please consider everything I am about to say as metaphoric. When I refer to group thinking, please consider this a metaphor for "a group activity that tends over time to influence the way that a majority of group members tends to think." I will then say that, for flesh-and-blood individuals, acts of thinking are recorded in (or in relation to) consciousness. For groups, we may say that acts of thinking are recorded in language.

Language: Language is the vehicle of communication and, thereby, of relation among members of a group. A group is characterized by its language. *Language use* or *speech* or *writing* is a means through which different members of a group, or different groups, influence each other. To hear or read speech or writing is to sense or perceive this influence. *Words* or *signs* are elemental units of speech or writing. *Meaning* refers to how the influences of such units are perceived. *Interpretation* is the means through which those who read or hear perceive different types and levels of meaning. They may, for example, distinguish *intended meaning* from *received meaning* and distinguish many levels of each (literal, allegorical, metaphoric, spiritual, and so on). They may also identify *performative meanings*—meanings that direct readers and listeners to *do* something—and distinguish many kinds, from physical actions to contemplative and interpretive behaviors, and many modalities, from subtle hints to interrogatives to commands.

As a rule, I will attribute language-specific meanings and responses to *group behavior*, including the behavior of group members, and I will attribute cognition-specific meanings and responses to individuals considered independently of their group membership. I use the term *reasoning* to refer to "thinking about ways of thinking," which means to seek to influence or change individuals' ways of thinking. I apply the term *reasoning* only to the language-related behavior of groups and group members, because I do not know what it means for individuals to try, systematically, to influence the way they think without making use of language-use and the group dynamics that come with it. I assume that reasoning includes individual cognition, but not by itself alone. *Scriptural Reasoning* is therefore a language- and group-related behavior.

Inquiry: Inquiry—for example, academic or philosophic or pragmatic—refers to a specific discipline and practice of reasoning, which means an effort to influence patterns of thinking, in this case, to influence patterns of reasoning themselves. *This book* records an activity of inquiry that I, its author, pursue as a member of the Societies for Scriptural Reasoning (SSR) and (Jewish) Textual Reasoning and as a participant in the philosophic tradition of American pragmatism. Whether or not I am aware of them, I belong to many other groups whose influence may be displayed in my inquiry. In the terms I have introduced, this book therefore records my effort to influence patterns of reasoning about SR, from the perspectives of a scriptural reasoner, a Jewish text-philosopher, an American pragmatist, and more. I offer this inquiry neither as "mine" alone, since it pertains to these groups to which I belong, nor as some "official" statement of the SSR, since the inquiry displays the unique configuration of my perspectives. Consistent with the practice of SR, I do not try to overcome the Jewish perspectives from which I write. In pursuit of some more well-rounded introduction to SR, I do not, on the other hand, try to speak from the perspectives of my Christian and Muslim or now Asian colleagues. To get a fuller introduction to SR, readers will have to ask them what they think; they will need to write their own books. In sum, there is no way to speak one's own mind alone and there is no way to speak adequately for the group. There is no shortcut to the longer run of things, or to the complex give-and-take of many inner and inter-relations among groups and group members.

Pragmatic inquiry and pragmatism: As practiced by students of Peirce, James, and Dewey, "pragmatism" refers to an inquiry that seeks to correct what pragmatists consider several errors in modern academic inquiry. These errors include tendencies (a) to identify the goals of one's academic inquiry with the goals of a circle of specialized inquirers without testing the consequences of these goals for the broader work of the academy and of the societies it serves; (b) to evaluate the inquiry without testing its contribution to repairing whatever problematic situations may have given rise to it and without, (c) examining the societal setting of these situations. I understand

Scriptural Reasoning to contribute to pragmatic inquiry, not because its practitioners necessarily think of themselves as pragmatists, but because SR contributes to the work of correcting errors that are analogous to the errant tendencies that the classical pragmatists identified in academic inquiry. SR contributes to other forms of academic inquiry as well and to other forms of nonacademic inquiry. Outside the academy, SR inquiry also displays a pragmatic dimension: an effort to influence changes in some of the practices of religious and other societal institutions. On one level, it seeks to correct errant tendencies comparable to those the pragmatists observe in modern academic inquiry: tendencies (a) to serve the interests of specialized groups within these institutions without identifying and testing the consequences of their interests for the broader work of these institutions and of the societies they may serve; (b) to promote their interests without evaluating the contribution of their efforts to repairing whatever problematic situations (or conditions of suffering) may underlie those efforts, and without, (c) examining the societal settings of these problematic situations.

Pragmatism, philosophy, and the human heart: Since classic pragmatism was an academic inquiry, it is reasonable to ask what distinguished pragmatists from other academics. What enabled the pragmatists to see and, hopefully, correct errors that most other academics failed to see and correct? Beginning with the founding pragmatist, Charles Peirce, these thinkers identified philosophy as the academic practice singularly responsible for monitoring and correcting the errors that the pragmatists sought to correct. They claimed that the modern academy was in trouble because the discipline of philosophy had abandoned its singular responsibility.

Their theory went something like this. The academy's errant tendencies are no different than the errant tendencies one may observe in most activities of human thinking and reasoning: the tendencies of individuals and small groups to think and reason on behalf of their own interests and to separate these interests from those of the communities and societies they served. These errors are, one might say, inveterate features of the human heart. No human endeavors appear to be free of them, so that human efforts to purify the human heart appear to be self-defeating. Writ large, the pragmatists' goal is not, therefore, to purify the human heart per se, but to identify and strengthen human capacities to monitor the heart's errant tendencies and repair their ill effects. Writ small, pragmatism conducts this work only within the academy but with broader implications for those who seek to trace them.

Within the academy, pragmatism's task was strictly to repair the discipline of philosophy so that philosophers would once again have the capacity to monitor and repair the errant tendencies of the academy (as noted above). To take Peirce's terms as an illustration, philosophy would then continue its sub-disciplines of *phenomenology, normative science (aesthetics, ethics,* and *logic),* and *metaphysics.* The difference would be that each of the sub-disciplines would have the capacity to contribute to that work of repair. To achieve this, the major work was to rearticulate how all these sub-disciplines relate to each other: how phenomenology draws on mathematics, how normative science identifies and responds to the problematic situations that stimulate academic inquiry, and how metaphysics (a species of applied logic) monitors the specialized methods of each of the academic discipline, envisioning how each would contribute to repair of societal (and other) conditions of suffering or disruption. The reformation of modern logic is the single most significant goal of pragmatism, so that the norms and guidelines for every discipline of reasoning would always already include criteria for measuring how each inquiry responds to the deep-seated problems that underlie it.

As narrated so far, this account would appear to classify the goals of pragmatism as strictly prescriptive: delivering, from some otherwise unidentified source, the single academic commandment, "thou shalt not conduct inquiry for thine own interests alone, but for the sake of repairing the societal (or other) problems or sufferings that ultimately concern your community of inquirers and the broader institutions and societies it serves." In fact, Peirce's pragmatism was stimulated, first and foremost, by concerns about what he considered the inaccuracy of his contemporaries' scientific claims. He traced these to poor laboratory practices and, thence, to inadequate models of laboratory science and, thence, to an inadequate logic of science. In the process, he learned several lessons that eventually led him to formulate the "pragmatic method":

1. Questions of truth must include questions of practice: if your scientific claims turn out false, then you need to do more than looking harder at your data; you need to examine how you go about gathering your data and making your claims. In more technical philosophic terms, *truth* is not merely "what hits the mark"; it is also "what is reliable." True claims are not simply accurate (or "on the mark") representations of what is out there; they are expressions of reliable ways of encountering what is out there. Truth is a measure of the inquirer's relationship to what is out there: a measure not only of how one *sees,* but also of the past and future story of how one interacts.

2. Correcting error requires more than correcting some set of discrete claims; it requires correcting practices that result in such claims. In the terms of Peirce's early statement of *the pragmatic maxim,* beliefs

(or claims) are abbreviated statements of what we expect will happen if certain actions are undertaken. But what does this tell us about how to correct one's actions (practices) if one's beliefs (claims) are wrong? Since claims are not simply necessary consequences of a given action or practice, how do errant claims indicate how to go about correcting the practices that generated them?

3. Peirce's third lesson is genealogical: A given claim tends to display the consequences of a given practice as enacted in each setting. A practice is a kind of habit. Habits tend not to be either good or bad, but relatively reliable ways of acting, strengthened by the discovery of successful results and weakened by the discovery of disappointing results. A bad claim is, therefore, evidence that something in someone's practice is disappointing. The goal is not simply to get rid of the practice, since it may otherwise be reliable, but to learn how to revise the practice in order to avoid such errant claims in the future.

Peirce's genealogical method is, metaphorically, a way to peer behind a practice (P^1). Combining logical, comparative and historical analyses, the pragmatist seeks to locate or at least imagine a larger family of practices (P) from which a practice emerged. Do the errors of a current practice raise doubts about the efficacy of the entire family? Or might this family include a somewhat different practice (P^2) that would not generate the current, errant claims? The genealogical inquiry ends when the pragmatist locates a practice of this kind (P^2 or a series of potential P^2's), diagrams the practice as a rule for replacing/repairing the errant practice, and works with specialists within this practice to reformulate the rule as an hypothesis about how to repair the practice. These specialists then test the hypothesis.

4. Rules for correcting a practice may be located, therefore, only within the family of practices to which it belongs. The pragmatist thus contributes general (or context-independent) methods for locating those rules but cannot contribute the rules themselves. Informally stated, correction is always self-correction, which means that pragmatists disclaim any context-independent rule for correcting a practice.

PRAGMATISM, CARTESIANISM, AND SCRIPTURE

If pragmatism's immediate task is to correct modern philosophy and if correction is self-correction, does this mean that pragmatism is a lesson in how modern philosophy should correct itself? If so, where do Peirce and other pragmatists locate the pragmatic method within the genealogy of modern philosophy? I wrote a technical book to answer that question, and a long and technical answer would not serve the purpose of this book.[3] The following, four-step summary should suffice:

1. Before discovering that his pragmatism had to include that rule of self-correction, Peirce identified what he called "Cartesianism" as a prototype of the errant claims of modern philosophy.[4] The Cartesian, he argued, is a philosopher who seeks to correct philosophy by discovering a previously unidentified set of rules for the practice of philosophy, including its self-critique. But, he argued, this discovery is a sleight of hand, built on the false assumption that individual thinkers have the capacity to locate, among their individual judgments, judgments that are self-warranting: judgments of perception or cognition that both deliver some information *and* provide indubitable assurance that the information is correct. In his early critique of Cartesianism, Peirce provided several sources of evidence that this assumption is false and sought to replace this assumption with its contradictory: the claim that all our thoughts are signs of other thoughts, so that individuals have no capacity for indubitable assurance; assurance must come from elsewhere (for example, from various social practices).

2. A decade after his critique of Cartesianism, Peirce concluded that he too committed a Cartesian-like error in thinking that one false claim (the Cartesian one) could simply be replaced by its contradictory (his early theory of signs). Introducing his initial statement of the pragmatic method, he argued, instead, that if Cartesian claims are false, they must be products of unreliable practices, and to correct a claim is to correct the practices on which it is based. Peirce then initiated what would become a thirty-year search for the family of practices that includes both Cartesianism and appropriate rules for correcting it.

3. He concluded that, on one level, Cartesianism belongs to the modern philosophies of science, and its rules of correction may be identified with the logic of experimental science. From this perspective, Cartesianism errs by overlooking the central role of probability in this logic, thereby misrepresenting hypotheses (or probable judgments) as self-warranting judgments. It did not seem difficult to locate models

---

3. Ochs, *Peirce, Pragmatism, and the Logic of Scripture*.
4. Peirce offered these arguments in his 1868 *Journal of Speculative Philosophy* papers. See "Questions Concerning Certain Faculties Claimed for Man," CP 5.213–63, and "Consequences of Four Incapacities," CP 5.264–317.

of probabilistic reasoning within the genealogy of the philosophy of science, from ancient Greece through Descartes, Kant, and such contemporaries of Peirce's as J. S. Mill. These models could be brought forward as guidelines for Cartesianism's self-correction.

4. But how did Peirce's critique of Cartesianism serve his demand that academic inquiries respond to their problematic situations and societal settings? If the logic of experimental science corrects Cartesianism, does it also correct the academy's tendencies to serve its own interests alone? In the concluding chapters of my book on Peirce's pragmatism and in a subsequent series of essays, I argue that Peirce's mature pragmatism (which he dubbed "pragmaticism") contained all the elements needed to answer this question but did not yet fully integrate these into a coherent account of science and social service. This, I argue, is because he failed to integrate his claims about pragmatism's scriptural prototype with his pragmatic arguments for the logic of experimental science. I argue that a pragmatic critique of the academy achieves coherence when its genealogical analysis concludes with not only a logic of modern science but also a logic of Scripture. This argument links a genealogy of the pragmatists' logic of science to a genealogy of Scriptural Reasoning.

5. Peirce's logic of science is informed by a logic of Scripture. Here is a minimally technical summary of my argument in support of this claim.

    a. *Truth, faith, and action:* Peirce argued, strongly and clearly, that pragmatism was a corollary of Jesus's injunction, "that ye shall know them by their fruits" (Matt 7:16). In Matthew, this is Jesus's answer to the question, "how to judge the truth of prophecy?" For Peirce, this is the same as asking, "how to judge the truth of scientific claims?" For the pragmatic maxim, truth is a property of habits of action (or what Peirce called "would-be's"). If, according to Peirce's logic of science, this property measures probabilities, is Peirce claiming that Jesus attributed probability to prophecy? Yes. Does that mean that Peirce was skeptical about faith and injected scientific uncertainty into the truths of Christian religion? No. It means that, just like Pascal, Peirce claimed that religious faith shared with "wagering" the logic of chance. If faith implied cognitive certainty, then faith would share in the two-valued logic of propositions, according to which knowing something (X) means knowing something true *about* it (X is a) in a way that also entails knowing something that *is not true* about it (X is ~(~a)): that, for example, if the cat is up, then she is not not-up (for example, not-down). But faith means trust in something that lies in the dark, and what cannot be seen cannot be measured by these stark alternatives. The two-valued logic of propositions applies only to what we clearly see. Faith in the unseen is therefore about something else.

  b. *Faith in the unseen:* Prophecy is about the unseen, since it is about the future and we do not yet see that clearly. To have faith in the prophet is not yet to have knowledge of what will be; it is to have trust that the future will bear out the truth of the prophet's words.[5] But is this not the same as believing the details of what the prophet says? No, not if belief means seeing clearly, for we still cannot see what the prophet sees until the future brings it to pass. Is this because the prophet has not offered us words identifying what will be? Yes; the prophet has offered words expressing what the prophet sees but hearing those words from the prophet is not the same as seeing them. The prophet sees now in the present, and we have faith *that* we will see. You may say that to have faith is an either-or affair. But, in its logical form, this either-or is not the same as the either-or of what we claim to see now. The latter is a claim about the quality of what we see, what we predicate of it, and we know this quality intimately since it is a predicate of the way we perceive things: *we* are the judges of this, so if we say we see red, we are the ones who know that we do not-see not-red. This is a matter of sight, not faith.

  But to have faith in the prophet's words is to trust in something about which we have no control; it is a matter of relationship, not vision, and relationships involve dispositions, like fearing or not fearing, betting one's life on something or not betting it. Yes, you could say that faith is either-or in this sense, but this is an either-or that allows degrees of either and of or. One can have stronger or weaker faith, and that is why the truths of faith are informed by a logic of probability. If you see something clearly, you don't probably see it; you see it. If you see something unclearly, this means you don't fully trust what you see, or you don't have enough evidence to be; it may be that you see this or see that. The logic of probability does not apply to the content of your seeing, it

---

5. For an extended, complementary exploration of prophetic reasoning, see Weiss, *Paradox and the Prophets*.

is what it is. It applies to the degree of trust you may have in what you see or in the significance of what you see. This trust is not either-or but strong-or-weak, measured by scales of probability. In sum, faith in the unseen is a matter of probability; seeing is believing; faith is acting without seeing.

c. *Faith and the logic of experimental science:* Experimental science provides ways of testing hypotheses about what we do not see clearly. Assume, for example, that "particles" and "waves" behave in contrary ways. And say that physicists appear to have collected surprising evidence that light seems to act both like a wave (an electromagnetic wave) and like a particle (a packet of energy that interacts with things discretely). And say that someone—like Werner Heisenberg or, later, Richard Feynman—speculates on how this apparently contradictory fact could be true. The experimentalist's job is to imagine and construct instruments that interact with light in ways that would increase or decrease our trust in the hypothesis. In this case, in 1803, Thomas Young successfully constructed an experiment ("the double slit experiment") to demonstrate that light behaved like a wave and not only (or, in his view, not) like a particle (as most believed at that time). Adding to research by Max Plank, Albert Einstein, Nils Bohr and many others, Heisenberg (c. 1927) reinterpreted the double-slit experiment as evidence that light behaves as *both* wave and particle. Experimentalists *see* evidence in ways that follow the rules of either-or, two-valued logic, but they then *interpret* what they see in ways that either strengthen or weaken the scientific community's trust that a given hypothesis is a good one. To say an hypothesis is good is to say that we have reason to trust a given account of the world (in this case, of the phenomenon of light). According to the pragmatic maxim, an account of the world implies some set of expectations about how the world would behave in certain circumstances. If, for example, scientists followed the quantum theory of light, they would expect, among other things, that light would behave like a particle under certain circumstances and like a wave under other circumstances. These expectations would influence the ways that they—and members of society who trust them—act in a world of light and dark.

d. *Pragmatists like Peirce and William James understood faith in a way that complements the logic of experimental science.* Assume, for example, that events in the actual world display the effects of laws that govern this world and assume that what religious people call "miracles" would fail to display such effects. According to the pragmatists, it would be illogical to say that claims about miracles necessarily contradict the evidence natural scientists collect about the world, since "evidence" collects reports about what we see in the world while claims about miracles offer ways of interpreting that evidence. The pragmatists criticize claims that miracles contain empirical reports or sense data that necessarily differ from reports that could be made by natural scientists. The pragmatists reason that, since religious people associate "miracles" with matters of faith, and since matters of faith are matters of things unseen, claims about miracles are not claims of literal sight. What is "unseen" includes *the meaning* of what has been seen, *our relationship* to what has been seen, and *the effect of* what we see on *our degree of trust in any general account of the world*. For the pragmatists, "meaning," "relationship," "effects," "trust," and "general account" all belong to our dispositions to act in given ways in relation to the world.

In these terms, miracles indirectly name features of our dispositions to act. To have faith in a miracle (faith rather than belief) is to trust in some prophet's account of the meaning of what we see. What we *see* is a report of the senses, which belongs to the either-or of belief, not of faith. What we *trust* is a report of the habits of action (of relationship, disposition, faith). The proof of what we trust is not made visible to our human, non-prophetic eyes, since it will be made visible only in the future, when we come to see what we now trust. One reason so many of us confuse the eyes of belief with the trust (the hug) of faith is that we experience trust as directly as we experience sight: it *feels* like sight. *This is a key to what Peirce considered the error of Cartesianism: when we misinterpret intellectual perceptions as equivalent to "inner sense perceptions," we mistake strictly probabilistic wagers (predictions in which we trust) for self-certain or indubitable beliefs. The pragmatists do not, therefore, reject Cartesian observations; they simply (and urgently) re-identify them with hypotheses whose warrant-or-disproof lies only in the future. This is a lesson of Peirce's, "A Neglected Argument for the Reality of God": that the logic of experimental science is the logic of faith.* Claims about religious miracles are not identical in content to claims about the physics of light, but they tend to be identical in logical form.

e. *Genealogy of the logic of experimental science as the logic of faith and the logic of Scripture:* Although Peirce did not know this, his understanding of faith corresponds to the meaning of the term in biblical and rabbinic Hebrew: *emunah* means "trust in" rather than "cognitive belief about," and trust is primarily a matter of one's relationship to persons. Faith in miracles, for example, is primarily faith in the prophets who tell us we have seen miracles. My interest in Peirce's logic begins with its service to what I consider the rabbinic logic of Scripture. On some other occasion, I hope to devote more attention to some scholars' claims that, by way of sixteenth-century *converso* scholars, rabbinic logic made a significant contribution to early modern reasoning about experimental science. On that occasion, I also hope to examine the comparable influences of medieval and early modern Muslim scholars of science. For the purposes of this book, however, the most efficient link between pragmatism and the logic of faith comes through a narrative about Patristic logic: Augustine's Trinitarian semiotic of Scripture. Drawn from my technical essay, "Reparative Reasoning: From Peirce's Pragmatism to Augustine Scriptural Semiotic," here is a summary of the critical steps in this narrative.[6]

Despite its errant dogmatism, Cartesianism also inherits patterns of self-criticism and repair: what we will label its inherent "reparative logic," whose first rule is that some occasions call for *constative claims* and other occasions call for *contested or reparative claims*. Constative claims are offered with the assumption that all listeners will share a set of linguistic conventions that enable them to understand the claim clearly. There are two types of constative claims.

Every day or common-sense claims are those that could potentially make sense to anyone in the larger language community: for example, when, at a dinner table in my own home, I say "The salt shaker is on the small cabinet," assuming that everyone at the table knows exactly where to look. *Scientific or specialized claims* are offered to sub-communities who share a specialized vocabulary that is usually adopted for the sake of analyzing and interpreting certain features of everyday discourse.

Reparative or contested claims are offered to change or repair specific conventions for formulating claims in either every day or specialized communities. Such claims are of necessity partly

---

6. Ochs, "Reparative Reasoning."

clear and partly ambiguous, since they both affirm and contest certain assumptions within a given set of linguistic conventions. They must be sufficiently clear to call the listener's attention to the range of conventional claims that are contested as well as to those that are not contested. The new claims they assert about the former must be ambiguous in varying degrees since the listener is being asked to entertain some new conventions of meaning.

f. *Peirce's theory of signs, or semiotics, offers a set of conventions for diagramming and distinguishing constative and reparative claims*: For his semiotics, the fundamental unit of reference is the sign: a *signifier* that displays its *object* (reference or meaning) only with respect to an *interpretant* (a context of meaning, interpretive mind-set, or system of deep-seated rules). Among types of sign, an *index* (symptom or mark) refers to its *object* by virtue of some direct force exerted by the object on the sign. In other words, an indexical sign is indifferent to its interpretant, the way a weather vane points north because the wind blows it that way. An *icon* (image) does not refer to its object explicitly; instead, it appears to its *interpretant* to share certain characters with its object. The icon therefore displays its meaning metaphorically, through similarity, the way a statue may represent some historical figure. A *symbol*, finally, refers to its *object* by virtue of some implicit law that causes the symbol to be *interpreted* as referring to that object. In other words, a symbol displays its meaning only to an interpretant, but it is not fully subject to the interpreter's attributions. Instead, a symbol *influences* the way its interpretant attributes meaning to it. The symbol engages its interpretant in some practice of meaning-making. Transferring agency to the interpreter, the symbol also grants the interpreter some freedom to transform the way in which that meaning will be retransmitted. *In this way, the symbol is the fundamental agent of pragmatic inquiry.* It is itself the interpretant of some tradition's deep-seated rules of practice, of which it serves as an agent. At the same time, the freedom it grants its own interpreter serves as a sign that these rules are also subject to and possibly in need of change. In sum, signification is the product of a three-part relation among *sign, object, and interpretant.*

In these terms, constative claims are verbal symbols that typically leave their interpretants unstated: as if these conditions for making meaning were self-evident. At times, however, a speaker may feel a need to articulate these interpretants, when speaking, for example, in a new social setting to a group of new acquaintances who may not take his or her words to mean what they meant back home. What, however, if some speakers feel they are virtually never able to communicate a certain set of judgments within a given sub-community of natural or scientific language-use? Or if the judgments they habitually make about a certain aspect of the world no longer seem to hold true and they feel taken aback, uncertain if the world changed or they changed? *These are conditions that may stimulate reparative claims, or efforts to repair or reframe the interpretants that would condition a given range of constative judgments.*

A reparative claim is *a complex series of symbols offered not to represent any object of meaning but to diagram a claim as some relation among sign-object-interpretant.* The purpose of a reparative claim is to draw the listener's attention to this three-part relation rather than to any object of meaning. Peirce's thesis is that our patterns or habits of action may adequately be diagrammed as three-part relations according to which certain stimuli in the world function as signs whose objects are certain ends of action and whose interpretants are certain reflex arcs.[7] An associated thesis is that habits may be communicated and taught through such diagrams. Reparative claims may therefore be represented as actions (of signification or communication) whose objects are repairs (and thus changes) in certain interpretants (the interpretants of certain habits of action whose apparent failings have stimulated the reparative claims). *Habit-change is the intended interpretant of a reparative claim.*

g. *Peirce's critique of Cartesianism is thus a reparative claim: an effort to recommend a habit-change in certain practices of modern philosophy. His critique is, more precisely, a critique of the modern Cartesian tendency to treat reparative claims as if they were constative claims and, therefore, unambiguous.* To repair modern Cartesianism, he must locate a prototype of Cartesianism that does not display this error. Searching back in time through Cartesianism's

---

7. As defined in Dewey, "Reflex Arc," drawing on James, *Principles*, I.12–80, the term "reflex arc" refers to the neural habits that associate certain "stimuli," or sensed events, with certain "responses," or muscular activity: the way our hands tend to pull back when we sense fire, or the way Pavlov's dogs salivate when they hear a bell.

antecedents, Peirce most likely located such a prototype in Augustine.[8]

AUGUSTINE'S LOGIC OF SCRIPTURE AS A PROTOTYPE FOR PEIRCE'S SEMIOTICS: A PRAGMATIC THOUGHT EXPERIMENT

Augustine's logic of Scripture may be a prototype for Peirce's effort to repair Cartesianism from within: While Peirce cites Augustine directly, my argument here is from analogy and typology rather than history.[9] I argue that, if you read *Trin.* and examine Peirce's triadic semiotics, you may observe the analogy I see between the one and the other. Latin scholar Robert Markus and Latin-inspired philosopher John Deely observe this as well and add that Peirce's semiotics completes the formal work that underlies Augustine's theo-philosophic studies. I add that, if Peirce completes Augustine's formal work, Augustine completes Peirce's theo-philosophic work. Peirce claimed that his pragmatism was nothing other than a corollary to Jesus's injunction "that ye may know them by their fruit,"[10] but he did not articulate what I take to be the hermeneutical implications of his claim: that what Peirce takes to be Jesus's pragmatic consequentialism is immanent in Jesus's reading of Scripture (OT), that Augustine reads Jesus's reading semiotically, and that the revelatory character of Scripture may lend pragmatic semiotics the imperative voice Peirce may otherwise seek in his proofs of pragmatism.

The following comments on Augustine should therefore be read as a thought experiment that illustrates how one could read *Trin.* as if it provided

---

8. I agree with Robert Markus, John Deely, and others, that the clearest logical analogue to Peirce's triadic semiotics is Augustine's semiotic in *Trin*. Roger Ward comments, for example, that "Peirce notes his benefit from a 'deeply pondering perusal' of Augustine and other Scholastics according to his report in 1867 (CP 1:560)": Ward, *Peirce and Religion*, 35. Ward adds:

> To make a further comparison, [Peirce's] Lowell lectures follow the path of the first half of *The Trinity* by examining practice based on faith as it seeks to understand the form that it contains. The Harvard lectures exhibit the scheme of the second half of *The Trinity* by taking up a claim to knowledge as already implicit, and then applying it to the practices of inquiry. The open-ended conclusion to the Harvard lectures . . . is parallel to the expansion in the conclusion of *The Trinity* of Augustine's argument into the continuing practice of the church. (Ward, *Peirce and Religion*, 36)

See also Burgess, *Play*.

9. For complementary approaches to Augustine, semiotics, and SR, see Ticciati, *Apophaticism*, 135–98.

10. Citing Matt 7:16. See above, p. 44n21.

scriptural grounds for a pragmatic semiotics. To repeat, I do not offer my comments as historically warranted but as analogically and hermeneutically suggestive.

Experiment 1:

Let us imagine that, from the perspective of logic, the "restlessness" that Augustine describes in *The Confessions* is a search for *Scripture's ratio*: a Greco-Roman logic that could identify patterns of reasoning that Augustine believes are immanent in scripture.[11] According to this thought experiment, Augustine is restless because the obvious candidates (Plato, the Manicheans, and so on) would classify scriptural reasoning as non-reasoning. He hopes to transform Stoic logic into a means of identifying the rationality of Scripture, which he comes to diagram in a three-part semiotic that is clarified, much later, through the semiotic work of John of Poinsot and adequately formalized only in Peirce's semiotic.

In these terms, *De doctrina christiana* would introduce—but only introduce—Augustine's place of rest: a scriptural semiotic that serves the norms of both Hellenic and scriptural inquiries by showing how the Bible's conventional signs can communicate the redemptive movement of God's Word in this world. From *Conf.* to *De doct.* to *Trin.*, Augustine would then trace the reparative work of the Word as it receives the fruit of Hellenic logical inquiry and transforms it into a vehicle for scriptural and Trinitarian semiotics. On this reading, Stoic logic would offer Augustine the most mature expression of Hellenic logical inquiry; *De. doct.* would show Augustine at work transforming Stoic logic into the triadic semiotic that, alone, can diagram the mediatory movement of intra-scriptural rationality; and *Trin.*—rather than *De doct.*—would display the mature expression of Augustine's semiotics.

Augustine does not display his semiotic explicitly, since too little of his mature semiotic appears in *De doct.*, and *Trin.* lacks formalization. The semiotic must be traced, instead, in the dialectic that animates three

---

11. While I interpret Augustine's restlessness solely for the sake of this thought experiment, I note that Ward's study of philosophic "conversion" in medieval thought follows a complementary line of interpretation. He writes, "I argue from the religious origin and concern of pragmatism that conversion provides a helpful framework for understanding and extending the American philosophic framework. Conversion entails a holistic change of life that follows a discovery of the truth about ourselves, our community, and God. Conversion also becomes a platform for reorienting practice and reflection.... For these reasons, I suggest that conversion forms a general aim of pragmatism's founding figures" (Ward, *Conversion*, xxxi).

competing tendencies in *Trin.* and in his later work more broadly. For the sake of our thought experiment, I identify these tendencies as *Objectivism, Internalism, and Reparative Rationality, each animated by competing subtendencies toward strictly biblical or logical inquiry.*[12] As I depict them here, these tendencies illustrate the struggle and dynamism that is immanent in a scripturally grounded pragmatic semiotics. The semiotics entails struggle, because it is stimulated by some loss, failure, or suffering whose hoped-for repair constitutes its *telos* and completion. The agent of this semiotics is some community of inquiry or any of its individual members. The agent struggles, both within and without, because the path of repair is inevident. The agent (within) may not necessarily know how relief will come, and the one (without) who suffers or fails may not necessarily be healed. The objectivism I attribute to Augustine illustrates the outer struggle; his internalism illustrates the inner struggle, and his reparative rationality illustrates the uncertain yet hopeful movement toward repair.

Augustine's restless search for a rational model of Scripture is displayed in the dialectic between his objectivism and internalism. I imagine that Augustine's objectivism propels him to look in the world for signs of direct encounter with what may be named "being itself" or "God." I imagine that his internalism draws him to look within for intimate acquaintance with the characteristics of this God or this being.[13] I imagine that Augustine finds rest only through a third tendency, which outweighs and integrates the others in *Trin.* I label this *Reparative Rationality: a tendency to participate in certain semiotic processes as means of redeeming sin and (non-identically) imitating the actions of God in this world.* This rationality would be animated by three collaborative sub-tendencies. *Confessional Rationality* would refer to a capacity, in the face of Scripture's witness, to recognize and acknowledge marks of sinfulness in one's own habitus. This is a capacity to recognize that one's objectivism may mistake representations of the real for the real itself and that one's internalism may mistake the self for an unclouded image of the divine (or worse). *Transformative Rationality* would refer to a capacity

---

12. I offer an extensive treatment of these tendencies in Ochs, "Reparative Reasoning," 200–11.

13. In Ochs, "Reparative Reasoning," I argue that the dialectic between Augustine's objectivism and internalism generates four foci of inquiry, each of which fails to fulfill the desire that propels it, but all of which work together to advance the development of Augustine's habitus: *Biblical objectivism* (a tendency to categorize the Bible as a direct description of the life of God on earth); *Logical objectivism* (a tendency to categorize formal systems of logic as direct descriptions of the elemental characteristics of being itself as the real); *Biblical internalism* (a tendency to identify one's reception of the Bible with an icon of the divine presence); *Logical internalism* (a tendency to identify the *cogito* with the internalized character of the real, or being itself).

for radical habit-change. This is a capacity, by way of Scripture's witness, to recognize and internalize rules of *askesis* and, thereby, to transform objectivism and internalism into tendencies for confessional and transformative rationality. *Trinitarian Rationality* would refer to a capacity to engage intimately with the divine life and, thereby, to participate in God's love of and repair of the world. God alone is mediator and redeemer; no representation or agent substitutes for God in this work.

This thought experiment complements the scholarship of Robert Markus and his claim that what Augustine sought in his later work is made explicit only in the semiotic of Charles Peirce.[14] I would add that, for Peirce, to "make explicit" is to define something formally, as in his list of 144 implications of the elemental semiotic distinction among *sign*, *object*, and *interpretant*. Augustine lacks that formal definition, but he makes another dimension of his semiotic explicit in the dialectical character of *Trin.*: the "restless" movement from objectivist to internalist inquiry and then to the reparative inquiry that transforms this dialectic into a dynamic dialogue. This dialogue is always subject to interruption, whenever human tendencies to self-reference ("sin," in Augustine's vocabulary) redirect either pole away from the other. We speak here of tendencies, not necessary laws, so we do not presume that tendencies to self-reference will necessarily generate the dialectic of objectivism and internalism we encountered earlier.[15]

Experiment 2

By way of a second experiment, let us read Peirce's effort to construct a pragmatic semiotic as analogous to Augustine's effort to limn Scripture's reparative rationality. This experiment begins with an introduction to the Stoic logic that Peirce draws on and that Augustine reads and transforms into his Trinitarian and scriptural logic.[16] I imagine that the final stage of Augustine's restless search is his discovery of the Stoic logicians and their discovery of the logical function/turn that enabled Augustine to find his path between Greco-Roman and Scripture's own rationality. Augustine has hope in the capacity of Stoic logic to draw a formal distinction among a sign ("signifier," *semeinon*), the external object toward which we might say the

---

14. Markus, "St. Augustine on Signs."

15. Tendencies to dialogue and repair may be stronger in each environment than the tendencies against them. But they may also be weaker, when self-referential forces occlude the attractive powers of dialogue and inhibit the self-corrective process we have called reparative reasoning.

16. See, for example, citations of the Stoa in Peirce, "Sixty Lectures on Logic."

sign is pointing (the "name-bearer," *tugkainon*), and the meaning we might associate with the sign ("the signification," *semainomenon*), which meaning is also a "sayable" (*lekton*) or that which can be uttered. This is a distinction between something that may cause someone to utter a sign and how the community of listeners perceives the sign. Neither Aristotle's semiotic nor Augustine's own early semiotic made formal distinctions between what Frege called a sign's "reference" (as when someone says "eraser," referring to that felt thing) and its "sense" (what each listener associates with the sign, such as "one who takes something away from something"). Without that distinction, however, it is very difficult to make sense of the Bible, since so much of its genius is displayed in the way it gives new sense to old references.

Early in *Doctr. chr.*, before what I imagine to be his "conversion" to the Stoa, Augustine's account of signs remains Aristotelian: "signs (*signa*). . . are things used to signify something" (1.2) and "a sign is a thing (*res*) which causes us to think of something beyond the impression the thing itself makes upon the senses" (2.1). But then (as I speculate), he refashions Stoic logic into a scriptural semiotic, concluding that, as illustrated in the *Conf.*, the latter pages of *Doctr. chr.*, and indirectly in *Trin.*: "of symbols . . . we may distinguish the signifier (*signatum*); the intended meaning or object (*significatum*); and "the subject to whom the sign stands for the object signified."[17] The notion of *significatum* was the key addition, since it indicates Augustine's distinguishing between a sign's intentional object, or sense, and its external object (*res*), or reference. I imagine that Augustine's semiotic conversion enables him to complete his scriptural conversion (and vice versa): the *significatum* ("subject for whom the sign stands") belongs ultimately to the divine: "Come says the Lord, let us reason together, so that light may be made in the firmament of heaven [the Bible as firmament] and live over the earth" (*Conf.* 3.19, citing Isa 1:16–18). By way of reasoning together (with the Lord), reason finds it light from out of Scripture. Read within our thought experiment, *Conf.* implies that philosophers may discover reason's triadic semiotic only through the light of Scripture.[18]

> Turn us again, O Lord God of Hosts, cause Thy face to shine; and we shall be saved (Ps. 80:8). For wherever the soul of man turns itself, unless towards Thee, it is affixed to sorrows . . . And even thus is our speech accomplished by signs emitting a sound; but this, again, is not perfected unless one word pass away when

---

17. Markus, "St. Augustine on Signs," 74.

18. Chad Pecknold provides a reference to Bible as firmament in Pecknold, *Transforming*, 46.

it has sounded its part, in order that another may succeed it. (*Conf.* 4.10)

In light of his dual conversion, I imagine that Augustine perceives the emptiness of his previous account of words as merely natural things; he had failed to recognize the distinction among sign, sense, reference, and subject that characterizes biblical language and much inter-human communication as well.

According to our thought experiment, there are at least four ways that Scripture warrants Augustine's transformation of Stoic logic into a logic of Scripture: *(a) The objects or referents of Scripture's words are, at once, visible in the world and not visible; (b) Scripture's reader is a sinner, whose perception of the not-visible remains clouded by this sin; (c) The reader can pray; (d) The Author of Scripture is also Redeemer, by whose mercy the reader may be given eyes to see and, thereby, welcomed to participate in Scripture's semiosis.* Here are brief clarifications.

Scripture's dual[19] *reference: the objects of Scripture's words and verses are only partially observable in this world.* If the "objective" character of scriptural signs includes non-observable elements, then the latter are discernible only "within" the signifier. The Stoic distinction between a sign's "name-bearer" (*tugkainon*) and its "signification" (*semainomenon*) enables Augustine's semiotic distinction between Scripture's sense or intended object (*significatum*) and "the subject to whom the sign stands for the object signified."[20] But if all things in the world are potential signs, where is their intended and non-visible object to be seen? It is "within." In what I imagine to be his "internalist" tendency, Augustine would identify the sign's "within" with the interiority of the self:

> Verily within me, within the chamber of my thought, Truth, neither Hebrew, nor Greek, nor Latin, nor barbarian without the organs of voice and tongue, without the sound of syllables, would say "He speaks the truth," and I forthwith assured of it, confidently would say unto that man of Thine, "Thou speakest the truth." (*Conf.* 12.3.5)

But the reader is a sinner.

> For the soul, loving its own power, slips onwards from the whole which is common, to a part, which belongs especially to itself. [The result is] . . .apostatizing pride, which is called the beginning of sin, while [the soul] might have been most excellently

---

19. Or, in a postmodern vocabulary, "double-coded."
20. Markus, "St. Augustine on Signs," 74.

governed by the laws of God, if it had [instead] followed Him as its ruler.[21] (*Trin.* 12.14)

"But the light shines in darkness, and the darkness comprehended it not." Now the darkness is the foolish minds of men, made blind by vicious desires and unbelief. And that the Word, by whom all things were made, might care for these and heal them, The Word was made flesh, and dwelt among us. For our enlightening is the partaking of the Word, namely, of that life which is the light of men. But for this partaking we were utterly unfit, and fell short of it, on account of the uncleanness of sins. (*Trin.* 4.2)

Anticipating Peirce's critique of Descartes, we may observe that, for Augustine, doubt has its proper birth, not in scientific cognition, but in the recognition of error and sin: si fallor sum (If I am mistaken, I am).[22] "There is no one but you to whom I can say, 'If I have sinned unwittingly, do you absolve me. Keep me ever your own servant, far from pride' (Ps. 19:13–14)" (*Conf.* 1.5). "But, dust and ashes though I am let me appeal to your pity, since it is to you in your mercy that I speak, not to a man, who would simply laugh at me" (*Conf.* 1.6).[23] *In these terms, Augustine's semiotic begins, not with cognitive uncertainty in the face of uncertain judgments (Cartesian doubt), but with the confession of sin in the face of divine judgment.*

Yet, the reader may confess and pray for forgiveness. Instruction in petitionary prayer is disclosed in Scripture. Prayer intones the scriptural word's yearning for the divine word to return to the divine word.

Take a man who is been roused by the warmth of the Holy Spirit and has already woken up to God ... He has taken a look at himself in God's light ... and realizes that his own sickness cannot be

21. Augustine continues:

And it administers that whole, wherein it strives to do something of its own against the laws by which the whole is governed, by its own body, which it possesses only in part; and so being delighted by corporeal forms and motions, because it has not the things themselves within itself, and because it is wrapped up in their images, which it has fixed in the memory, and is foully polluted by fornication of the phantasy, while it refers all its functions to those ends, for which it curiously seeks corporeal and temporal things through the senses of the body, either it affects with swelling arrogance to be more excellent than other souls that are given up to the corporeal senses, or it is plunged into a foul whirlpool of carnal pleasure. (*Trin.* 12.14)

22. The phrase appears in many writings, for example *Civ.* XI: 26.

23. *Conf.* begins in this spirit and retains it to the end: "I am poor and needy and I am better only when in sorrow of heart I detest myself and seek your mercy, until what is faulty in me is repaired and made whole and finally I come to that state of peace which the eye of the proud cannot see" (*Conf.* 10.38).

compounded with God's cleanness. So he finds it a relief to weep and implore (*deprecare*) him ... to take pity and pull him altogether out of his pitiful condition, and he prays (*precari*) with all confidence once he has received the free gratuitous pledge of health through the one and only Savior. (*Trin.* 4 Prologue)

In Jonathan Teubner's reading of *Trin.*, there are two phases of this prayer. "*Deprecare* signifies a prayer for mercy . . ., for something to be taken away, and *precari* is more adequately understood as a kind of prayer . . . for something to be given. It is by *deprecare* that Augustine asks for pity, and only after he has received his pledge of health does he use *precari*."[24] *Precari* is therefore possible only if and when the redeeming Word removes the uncleanness that blocks humanity's participation in God's saving presence.[25] "In short, prayer (in all its varieties) is the embodied means by which the Christian *endures* the gap between this world and the *beata vita* in the next. Prayer allows the Christian to live into the future whilst remaining in the *tenebrae* now."[26]

God may hear the reader's prayer and grant forgiveness and knowing.

> And I sought a way of acquiring strength sufficient to enjoy Thee; but I found it not until I embraced that Mediator between God and man, the man Christ Jesus. . . . For the Word was made flesh, that Thy wisdom, by which Thou createdst all things, might provide milk for our infancy. (*Conf.* 7.18; 10.43; *Doctr. chr.* 1.34)

> My soul resisted your healing hand, for it was you who prepared and dispenses the medicine of faith and made it so potent a remedy for the diseases of the world. . . . Since we were too weak to discover the truth by pure reasoning and therefore needed the authority of the sacred writings, I now began to believe that you would never have conferred such preeminent authority on the scripture, now disused through all the lands, unless you had willed that it would be a means of seeking to know you. (*Conf.* 6.4–5)

---

24. Teubner, *Prayer After Augustine*, 85

25. "Humanity's uncleanness is blocking this participation, which is also anticipated by Augustine's use of *deprecare* in the prologue. *Deprecare* is . . . a prayer for purification . . . a stripping away of uncleanness" (Teubner, *Prayer After Augustine*, 97).

26. Teubner, *Prayer After Augustine*, 115. For Augustine, such prayer is not against original sin but against one's inability to hear the Word that would repair original sin. This difference is critical for our thought experiment.

I imagine that, in the light of his conversion, Augustine would perceive the emptiness of his previous use of words as merely natural things that lacked the interpretant with respect to which they symbolized one reality rather than a myriad of ephemeral possibilities. Looking back at the foundationalist tendencies in his early critique of Descartes, Peirce wrote in comparable ways about the interpretant that was lacking in his work: what he often named the "key" to unlocking the mysteries of the universe. For Augustine, incarnation represented this key.

> And I sought a way of acquiring strength sufficient to enjoy Thee; but I found it not until I embraced that Mediator between God and man, the man Christ Jesus . . . . For the Word was made flesh, that Thy wisdom, by which Thou createdst all things, might provide milk for our infancy. (*Conf.* 7.18; 10.43; *De doct.* 1.34)

For Marcia Colish, "The doctrine of the Incarnation and the manner in which Augustine understands his conversion to it are . . . essential to his conception of the redemption of language, which, he holds, makes theology possible."[27] "The redemption of language" is perhaps the best way to characterize a capacity to repair not only distressed practices in everyday life, but also distressed practices of repair. Augustine's text attributes this capacity to the Word alone.

Experiment 3: Extending the term *Cartesianism*

Experiments 1 and 2 enable us to offer a concluding experimental thought: to readopt the term *Cartesianism* to refer not only to the errant dimension of modernism that early postmodernists attribute to René Descartes, but also to the much longer tradition, largely Neoplatonic, that extends from Augustine through various medieval and scholastic readers to Descartes, Kant, and then Peirce and beyond. This expansive sense of Cartesianism enables us to acknowledge the dynamism, uncertainty, and struggle that accompanies the work of each participant in this chain of transmission. It also enables us to account for each participant's capacity to contribute something to other participants. Along with his optics and scientific rigor, for example, Descartes's *Discourses* bring to light the rationalist and internalist tendencies that are always already immanent in the work of his antecedents (like Augustine) and decedents (like Peirce). A complementary thought experiment is to think of the "Cartesian" as a trans-historical type who bears all of

---

27. Colish, *Mirror of Language*, 22.

the traits of all of the participants, each with varying degrees of errant and of reparative tendencies, all participating in a division of labor that enables each to contribute something urgent and unique, where each contribution brings its own challenges and dangers as well as strengths.

The genealogical critique of Cartesianism ends here, with the claim that Augustine's scriptural and Trinitarian semiotic displays the effects of a three-part or triadic pattern of reasoning (*habitus* in Colish's terms) and that this pattern serves as prototype for the tradition that generates Cartesianism. This tradition inherits both a dialectic of objectivism and internalism, as exhibited in Augustine's pre-Stoic semiotic, and a norm for repairing that dialectic, as exhibited in Augustine's Stoic-and-scriptural semiotic. Peirce's pragmatism inherits a pattern of reparative reasoning comparable to the latter. For this reason, we should take seriously Peirce's own claim about pragmatism: that it is very intimately allied with the ideas of the gospel and that an effective logic of experimental science may therefore, indeed, name Scripture as its interpretant.

Cartesian doubt finds no relief in the dogmatic practice of Cartesian reasoning, because this doubt misrepresents itself as objective uncertainty, rather than as the separation of self from the Word that gives birth to it. Augustine's semiotic is fulfilled in an account of redemption that does not replace scientific with religious reasoning, but that situates all projects of human reasoning within the deeper context (or, we might now say, the transcendental conditions) of humanity's search for redemption from sin.

> "Turn us again, O Lord God of Hosts, cause Thy face to shine; and we shall be saved" (Ps. 80:8). For wherever the soul of man turns itself, unless towards Thee, it is affixed to sorrows.... And even thus is our speech accomplished by signs emitting a sound; but this, again, is not perfected unless one word pass away when it has sounded its part, in order that another may succeed it. (*Conf.* 4.10)

PRAGMATISM AS A SCRIPTURAL HERMENEUTICS

In these terms, one philosophic root of SR is a rediscovery of pragmatism as a scriptural hermeneutic. I say "rediscovery," because current scholars of philosophy disregard Peirce's claims about pragmatism's scriptural sources. But Peirce's pragmatism is a critique of Cartesian tendencies in the modern academy and, as I have argued in this chapter, pragmatic repair of those tendencies is grounded in a distinctly scriptural semiotic. Without that ground, pragmatism either stands on the kind of foundationalist argument Peirce's pragmatism was designed to repair, or it remains ungrounded. "Neo-pragmatists" have in fact taken the latter option, as illustrated in Cornel West's image of Emerson's "self-begotten sailor" as prototype for pragmatism's ungrounded ground.[28] For Peirce, however, foundationalism cannot be repaired by its logical contradictory; groundlessness is merely the flip side of foundationalism. Foundationalism can be repaired if and only if Cartesianism inherits a normative and logical ground that is not self-begotten. This ground is Scripture: not as mere text, but as the specific textual tradition that reads verses like "love your neighbor as yourself" and "ye shall know them by their fruit" as displaying the Creator's imperative voice. In these terms, the ground of pragmatism is not "Scripture itself," or "God's word itself." It is the ongoing life of scriptural tradition as a trans-historical activity that helps order, renew and repair the normative dimensions of societal life from one generation to another.

As it appears in the term "Scriptural Reasoning," reasoning refers to any network or process of cognitive activities that, attentive to some surprising or unexpected phenomenon, recommends some form of action in response or in relation to that phenomenon. In more specific terms, reasoning appears as "reparative reasoning": any network or process of cognitive activities that, attentive to conditions of suffering or error or simply "something that is not right," recommends some manner of action to repair those conditions. Reparative reasoning is pragmatic reasoning when it recommends repairs to the practice of philosophic reasoning in the modern academy: specifically, when it obliges philosophy to repair errant modern tendencies to separate academic reasoning from the responsibilities of reparative reasoning. Pragmatic reasoning is Scriptural Reasoning when it recommends repairs to the practice of pragmatic reasoning itself: today, for example, when pragmatism tends to be practiced like any other form of modern philosophy, separating itself from the imperatives and patterns of reparative reasoning. In this case, pragmatic reasoning is Scriptural Reasoning because Scripture, alone, obliges reasoning to serve the ultimate ends of reparative reasoning. Pragmatism has normative force only as Scriptural Reasoning; otherwise, it serves the norms and ends of whatever philosophic sub-community recommends it. Precisely how does pragmatism find its norms in Scripture? Chapter 2 introduced a rabbinic approach to this question. This chapter has introduced an Augustinian approach. There will be little room in this book to go beyond either introduction.

The way I have just defined Scriptural Reasoning is meant only to explain some of the broader philosophic interests of the founding scholars of

---

28. West, *American Evasion*, 166.

SR. When facilitating SR as a practice of intra-or interreligious text study, or when teaching students of religious studies, theology, or comparative traditions, I define "Scriptural Reasoning" in complementary but different ways. I do not treat any of these definitions as primary or privileged, since SR appears differently to me in different contexts of life and study:

Formational SR: As introduced in chapter 1, this refers to the "gateway" practice of SR: small group, inter-traditional study that serves as the common denominator for all participants in Scriptural Reasoning projects. Participants discuss the plain sense of different scriptural verses *as if* they shared equal facility in reading those words. They gradually turn to discussing what seems most challenging or surprising in those verses. The discussion continues around and around the table, often generating one or two lines of discussion, as participants respond not only to the verses but also to one another's readings. Over time, as discussion tends to hover around certain issues or topics that have arisen within the readings and that tend to capture the group's interest and imagination, one job of the facilitator is to allow one or two discussions of this kind to continue, while at the same time guiding participants back to the texts before them, making sure that discussions are continually refreshed and nourished by the verses on the table. *Scriptural Reasoning refers to a phenomena that often arises when groups like these have continued for many successive sessions (for example, for perhaps five one and a half hour sessions over a one and a half day period, or briefer meetings held regularly, biweekly or monthly): continuing across several sessions, one, two, or sometimes three lines of discussion, in parallel, gradually give rise to a type of reasoning unique to the texts and participants gathered.* New participants may not necessarily perceive such "reasonings" to have emerged. But experienced facilitators describe consistent patterns of reading-dialogue-interpretation emerge around the table. These patterns reflect features of the participants' traditions of scriptural study as well as the styles or schools of reasoning and interpretation they bring to the table. But the patterns are irreducible to any of these. "Scriptural Reasoning" refers to forms of reasoning that arise within an SR group, in ways that are specific to that group at that time, and that may not appear in that particular way again.

Inter-scriptural reasoning in general: As displayed in Formational SR, "Scriptural Reasoning" also refers more broadly to patterns of reasoning that emerge out of additional kinds of text-based interreligious study. The texts are prototypically scriptural, but the phenomena may also be observed in groups studying scriptural commentaries or cognate literatures or non-literary practices. The characteristic features of SR in these cases are patterns of reading, discussion, and interpretation that may characterize events of interreligious (or also interdenominational) encounter.

Reasoning that emerges out of single text traditions. As noted in chapter 2, I consider TR and SR types of a more general pattern of reasoning I am content to label "Scriptural Reasoning." In TR groups, individual and denominational differences tend to animate group reasoning in a way that appears fully analogous to the differences that animate reasoning in SR.

Text- or Scripture-based reasoning most broadly conceived. Some authors apply the term SR to refer to any kind of reasoning that seems to emerge from out of scriptural or Scripture-like texts. These might include reasonings from out of a single canon (such as the Bible), or out of a single document, or an entire tradition. It is best to accept these usages as offered on analogy with SR. But we do not expect such uses to reflect the more precise logical characteristics we attribute to SR.

Civilizational dialogues between scriptural traditions and across many generations. At Minzu University in Beijing, Bin You[29] defines Scriptural Reasoning as a civilizational dialogue between scripturally based religions. His prototype is dialogue between Jesuit Catholicism and Confucianism during the Ming dynasty, displayed prototypically in Matteo Ricci's extensive project of translating Confucian classics.[30] You recognizes Formational SR; he engaged David Ford and later, in 2011, he invited me to introduce our approach to SR. In 2012, he invited fifty young Chinese scholars to join a week of SR study with seven SR scholars. But he prefers the civilizational approach. During the week of study, I lectured on the importance of the SR table, around which the reasoning of SR flows. You commented to the audience, "At Minzu, the Ming dynasty is the table, around which Catholic and Confucian Scriptures reason with each other through the centuries."

SR as literary theory. At Renmin University in Beijing, Huilin Yang[31] acknowledges the work we have done in Abrahamic SR but suggests that there is much more to be learned when SR is moved to the Chinese context. He writes:

> The Scriptural Reasoning movement, promoted by many religious scholars in the West, has incorporated a series of crucial hermeneutical propositions. If we extend the movement from the dialogues within the Abrahamic traditions to the dialogue

---

29. At Minzu University, he is Professor of Christianity and Biblical Studies and Founding Director, Institute of Comparative Scripture and Interreligious Dialogue.

30. See, for example, You, "To Be Harmonious." You also examines civilizational dialogue in contemporary China: see You, "Literacy, Canon."

31. He is Academic Vice-President of the University, founding editor of the *Journal of Christian Cultural Studies,* and director of Renmin University China's Center.

between East and West, then the translation and interpretation of Chinese classics by Western missionaries can be regarded as profitable case studies. If we want to solve the problems of the "constitutive subject" and the "projected others" completely, we must thoroughly get rid of the discourse logic of "determinate meaning" and "cultural identity." Here the "hermeneutical circle" and the "impossible possibility" can provide a necessary supplement to the current theories of Scriptural Reasoning. In the process of translating and interpreting the Chinese classics, the missionaries underwent a shift of identity. The missionaries used Western concepts to name Chinese ideas and thus paradoxically brought Chinese ideas into Western conceptual systems, providing a lively experience of understanding common values anew in a pluralistic context.[32]

One lesson is to read SR as a civilizational dialogue; like You, Yang writes and teaches about the dialogue of scriptural religions throughout the various dynasties of China.[33] A broader lesson is to read SR as a literary dialogue: a postmodern account of the way literary texts, and not only Scriptures, enter into dialogue, one with the other, from document to document or genre to genre or literary period to literary period.[34] Here, SR becomes a method of comparative literature. Another lesson is to read SR as a way of studying dialogue among all religions: a postmodern account of interreligious reciprocity beyond the limits of personal and group identities. In 2013, Yang hosted a daylong session on SR as literary theory: a section of the annual conference of the Association Internationale de Littérature Comparée (AILC) in Paris. Our discussions that day resembled features of TR, SR, and more traditional academic debate.

Hearth to Hearth Interreligious Dialogue: In 2012, I undertook several projects in "Hearth to Hearth Dialogue (H2H)": efforts to enlist SR

32. Yang, "Scriptural Reasoning."

33. Yang writes, for example, "Possibly, an unintentional 'scriptural reasoning' started quite early when Chinese culture and ideology began to come in contact and collide with those of the West" ("The Possibilities and Values of 'Scriptural Reasoning' between China and the West," in Yang, *China, Christianity,* 164). See also "Language and Missionary Universities in China" (chapter 1); and, for contemporary civilizational studies, "'Ethicized' Chinese-Language Christianity and the Meaning of Christian Ethics" (chapter 4). For a recent study of Yang's engagement with Scriptural Reasoning, see Starr, *Chinese Theology,* 252–59.

34. See, for example, how he examines literary features of religious narratives concerning "the Other": "By questioning the 'subject' of human cognitive activities and the central 'discourse,' this insistence on absolute 'difference' and 'uniqueness' ensures mutual inspirations among different narrations." ("Possibilities and Values," in Yang, *China, Christianity,* 183).

reasonings as resources for diagnosing and responding to various types of interreligious violent conflict. The goal was not to bring FSR into war zones, but to draw out of FSR certain language-based practices of engagement and reasoning that might assist in peacebuilding work.

Having concluded an overview of the history and theory of SR, I turn, in chapter 4, to the practical focus of this book: how to teach and study SR and how these practices introduce a "logic of SR" that has applications beyond the table of SR study.

CHAPTER 4

Teaching SR
Classroom Narratives

How, then, to teach SR and how to set up an SR classroom? In this chapter, my answer is strictly empirical: illustrative narratives of classes I have taught, with summaries of some of my techniques. In chapter 5, I offer philosophic, semiotic, and pragmatic analyses of "what is going on" in these classes.

ILLUSTRATING HOW TO READ SCRIPTURE IN SR: A COURSE ON "JUDAISM AND ABRAHAMIC SR"

For the past fifteen years, I have offered an undergraduate Scriptural Reasoning course about every two years, sometimes focusing on politics but often on other areas, such as ethnography or text-interpretation. All these courses have been successful, except for the year that, for various reasons, the enrollment in an Abrahamic SR course was only seven students (as opposed to the usual twenty), without any students from Jewish or Muslim backgrounds. I learned that some significant religious differences *inside the classroom* are requisite for teaching the process of SR. Should I encounter such an enrollment on a future occasion, I would, with students' permission, change the class to a study of TR within the one tradition most familiar to the students. In that way, students could study across differences of denomination or proclivity that appear *within* a given tradition. At the same time, I have had success introducing SR *through* the study of TR, such as in my course on "Judaism and Abrahamic Scriptural Reasoning," the subject of this first course narrative.

The first half of this course addresses Jewish Textual Reasoning; the second half addresses Abrahamic Scriptural Reasoning. In between, I ask how reading practices in one tradition may or may not prepare members of this tradition to encounter readers from other traditions.

Part I of the course opens with an introduction to biblical and rabbinic Judaism, some history, and extended literary study. We focus on recent, readable scholarship on classical rabbinic practices of rereading and interpreting Scripture for the sake of guiding religious action in the world. I find the study of rabbinic scriptural interpretation, or *midrash*, an effective means of introducing not only classical Jewish faith and practice, but also some of the interpretive methods of Abrahamic Scriptural Reasoning. The following features of rabbinic midrash also correlate with features of classical Christian and Muslim practices of scriptural interpretation. I consider these features to have great significance for the practice of SR:

- *Attention to the scriptural text as the primary teacher:* An asymmetrical relation defines all SR: between the scriptural word (as given, revealed, gifted, commanded, or spoken) and communities of human readers who receive Scripture's word.[1]

- *Attention to the plain sense as gateway to all scriptural reading and interpretation:* For most Abrahamic traditions, Scripture teaches, first, through the black-on-white of its words and the plain sense of each scriptural text, as defined by each scriptural tradition and community. These are gateways to all knowledge of Scripture. They are therefore authoritative and relatively unchanging, but they are gateways, alone. To live the scriptural word, readers must come through the gates. For most Abrahamic traditions, this means sharing in the communal practices and experiences with respect to which Scripture's plain sense displays its performative meanings. What does it mean for participants in TR and SR study?

    Participants in a circle of TR study tend to enter through a single gateway: the text and plain sense of a single canon of scripture. They differ and debate about what they find inside the gates: different accounts of the meaning of scripture's plain sense, shaped by differing

---

1. The "Ten Words [commandments]" (*eseret hadibrot*) of Exodus serve as a prototype of Scripture's self-authorization: "God spoke all these words saying, 'I am the Lord your God who brought you out of the land of Egypt. . . . You shall have no other gods before Me'" (Exod 20). Another prototype is Qur'an 2:2, "This is the Book about which there is no doubt, a guidance for those conscious of Allah" (Salih International).

individual histories and experiences. Participants in a circle of SR study enter, on the other hand, through the gateways of several different scriptural canons, each of whose sets of words command equal authority around the SR table. SR discussion is animated by the different meanings participants derive from each and all of these sets of words, generating SR's characteristic back and forth[2] between singularity and plurality: the singular authority of each canon and of each set of texts selected for study, the plurality of canons and of text sets, the plurality of meanings attributed to each text, the singularity of each participant's text interpretation, the singularity and multivocity of the reasoning that may flow around the SR table.

- *Attention to the interpreted sense as Scripture's enacted word:* Scripture lives only for those who come through the gates, but this is not an eternal life; it is life's meaning for that occasion of reading, but not for the next one. The gateways of word and text must be entered anew for each occasion of reading. I take this as a rule of classical rabbinic *midrash*. While it was not as definitive a rule for the early communities of Christian and Muslim readers, it remained a recognizable option. Muslim and Christian scholars of SR have adopted that option as a legitimate direction in traditional reading and as the defining option for SR (although not necessarily for TR). SR is possible only if participants recognize the gateways of Scripture, keep those gateways open, and pass through them again on each occasion of reading.

- *Challenges to the plain sense are windows to the interpreted sense:* The Talmudist David Weiss Halivni refers to challenges in the scriptural texts as "maculations."[3] These, he argues, are imperfections (or "non-immaculate" moments in the text), but imperfections that serve the divine will, since they challenge ("goad" in the language of a famous Talmudic passage[4]) rabbinic readers to reread the plain sense in ways

2. Halivni refers to the *shakla vetarya*, "give and take," of the rabbinic sages' deliberations over religious law/ethics. Borrowing Bakhtin's term "shuttling," Fraade writes that rabbinic commentaries "have the effect of repeatedly shuttling its students between the scriptural prophecies and their sociopolitical fulfillment in their collective life" (Fraade, *Tradition*, 5).

3. Halivni, *Peshat and Derash*. See also Halivni, *Revelation Restored*.

4. "[R. Elazar] lectured again: It is written: 'The words of the wise are as goads, and as nails well planted are the words of masters of Assemblies, which are given from one Shepherd' (Eccl. 12:11). Why are the words of the Torah likened to a goad? To teach you that just as the goad directs the heifer along its furrow in order to bring forth life to the world, so the words of the Torah direct those who study them from the paths of death to the paths of life. But [should you think] that just as the goad is movable so the words of the Torah are movable; therefore the text says: 'nails'" (*Ḥag.* 3b).

that carry deep performative meanings for life in the readers' contemporary community. If so, do these messages bypass the plain sense? Following the Talmudic dictum, "the interpreted meaning never departs from the plain sense," Halivni replies that maculations summon rabbinic readers to reread troubling texts as correlative to troubles in their particular contexts of life and reading: in this sense, a maculation is not merely in the text but also in the community of readers; to repair one is also to repair the other. I do not presume that Halivni's Talmudic hermeneutic has direct analogues in classical Christian and Muslim scriptural hermeneutics. But I have observed that Christian and Muslim scholars of SR identify warrants for such a rule of reading within their traditions and that, like me, they value this rule as a significant element of SR: textual challenges are also signs of societal challenges and vice-versa. A movement between textual and societal reading is a signature of many successful practices of SR.

- *To read deeply is to open degrees of polysemy in Scripture's words and texts.* A famous Talmudic midrash rereads Psalm 62:12, "God has spoken once, twice have I heard this: that strength belongs to God," to mean that "a single verse results in many meanings, but a single meaning does not result from many verses."[5] For traditional rabbinic scholars, this does not mean that the plain sense necessarily keeps changing. It implies, instead, that interpretive rereading will not ignore the plain sense but will draw on semantic possibilities that are warranted by Scripture's words whether or not a given possibility governs the tradition's plain sense. SR may seem impossible for readers who are unprepared to entertain the notion of scriptural polysemy even for Scripture's interpreted and performative senses. Different SR scholars favor different degrees of polysemy; but I have not yet met an SR scholar who insists that each word and text of Scripture speaks monovalently.

To return, then, to Part I of my course. Our review of recent rabbinic scholarship culminates in class study of the online *Journal of Textual Reasoning*.[6] My goal is to have students examine the scriptural passages on which journal authors comment and, thereby, enter into the flow of scriptural reading and interpretation that weaves the individual essays of a journal issue into a circle of TR study. Once the class enters into this flow, we

---

5. *Sanh.* 34a.
6. Which I founded in 1989 and which is published since 2000 by the Library of the University of Virginia. It is now coedited by Mark James and Deborah Barer. http://jtr.shanti.virginia.edu/. For recent work related to TR, see Barer, "Law, Ethics."

conclude the first half of the semester by dividing into small study groups of four to six students and completing the following activities.

First, over several classes, each group performs its own variety of Jewish TR: reviewing the plain sense of a set of biblical passages, discussing challenges in the plain sense, and then discussing how a modest set of rabbinic commentaries addresses these passages and any challenges in them. The first time I introduced this exercise, I thought we would spend only half of a first day in these small groups before I returned to my lecture. But students enjoyed their small group study too much for me even to consider interrupting it. I learned that students do very well educating themselves in this fashion for three or more full class sessions, and I came to appreciate the energy and joy that is released in good, small-group sessions of TR or SR, opening pathways for deeper study of Scripture and commentary and for deeper fellowships of study: opening what the theologian Daniel Hardy called the "attractive powers" of Scripture.[7] *Second*, for their midterm activity, each group undertakes a shared writing project. After selecting and studying an issue of the *Journal of Textual Reasoning*, each group searches for additional scriptural and commentarial sources that would speak to the themes of that issue. Each group then composes its own issue of the *Journal* in miniature: introducing scriptural texts and analyzing rabbinic commentaries.

For Part II of the course, we turn to Abrahamic Scriptural Reasoning. Having already introduced Jewish traditions of reading, we spend four classes introducing Christian and Muslim traditions of Scripture reading and commentary, aided by guest lecturers. Then, for two weeks, we read through several issues of the online *Journal of Scriptural Reasoning*.[8] We conclude by studying one *Journal* issue in detail, debating how the authors reread texts of Scripture and commentary in light of the overall theme of the issue. This discussion sets the stage for the final month of class work, during which the class divides into new study groups, each of which will compose its own version of a full issue for the *Journal of Scriptural Reasoning*. This time, the goal is not to re-examine the sources of a past issue but to choose a new topic and new sets of scripture to study, compare, and interpret. Each student composes a journal chapter of about eighteen pages, and one student serves as editor, organizing the chapters and composing an introduction and conclusion in place of a separate chapter. If the final

---

7. Hardy et al., *Wording a Radiance*, 45–50.

8. Which I founded in 2001, published by the University of Virginia. http://jsr.shanti.virginia.edu/. The current editor is Jacob Goodson (see Goodson, *Narrative*). The associate editor is Simeon Zahl (see Zahl, "Tradition").

product is worthy, it is published as an issue of UVA's online *Student Journal of Scriptural Reasoning*.⁹

Additional Lesson: TR as an in-class teaching and learning practice. As in my Judaism and Abrahamic SR class, it may be useful to include sessions of both tradition-specific TR and cross-tradition SR in the same course. Study sessions might focus, for example, on a single scriptural pericope, on a set of brief texts, on a brief scriptural text with later text commentary, on a text followed by a string of commentaries, or on several lines of commentary on different texts. A teacher may facilitate such studies as in SR, following this sequence, for example: ask the group to read a scriptural text aloud, invite individuals to comment on challenging features of the text, invite others to add to the commentary, move to other verses and, after addressing several verses, move to a text commentary. I often find TR sessions useful, as well, within a course or group study in SR. After studying and comparing Qur'anic and biblical texts for a couple of weeks, for example, the group might devote a week to Muslim-specific text commentaries before returning to another tradition or comparison. Teachers might also follow their sense of adventure to explore unexpected types of text reasoning in service to the course theme: for example, facilitating TR or SR study of liturgical or other ritual texts, or even study of videos of certain rituals.

TR also works well as an instrument for teaching individual religious traditions. Minimally, it is helpful to offer students opportunities to study scriptural texts and commentaries in small group TR circles during class time. This works well even as part of the give-and-take of a lecture discussion. Robert Wilken and I enjoyed the results when we employed TR circles within a course we co-taught on rabbinic and Patristic commentaries. We found it helpful, for example, to break for twenty minutes of TR group study one half of the way through a one-hour lecture on rabbinic midrash or Patristic allegory. Such study opened student eyes to the inner steps of text interpretation, as if something barely visible now appeared enormous. Maximally, TR could serve as the primary focus for an entire course. Several of my courses on Judaism and interpretation or on Abrahamic traditions come close to this model.

ILLUSTRATING HOW TO FACILITATE FORMATIONAL SR IN THE CLASSROOM

Formational SR as an In-class Practice: In previous chapters, I have described the gateway practice of Formational SR (FS). Here, I illustrate how

9. http://abraham.lib.virginia.edu/sjsr/.

this practice can be integrated into an SR course. In an individual session of FS, the teacher offers a brief introduction to a given scriptural passage. Students divide into groups of two, rereading the passage aloud to each other and conducting about fifteen minutes of one-on-one discussion and debate about the character and meaning of that passage. The teacher then invites the pairs to reassemble as a single class, of ideally a maximum of fifteen students. The teacher facilitates a plenary discussion of the same passage, anticipating that students will have a lot to say about the kinds of reading and debate they exercised one on one. After a certain time, the teacher introduces a second scriptural text, to be studied in pairs and then in plenary session. In this second round, however, students discuss both the second text and aspects of the first text that arise naturally in discussion. One may expect the second plenary discussion to generate comments not only on the second text, but also on the relation between the first text and the second text. The teacher's final activity is to introduce more general discussion of how different scriptural texts relate one to the other, noting, for example, how one text may appear to reinterpret another. Concluding the session, the teacher may teach a hermeneutical lesson: that Scripture "speaks" not only through the meaning of individual verses or passages, but also through observable differences among different verses and passages. Since these differences cannot be seen without the reader's active participation, the teacher should explain that Scripture is a kind of literature whose reading requires its readers' active engagement. Students should learn that this engagement includes taking the risk of offering educated guesses about what Scripture may be doing when it presents different verses. A good lesson for final discussion is that good scriptural reading allows for the possibility of mistakes and of a range of imaginings, on top of attention to rhetoric, grammar, and intertextual reading. For subsequent class meetings, students should now be ready to perform FS study in small groups of four to six.[10]

SR Lessons to Teach by way of FS Study: Here is a sample of the SR lessons a teacher might deliver through exercises in small-group FS study followed by plenary teaching and discussion.

1. *Intra-scriptural interpretation*: a lesson about how Scripture instructs its readers through the way one text cites, extends, or comments on another.[11] For example, in-class small groups might study Genesis 1:1–2:4 ("In the beginning God created the heavens and earth. . . . When they were created . . .") followed by brief plenary discussion of

---

10. While a UVA PhD student, Emily Filler composed SR guidelines that remain a helpful resource for FS study. For related work on TR, see Filler, *Total Textual*.

11. See Fishbane, *Biblical Interpretation*, 322.

the text's range of possible meanings. The groups then discuss Isaiah 26:4 ("For in Yah the Lord you have an everlasting Rock"), after which they read Isaiah 26:4 as if it were a commentary on Genesis 1:1–2:4. Among questions to ask the groups are: "After the exercise, what do you think about your initial plain sense readings of Genesis 1–2? Are certain readings of Genesis more/less compatible with Isaiah 6:4? Take time, now, to locate and study a third text that you might read as a different commentary on Genesis 1–2. Which readings of Genesis are more/less compatible with this third text? Now, imagine that some community of readers prefers reading Genesis by way of Isaiah and another prefers reading Genesis by way of your third text. Speculate a little: could these preferences suggest any differences between the two communities' styles of interpretation or belief?"

2. *Scriptural Religion*: Based on the first lesson, another lesson is to show how a scriptural tradition *works*. As illustrated in the FS method of study, a scriptural tradition reproduces itself by teaching its students not only to read Scripture in a certain way but also to reason thereby in certain ways, and to do this in the fellowship of certain communities of fellow students. In this way, the tradition teaches its students certain ways of *reasoning*, which are, at the same time, ways of *relating to other human beings* (at least those with whom one studies) and of *interpreting texts* (texts of Scripture, but the class has not yet discussed what Scripture "means" in general). In a course on SR, a teacher might guide students through several sessions of this kind: treating a range of different texts that display different themes and, more importantly, that illustrate different ways that scriptural passages might relate one to the other. What lessons can reflective readers "read into" these differences? Once students get accustomed to combining close textual reading with imaginative reflection on the verses, the teacher may then introduce them to deeper levels of reflection about patterns of scriptural hermeneutics and the varieties of thinking to which these give rise.

3. *Interreligious study*: A third lesson is to demonstrate a distinct approach to comparative religious study: one that works from the "inside" of a religion while also speaking to the commonalities and differences among a set of different religions. Consider, for example, a course that teaches two or three scriptural traditions simultaneously. As discussed under intra-scriptural study, students spend a session on the biblical story of Adam and Eve. In a lengthier session, they study a few passages on the creation of Adam from the Qur'an (for example from Surah 3:58 ff.), exploring several possible readings of the Qur'anic text, while also

looking back and forth at the Qur'anic and biblical accounts. When I continue this process for several weeks, students report that they tend, first, to compare one scriptural canon to another and, later, to hear the canons *speak* one to the other. The canons speak, for example, through the way students examine accounts of Adam in several different texts: reading one Qur'anic text, they debate Adam's relation to angels; reading one biblical text, they debate Adam's accepting what Eve gives him; reading a second Qur'anic text, they debate God's educating Adam, which leads to a discussion of the Psalmist's asking of the Lord, "What is Adam/humanity that you are mindful of him/them?"(Ps 8:5), which leads to another reading, and so on. In this manner, FS invites students to conceive of certain religious traditions, first, as processes of scriptural reading and interpretation. FS then invites students to *participate* in exercises of scriptural reading and interpretation so that they might better imagine what it might be like to practice this one aspect of religious traditions. FS then introduces students to interreligious difference by inviting them to participate in different processes of reading and interpretation. To be sure, the exercise I have described is not a gateway to comparing the practices of various traditions but a means of broadening participants' range of experiences so they could imagine how different scriptural traditions could conceivably receive and interpret different texts in different ways. The next step is examining individual religious communities, encountering their members, and studying their beliefs and practices—including practices of reading and interpretation.

This lesson illustrates how the FS approach differs from modern academic practices of comparative religion. In modern practices, one typically begins with purportedly universal concepts—such as "the sacred" or "reference to gods"— with respect to which theorists seek to compare different religions. In FS, however, only two or three religions are compared at a time, and the terms of comparison emerge from out of relations among practices of religious groups. These relations include interactions across the groups or across group practices, including practices of reading and interpretation. But how can theorists compare religions if there is no neutral or third language through which to compare them? In FS, the third term is not a linguistic or conceptual construct but a human practice. Some community of study serves as the third something through which two or more religions engage one another. *The crucial lesson is this:* The product of communal study is not some set of sentences taken to *represent* similarities and differences across the religious groups.[12] *The product is, instead, the process of interaction and dialogue among members of the community of study as they engage and interpret and re-engage the religious groups' practices. This process of interaction and dialogue becomes the third something with respect to which the community measures relations among a set of religious group practices.* Inter-group relations are measured only through the questions, answers, dialogues, and discoveries that emerge through the activities of the community/team that desires such measurement; chief among these activities are interactions with a set of religious group practices in each time and place. By way of FS, comparative religion becomes a context-specific event of relation among a set of religious group practices and the community/team that desires this comparison. By way of the event, the community/team will most likely experience a change in its desires.

4. *Studying Change within a Given Religion:* A fourth lesson is to apply the preceding approach to the study of changes within a single scriptural tradition. Students first study a set of scriptural passages within one tradition and then examine commentaries on selected passages, drawing the commentaries from a specific stage of the tradition's reception history. Students study both base-text and commentaries, first, as independent texts and, then, as relating in various ways one to the other. Next, students examine an historically third layer of commentary/text reception and then a fourth and so on. Teachers may find it useful to introduce socio-historical studies as well. I have found it helpful if students study the texts apart from social history, to get a sense of the tradition's intertextual dynamic, before they turn to the social histories. The goal is to have students learn enough social history that they can offer hypotheses about the conditions of life that could possibly have moved a community to reread an ancient text in a specific way. The goal is not to master the histories but to practice the approach of reading enough to offer reasonable hypotheses and debate their strengths and weaknesses in class. Students learn that their claims operate within the class fellowship of study rather than in some neutral space.

5. *SR and Religious Belief: Eschatological, Congregational, and Earthly Types of FS:* As theorist (but not as facilitator), I like to gaze imaginatively at FS as an ideal type to be realized differently in different contexts. I perceive this FS as realized fully only in some end-time scenario in which small circles of participants share their explorations of the possible

12. See James, "Communal Thinking."

meanings of selected verses from several scriptural canons. In this vision, all participants are religiously observant within various traditions, yet they all read the primary languages of each other's scriptural canons. They treat each hour and a half session of SR as a ritual space: a time set apart to share modes of consciousness unlike those that typify their everyday lives and sacred spacetimes. Before and after the shared time, they inhabit their normal bodies, interacting as participants from distinctly different religious traditions. Within that ritual time, they allow each other to explore both traditional and innovative ways of interpreting verses within and across the borders of sacred canons: rediscovering the literary power of various traditions of reading, and of challenges latent within given texts (grammatical or performative), and of imaginings that seem to rest unseen under everyday habits of reading. In this vision, several sessions of study lead participants into increasingly uncharted levels of engagement.

The vision interests me as a way to imagine the elemental pattern of SR as, at once, a way of reasoning and a way of engaging the divine word. In the latter sense, I imagine the divine voice in its multiplicity as a community of voices brought into direct and elemental conversation. This is a thought experiment that I introduce to advanced graduate students of SR, to open logical and eschatological imaginings, without, I hope, seeding unrealizable or inappropriate goals for on-the-ground SR planning and facilitation. I need to work harder to distinguish the thought experiment from more earthbound educational planning. Toward that end, I re-imagine the scenario of FS in three other ways, which I shall label, "One step short of eschatological," "Congregational" and "Earthly" SR.

FS: one step short of eschatological SR. This is a type of FS I often encounter when working among academic peers and advanced students. It is close to my eschatological ideal, except that participants bring different levels of familiarity with the scriptural canons, most know only one scriptural language, and different individuals have different goals of study. The best way to facilitate this type of FS is to enjoy the event of study heartily, to display one's enjoyment, to encourage participants to read and comment freely in their different ways, but also to remain alert as facilitator: noticing what is happening, who is speaking too much or too little, which texts are getting under- or over-read, which lines of interpretation are worth extending, and which have gone on long enough, and, all the while, standing ready to act, subtly and quietly, to keep the various aspects of this study in balance.

FS: the congregational ideal type. This scenario comes closest to the expectations of most congregations when they prepare for interreligious study. For most congregants I have observed, the goal of interreligious study is to enable members of different religious groups to get to know each other's beliefs and practices in an amicable setting of fellowship and discussion. When SR study is identified with this kind of interreligious study, members of each group learn, simultaneously, about the other group's practices of study and belief. In this kind of congregational study, each group preserves the integrity of its traditions of study. Some SR scholars characterize this approach as "parallel TR," since members of the two groups retain their tradition-specific identities and rules of practice while sharing in a single session of study.

FS: the earthly type. This is the type I usually observe rather than imagine. It is the way the human beings who join a SR fellowship tend most often to engage each other across the borders of various scriptural canons. Sometimes the engagement tends toward the eschatological type, sometimes toward the congregational type. When I plan SR sessions, as teacher or facilitator, I tend not to hold either pure type in my mind but to maintain this in-between type as kind of earthly ideal. Keeping the two ideal types in mind as limit cases of SR, I tend to engage a setting of SR with only a vague plan, which acquires definition only once I see who has joined the group and how they are responding to the readings and to one another. I might, for example, begin with a plan closer to the eschatological type but then change directions if I sense that things are going slowly. I might say to the group, "Well, let's stop for a minute and try something: let's go around the circle and have everyone talk a bit about how they read this particular verse." If discussion warms up, I might (or might not) then facilitate back toward the eschatological type. On another occasion, I might begin with a plan closer to the congregational type but then change directions if I observe participants racing ahead with a greater play of interpretive possibilities. In this case, I might stop and ask the group, "Do you sense where we're going?" I would then evaluate if most of the group is uneasy about the move (in which case I would nudge discussion back toward congregational SR) or if most of the group is ready for more radical SR (in which case I would reassure them about the temporary character of what we are about to do). As teacher/facilitator of FS, I need to be quiet much of the time, but I also need to know when it is time for intervention. The deepest movement of SR reasoning happens "on its own" only in rare cases or among deeply experienced participants. Most of the time, thoughtful and prudent facilitation is a must. SR is not, after all, something these traditions have seen before: it is compatible with the traditions and can be performed among the most orthodox believers, but it asks these traditions to do something they have simply not been asked to do before. A general lesson: when introducing FS into any course, it is best if the teacher has some ideal type in mind while also being prepared to make ad hoc decisions as needed.

ILLUSTRATING HOW TO TEACH SR AND SERVICE LEARNING

As originally conceived, SR is not an ivory tower activity but a practice that moves from text study to reparative work in the world.[13] Nonetheless, we founders of SR were wary of the dangers of moving prematurely from text to world. We recognized that SR challenged ingrained habits that favored individualized and intra-disciplinary thinking within the academy and doctrinal and intra-denominational thinking within the religious traditions. We therefore urged participants to delay their turn to reparative work until they had taken time to acquire SR habits of relational thinking. But the founding SR groups have tended to delay this turn too long. By 2010, I felt it was high time to explore what it means to move from SR study to action. One of my first steps was to transform the Abrahamic SR course I taught for many years into a community service learning course: "Faith and Community in the Abrahamic Religions."[14]

Habitat for Humanity: Reviewing various options in Charlottesville, an assistant and I decided to work with Habitat for Humanity of Greater

---

13. For illustrations of Jewish TR in the world, see Zoloth, *Health Care*; Cohen, *Justice*; Epstein-Levi, "Polyvocal"; and of Christian TR, Ford, *Upside-downness*.

14. UVA Fall 2011. In this effort, I understood "service learning" to mean course work that includes service work in community-based projects in our environing town of Charlottesville. The director of the University of Virginia's Office of University Community Partnerships (Megan Raymond) guided me in the process. I received one of the Office's Academic Community Engagement grants to cover some class preparation time, an honorarium for a graduate assistant, and course expenses (transportation and the cost of monthly suppers that we provided for students and the Charlottesville families with whom they worked). I worked with a sophisticated community service employee (Katie Geisshuessler), who provided extensive advice on how to locate a partner institution in the community and who co-designed the project and co-wrote our grant application. We began this work more than a year before the course was to meet, and I spent two hours a week on this work throughout the entire year, on occasion many more hours.

Charlottesville, which often attracts student volunteers and which was embarking on a project of special interest: planning and building an entire city block of homes. The project added "community building" to Habitat's bread-and-butter work of house building. Partner families who sought to live in this city block would need to cooperate with one another not only as neighbors but also as members of a homeowner's association. We judged that "poverty, housing, and charity" would serve as a good theme for scriptural study, and the Habitat director judged that our fellowships of SR might contribute a resource for community building among partner families.[15] After several months of preparatory discussions, we drew up a partnership plan: Habitat would welcome our students as monthly home construction volunteers, invite us to host the Partner Families' monthly pizza suppers, and send Habitat staff on occasion to present class lectures and join in class discussion of issues on housing and poverty.

We characterized the course as a reparative response both to conflict among the Abrahamic religions and to housing needs in our town: "In a time of violence among the three Abrahamic communities, this course examines two potential practices of peace: shared study across religious borders and shared efforts to repair society. Students will study Abrahamic traditions about shelter. And they will join Habitat for Humanity's effort to help families in need build their own homes." As characterized in the following excerpts from students' final reports, the course integrated five styles of teaching and learning:

1. *Readings, lectures and class discussion on the three Abrahamic scriptural traditions. Faith from the classroom or the pulpit?*

> We talked about how study of Scripture on charity relates to doing charity, how words can relate to reality. This is a new concept for me. I have always thought of religions as something to be studied and investigated, but never have I let it reach out from behind the glass of my clinical observation and into my daily life. . . . There is something empowering in the way we study Scripture. Our small group, exploring and picking apart meaning together, feels like an adventure. Kelly (a grad mentor[16]) described it as "gentle" and I think it is—with no outside "truth" demanding acceptance or validation. No assumptions of what I must believe. It is easier to take it seriously, to see as Scripture as more than something to be held at arm's length. And so I

---

15. The Habitat Director was Daniel Rosensweig, the Partner Family coordinator Shelley Winter.

16. While a graduate student, Kelly Figueroa-Ray (UVA PhD 2018) mentored SR groups and began to write on SR. See Figueroa-Ray, "Lady."

begin to see faith in life, as I respond to cries where I can. (Anna Boynton)

2. *Revelation and Poverty*

We read that Revelation is not confined to the Qur'an because Allah is revealed in the cosmos as well: "As the universe is the Creator's speech through deed, so the Qur'an is His speech through word."[17] I took this to mean that just as the Qur'an "cries out" for charity and care for the poor and the orphaned, the actual cries of those who are suffering should also be heard as revelation.... Cohen explains how, in the Jewish community, "poverty was more economic than social, [because poverty] knows no social barriers": the poor and rich alike are vulnerable to affliction and thus potential recipients of charity.[18] For me, this way of looking at poverty greatly challenges American society, where poverty is both an economic and a social condition. The gap that divides rich and poor is very wide and the barriers that prevent movement between the two states are in some instances insurmountable.... While it seems contradictory, could it be the case that giving virtue to poverty decreases solidarity among the poor and rich, while stigmatizing poverty (not necessarily the poor) does just the opposite?" (Ashley McKinless)

3. *In-class SR*

In the beginning of the semester, Scriptural Reasoning was seen as a method to bridge the gap between a believer and a scholar; ... perhaps even the three Abrahamic traditions could be studied together.... We often concluded that Scripture did not have just one meaning, but infinite meanings.... By the end of the semester, [we observed something] slightly different.... The act of Scriptural Reasoning was like a tent surrounding the participants ... [so] that they might be protected as a community.... By the end of the semester [we concluded] ... that the goal of practicing SR was not to attempt to make the three traditions agree with each other... but only to give them a place and time in which they may study each other's Scriptures together in a friendly manner. What an important and valuable practice in today's world! (Anonymous)

4. *The Class as a Lab*

---

17. Mermer, "Principles of Qur'anic Hermeneutics."
18. Cohen, *Poverty and Charity*, 68.

Something powerful happens when people combine physical volunteering with learning. It is like the "word and deed" combination that Millard Fuller extols in *Theology of the Hammer*.[19] The deeds we did outside of the classroom (building, partner family dinners, dialoguing with other scholars) made sense of the words we formulated and exchanged inside the classroom. Instead of being passive learners, we become active agents in creating something. The classroom lab was a place of baptism by fire, where theory was converted to action and tested and refined by the ever-present cries of the real world—cries elicited by actual people with names in an actual town. Students were forced to take ownership of their hypotheses. We could not merely absorb information as passive consumers in the classroom. In the lab, we were forced to become stakeholders in the marketplace of learning. (John Gayle, graduate mentor).

5. *Narrative Reasoning with Partner Families*

The Habitat administration was concerned that a Scripture-based approach like SR might make partner families uncomfortable, since we could not presume what attitudes they might have toward religion. As an alternative, the class developed a practice we called "narrative reasoning," inviting Partner Families and students to write brief narratives about topics related to the search for housing: personal accounts, for example, about "houses I have lived in, and the home I hope for." After collecting and editing the narratives, class members selected brief selections for each circle of partner families/students to discuss over our monthly pizza suppers.

> The principle of reading Scripture is that, through study, we must let the past inform our present. In the move from Scriptural Reasoning to narrative reasoning, . . . this principle is not lost but preserved, even enhanced. . . . To describe their first memory of a home, partner families recall the worn floors of childhood, the smells of their favorite foods, the sounds of their crying sister, a rumbling television set, the feeling of arriving home from school and the screams of the children next door. . . . Each family comes to the pizza-laden tables with a history marked by difficulty, but also with hope. . . . The narratives collected are eclectic, idiosyncratic, scatter-brained, and precious: the histories of people, to be studied with care, acuity, and a desire to understand. (Evie Kling)[20]

19. Fuller, *Theology of the Hammer*.
20. Another pertinent entry: *Narrative Reasoning*.

ILLUSTRATING HOW TO APPLY SR TO PEACE AND CONFLICT STUDIES

Since 2010, I have explored ways of applying SR more directly to projects in foreign affairs, peace and conflict resolution. All our work in SR has concerned conflict resolution to the extent that every SR dialogue is study across difference and, in that sense, addresses ways of repairing relations of potential mistrust, misunderstanding, or hate. We extended this kind of SR dialogue to international settings, where differences among participants may be greater than they are within some of our local community and academic settings. Examples include our SR project in Cape Town (described in chapter 1), SR fellowships in Beijing China, Dubai, Oman, Jerusalem, Berlin and several other cities. The "1000 Cities Project" in North America extended SR fellowships to approximately thirty environments of religious

> In both narrative and Scriptural Reasoning, it [may be] easy to identify the plain sense of the text, but it is difficult to uncover the interpreted sense, asking "why did the author write this way?" and "how can I relate this to my situation?" But [the challenge of responding to] this difficulty is what brings different people together and helps communicate across religious and cultural barriers. Here, for example, are excerpts from two partner family narratives.
> 1. Home for me is . . . my country . . . , people who share my same culture and grew up in the same or very similar contexts as I did. Those experiences shape people in similar ways. Culture includes language, religion, attitudes toward life in general, beliefs, education, tradition, foods and more. I think that home for me also includes the house that I live in today, and the people who live in it.
> 2. Home is both a dream and a goal. It brings independence. A home is a peaceful environment, full of light and space. Home takes preparation. Sometimes our house would get cluttered with stuff, making it less of a home! Homes need purging. Purging requires help!
>
> In Scriptural Reasoning, we interpreted texts as displaying "cries," or signs of the need for social repair. The two narratives may be interpreted in the same way, displaying cries that call for reparative responses. #2 states, "Homes need purging. Purging requires help!" Here, the author's cry is literal; responsibility is left to the reader to help those in need of better shelter. . . . #1 offers another form of response to this cry for help: "Friends can sometimes help you, but no one cares for you as much as your family does, especially when you have a problem." . . . [But what of family members who] remove themselves from the desperate needs of their relatives? This kind of question generates good narrative reasoning, as participants enter lively discussion about best ways to respond to a family's needs. Here, participants learn lessons from each other that could also be applied to their own lives. . . . Narrative reasoning, using techniques like those of Scriptural Reasoning, allows participants to form a community of dialogue out of which the narratives they read become sources of teaching they may apply to their everyday lives (From Daniel Novick's final essay, "Theories of Narrative Reasoning: Applying Scriptural Reasoning Techniques to Narrative Reasoning").

difference. The most significant outreach to public SR was in the UK where, under the leadership of David Ford, the Cambridge Interfaith Program (CIP) received significant sponsorship from public and private institutions to promote societal as well as academic SR. More recently, I turned to areas of international relations, diplomacy, and peace building, beginning with a Henry Luce Foundation project testing the usefulness SR techniques in Middle East peace building, a U.S. State Department-related project on SR-related training methods in interreligious conflict-transformation, and the development of a UVA Research Initiative on Religion, Politics, and Conflict (RPC). RPC's first educational program was a graduate course on "Religion and Foreign Affairs."

Graduate Studies in Peace and Conflict: "Religion and Foreign Affairs" examines the recent turn to religion as a focus of attention in US foreign affairs. Why did religion receive relatively little attention before 9/11 in the US Department of State and in university programs in international affairs and diplomacy? The course begins with a survey of US government reports and foreign affairs literature on religion over five decades before 9/11. What happened in the early twenty-first century to make religion a front-page international news topic and a topic of at least modest concern in international affairs think tanks and agencies? The course examines the role of religion in political and military conflicts over the past decade, including detailed case studies of religion and conflict in the Middle East and South Asia. The course also addresses recent academic writing and DOS policy on the probable role of religion in conflict and peace in the coming decade. Classwork is supplemented by field visits to pertinent governmental agencies and NGOs. The last third of the course examines current work by the DOS Bureau of Conflict Stabilization Operations (CSO), focusing on programs overseen by then Deputy Assistant Secretary for Partnerships and Learning, Jerry White, including ongoing work on conflicts in Burma, Libya, Israel/Palestine, Kenya, and Nigeria.[21] This is not a course for beginners but presumes prior course work in at least two of the Abrahamic traditions. Course study emphasizes both indigenous and academic accounts of the political force of traditional beliefs and of the role of traditional religious beliefs in what foreign affairs officers identify as "religious conflicts."

SR practice makes its appearance in the second month of the course as one of the current approaches to interreligious conflict transformation. Students read published collections on SR and practice SR study in-class to experience how SR stimulates dialogue across difference. In the third month of the course, students are introduced to "Hearth to Hearth Peace

21. See chapter 6, 155–58.

Building" (H2H), the SR-inspired approach to peace building that I have developed with UVA graduate students in the context of our work with CSO and several NGOs. As introduced in chapter 1,[22] I think of the hearth of a religion as what is most valued in a religious group's beliefs and practices: those dimensions of life that group members turn to in times of crisis, tension, or uncertainty in the hope of drawing nearer to the source of their deepest values and identities. Scriptural Reasoning acquires its name from a conspicuous practice in Abrahamic traditions of turning to scriptural texts as a primary means of accessing the hearth of a given religious community. When I refer to the hearth of a religion, I am not making any claim about what religion or a religion really is. I am, instead, offering a pragmatic or operational claim: that the notion of hearth is useful if, for whatever reason, it helps SR scholars or peacebuilders successfully anticipate how a given religious group might respond to a given environment, including the behaviors of other neighboring groups. In chapter 6, I offer a detailed account of how H2H works. As a sampling, here are three features of H2H I introduce in the concluding weeks of Religion and Foreign Affairs:

H2H in SR and beyond: After reintroducing SR as a practice of H2H, I illustrate how to identify "hearths" in non-scriptural religious groups. The class reads accounts, for example, of the place of traditional oral navigational lore in pre-Westernized Micronesian island societies. Transmitted through generations of revered navigator-captains, the lore is a poetic repository of proven navigational directions, interwoven with accounts of the gods, political wisdoms, and instructions for the ritual practices that accompany sailors' preparation before dangerous ocean journeys. I ask the class to consider whether or not Micronesian navigators and sailors might gather around the lore and the rituals of sailing the way members of Abrahamic groups gather around Scripture and its accompanying rituals. I then ask: If there are analogies, could inter-island discussions of navigational lore bear any analogies to SR? If so, could such discussions parallel H2H engagements among Abrahamic groups? The class then explores potentially hearth-like features of other non-scriptural traditions.

Symptoms of potential conflict: During the final two weeks of the course, students discuss four lessons in H2H diagnostics: the importance of group language use as a source of symptoms of potential conflict between one group and another; how to read group value judgments, spoken or written, as highly sensitive sources of such symptoms; the importance of identifying value terms that appear in such judgments and of measuring the range of meanings (what we call "semantic range") that a group associates

---

22. See chapter 1, 18–24.

with such terms; and how to trace probable correlations between changes in semantic range and changes in a group's probable future behavior toward other groups.

H2H and peacebuilding policy: The course concludes with a discussion of how training in approaches like H2H might or might not help government and NGO policymakers improve their capacities to diagnose and respond to potential religion-related conflicts.

SR in Peace and Conflict Studies: An Undergraduate Course: First offered in 2004, my UVA undergraduate course in Abrahamic SR addresses the subtopic of international politics, diplomacy and religion. The course asks what the consequences for peace would be if diplomats and foreign policy analysts took religion seriously: first, as a subject of ethnographic study to understand the actual context of a given conflict and, second, as a resource for better understanding the conditions for peace in a geographic and cultural region. The course began with two weeks of introduction to the scriptural traditions and two weeks exploring earlier histories of challenge and conflict among the traditions. The class then discusses several books on religion and conflict, culminating in extensive discussion of the argument that it is high time for diplomats to take religion seriously as a source as well as subject for peace negotiations. We then turn to the meat of the course: intensive small group research and writing on one major conflict that involves communities from at least two different Abrahamic traditions: for example, war in Bosnia, conflict in Ireland, or South Africa, or Israel-Palestine. We generate bibliographies for each student's research work and devote class periods to small group discussion of related areas of research and fellowships of SR study.

One of my favorite quotes from the 2004 class came as a student finished her report on war in the Balkans. She said in a tone of polite amusement, "Really, you don't think Scriptural Reasoning scholars are ready to sit down in places of actual armed conflict, do you? Let's get real!" The class agreed with the sentiment, but most also agreed that, before and after episodes of violent conflict, religious traditions should be a source of background study as well as a resource for diplomacy. The course included guest presentations by UVA faculty in international politics, including former ambassadors. Faculty guests also served as the audience for final reports from the student teams. The overall theme for the day was, "How might knowledge of religion have contributed to peace building efforts in these various conflicts?"

ILLUSTRATING HOW TO TEACH SR THEORY TO GRADUATE STUDENTS

In the early years of SSR, we SR founders sought to generate theoretical models by interpreting the practice of SR with the tools of our favorite sub-disciplines of philosophic, hermeneutical, and theological analysis.[23] We had some success, particularly with applications of Charles Peirce's semiotic and pragmatic theory. But at times we found ourselves pursuing contradictory ends. SR refers to reasonings that arise out of fellowships of SR study, not to ways of reasoning *about* Scripture from out of established, usually Western, models of reasoning. In this way, SR assumes certain postmodern and postliberal wisdoms about the limits of humanly constructed conceptual systems and processes of concept formation. As a constructive project, SR is not, however, skeptical about human capacities to participate in processes of reasoning that perform what humanly constructed processes cannot: we can reason beyond the limits of conceptual systems of reasoning, and fellowships of scriptural study can engage us in this kind of reasoning beyond limits. If we can participate in trans-historical traditions of reasoning after revelation, then we might imagine sharing in other kinds of reasoning that SSR has not yet explored: the reasonings of love relations; the reasonings of practices of justice, charity, or mercy; communal and societal reasonings; the reasonings of any natural processes, from the flight of bees to the movements of subatomic particles.

The latter example brings to mind the pertinence of SR to scientific studies as well as literary ones, and that means the pertinence of twentieth- and twenty-first-century probability theory, including statistics, quantum mechanics, and recent developments in systems theory. Probability thinking may prove central to future SR theory. I would put it this way: when Scripture offers us a verb stem with a wide range of probable meanings, then the meaning enacted in a particular reading in a particular context will fall within that range of probability. If we identify that range with the *interpretive meanings*, rather than *plain sense meanings* of Scripture, then it might be more accurate to trace the probable meanings of a scriptural term or pericope through a set of probability curves, rather than through some language- or literary-specific set of tropes. Readers might challenge me by saying, "But to build probability curves is to make use of a system of humanly constructed concepts!" In response, I would offer this narrative. One of my favorite class visitors at UVA is Olivier Pfister, Professor of Physics and director of UVA's quantum computer laboratory (computers made

---

23. More recently, see Goodson, *Narrative Theology*.

more intelligent by splitting streams of photons). Professor Pfister tells students in my "Scripture and Quantum Science" class how he uses Newtonian physics to construct his laboratory apparatus and quantum mathematics to construct his theories of how the photons will behave, but how he stands in wonder each day when he turns his laser apparatus on: "I am probably in a state," he says, "similar to what you call prayer and faith, because I have no way of fully anticipating what the photons will do, and I am able to complete each day's mathematical model only on the basis of what happens after the laser turns on; the results are different each day, and the final details of the mathematics are different each day."

The lesson I learn from Professor Pfister begins with his reference to the "final details" that differ each day. The difference between conceptual systems and probability systems is the degree of uncertainty that accompanies any probability: a measurable uncertainty. To participate in reasonings greater than our concepts is to construct the best we can but with a degree of uncertainty built into the construction, refining our construction and re-measuring its uncertainty at the end of each day, based on what our actual experience in the world discloses. These last sentences apply to the SR approach to Scripture as much as they do to quantum physics. There is much to say about Scripture prior to each day's reading, but a degree of uncertainty is built into each reading and there is no way of predicting the final details of what each day's reading will bring.

SR thickens the final details, makes it roomier by gathering many minds as well as traditions around the reading table and by enabling readers to move from reading to occasion-specific interpretation to circles of rereading and reinterpretation. SR reasoning is a name for lines of movement that emerge and may be observed among those circles: not individual thoughts, but patterns traced across a flow of utterances that moves from speech act to speech act around the circle. The defining question is "Patterns according to whom?" Reflecting on such patterns is not a part of SR practice per se; it is the stuff of secondary reflection *on* a fellowship of study, but I imagine that participants in strong SR circles sense and participate in such patterns in a pre-reflective way. I imagine this because I have seen such patterns strengthened through the hours of an SR fellowship of reading, as if, underneath the explicit work of reasoning about the meanings of words, subliminal choices are being enacted that strengthen, weaken, or redirect the collective product of so many hours of dialogue.

One type of SR theory emerges when members of an SR fellowship devote themselves, after sessions of study, to sessions of intentional reflection on the patterns of SR. SR theorists recall series of speech acts that appear (per hypothesis) to have contributed to a pattern of SR reasoning. The first task is to map the series. On the model of calculations in the quantum laboratory, the map is a probability function, mapping the relative likelihoods that a set of scriptural texts would be read by a set of readers as displaying a certain range of meanings. The next task is to test the usefulness of this map by adopting it, per hypothesis, as a rule for future readings. The test is to practice SR and then map apparent patterns, repeating this sequence over several sessions. The resulting maps are compared with the original map: if the maps are comparable, then the SR theorists have evidence that they have mapped a rule/pattern of SR. If so, the next task is to measure other behavioral consequences of this particular pattern, such as types of intragroup social relations, preferred study texts, recurrent conversations about belief, ethics, or hermeneutics.

Well, I am only speculating. We have not yet conducted this kind of theory-building on a scale large enough to generate testable theories. For this reason I thought it was time to frame a graduate course to introduce the process, refine and test it among students already experienced in SR: students of UVA's graduate program in "Scripture, Interpretation, and Practice."[24] This unique class is a laboratory-like activity in which much of the content is in the process, and the process is specific to the students who take the class at some time and place; the syllabus is regularly rewritten to reflect the results of in-class learning; and things happen in the class that I could not anticipate, much of it generating theoretical practices I had not anticipated. I name the class "What is Scripture?" and describe it this way:

> "What is Scripture?" That is the defining question for a core seminar in the UVA graduate program in Scripture, Interpretation, and Practice (SIP). While SIP prides itself in not asking essentialist questions like "what is?" this course risks the question but only as a source of context-specific, personal and tradition-based reasonings. I offer the course not only to prepare SIP students to perform SR theory, but also to enlist their assistance in identifying what SR theory should be.

How we conducted "What is Scripture?" in spring 2013. I began the course in a way I rarely do: offering broad introductory lectures. The first lecture was on the long history of postliberal thinking pertinent to the course topic: from sources cited in modernist theories of scripture (Descartes, Durkheim/Feuerbach, Wellhausen), to postmodern criticism of

---

24. See the program website, http://religiousstudies.as.virginia.edu/content/comparative-scripture-interpretation-and-practice. The focus is on comparative Abrahamic studies. Over its twelve-year history, the program has produced a good number of MA graduates and twenty PhDs all currently teaching at various universities internationally.

such sources (Lyotard, Foucault, Derrida, Wittgenstein), to illustrations of the postliberal critique (Barth, Rosenzweig, Muhammad Iqbal, Hans Frei/ George Lindbeck). For the second lecture, I reviewed these antecedents to SR theory: writings from the Society for Textual Reasoning and the Society for Scriptural Reasoning; postliberalism as "Another Reformation": resetting conditions for inter-traditional reasoning; post-postliberalism as "Another Enlightenment": resetting conditions for another kind of Enlightenment project; Descartes reformed: communities of reasoning (beyond the cogito); inter-tradition fellowships of contemplative reasoning; reformed rules of reasoning: multi-valued logics, relational logics, quantum logics; reformed reasonings: the logics and mathematics of scripture; a reformed organon: reformed categoriologies, philosophies, ontologies, practices; reformed disciplines; "Another Civilization": an unhumble thought game about what Western civilization would look like if the organon of academic reasoning were Scriptural Reasoning. In the third lecture, I introduced the primary work of the course: identifying the "reasoning" of Scripture as a way to answer the question of what Scripture is. I suggested that to identify reasoning is to identify and diagram observed patterns, in this case patterns of reading and interpreting Scripture, or what W. C. Smith calls "scripturing." Drawing on the wisdom of John Deely,[25] I surveyed several philosophic models that might contribute to our practice of diagramming: Pre-Socratics and the cosmos, Plato (Socrates) and Athens, Aristotle and the societal/natural world, Roman Stoics and early semiotics, Augustine and beginnings of our semiotics, John of Poinsot, Descartes to Locke to Hume to Kant, Peirce, Heisenberg.

Setting up the Course as a Laboratory: The plan for the course was to induce a laboratory environment in which students would discover ways of mapping different kinds of scripturally based reasonings. Such reasonings are not disclosed "in" Scripture but in activities of reading and interpreting Scripture: that is, "ye shall see them in their fruit." The goal for the course was not to produce any testable claims but to engage in a variety of exercises that would test our ability to make claims. I thought a good way to begin was to analyze three examples of what I take considered either ethnographic or postliberal scholarly readings of scriptural traditions. I chose W. C. Smith's readings of various scriptural traditions in *What Is Scripture*; Muhammad Iqbal, *The Reconstruction of Religious Thought in Islam*; Georges Dreyfus, *The Sound of Two Hands Clapping: The Education of a Tibetan Buddhist Monk*. I introduced a vaguely defined method for students to map patterns of Scriptural Reasoning in sample chapters of each of these texts.

---

25. Among many writings, see for example Deely, *New Beginnings*.

In class, the students and I revised and completed the method, revising it again throughout the course. After trying the method out on these three texts, we divided the class into small working teams that would re-analyze the results of these initial mappings, generating successively more abstract maps of the patterns of reasoning. Over several weeks of in-class lab work by these teams, we experimented with new kinds of teamwork. Some teams analyzed new readings, some teams mapped sessions of formational Scriptural Reasoning and then mapped the results and so on. Midway, we varied team membership, so that our final teams tended to include like-minded thinkers who would produce series of reports submitted in writing and orally to the class. Each report summarized three to five levels of progressively abstracted analyses of a pattern of Scriptural Reasoning, so that the first level illustrated what we called "empirical data" (discrete observations of individual acts of reading or interpretation) and the last levels illustrated the team's concluding claim about "what Scriptural Reasoning is" in a document or practice or text. We all agreed that our non-foundationalist use of the term "is" was to energize the team's effort to make a final claim about some specimen of reasoning. We knew that, after the fact, we would replace each "is" with "is for this specimen of reading/interpretation as analyzed by this team on this occasion" (functionally the same as "appears to be" or "could be mapped as," but most of us felt that "is for x at time y" better describes an actual state of belief or observation).

Laboratory Conclusions and Some Lessons from Charles Peirce: As I argue in chapters 1–3, Peirce's pragmatic logic and semiotic could be read coherently as a map of Scriptural Reasoning, following a method introduced by Augustine, explored through the Cartesian-Kantian tradition, and refined and formalized by Peirce. Peirce's map is not the only effective way of mapping Scriptural Reasoning; but, within the limits of a finite lifetime, I may have opportunity to refine only one model, so I have chosen to specialize in this one. (Among my students, those who are more oriented to scientific reasoning often want to learn Peircean ways of mapping; others choose hermeneutical or phenomenological or other models.)[26] As the class's laboratory work progressed, I therefore wanted them to test the students' maps against Peirce's. For my sake, I was curious to see if the student teams would rediscover what Augustine and Peirce discovered. For the students' sake, I hoped they would attempt to compete with Peirce: raising their game to catch up with Peirce's refinement and then stake out new analytic territory that I could not even imagine. I was very pleased with the results. Students

---

26. I hope that they think probabilistically even about their graduate learning, continually refining methods of inquiry in response to their experiences in the profession.

offered lengthy and complex reports, from which I will illustrate a few concluding excerpts:[27]

Team I reached this conclusion:[28] "Scripture occurs wherever there is mediation between a community and what is considered 'other' to the community. Scripture refers to the sign vehicle through which a community seeks this other." After class discussion and more work, Team I restated its conclusion: "Scripture is sign and action. Scripture is sign as it mediates between community and Other; it is action as it preserves, retells, and carries on that mediation. Definition of terms: Sign refers to the middle term of a triadic relationship; Action refers to the traceable movements of an agent; Mediation refers to the interaction between community and other."

Team II reached this conclusion:[29] "Scripture is the text/practice that members of a community consider objectively authoritative, but that those outside the community consider only subjectively authoritative." After class discussion and more work, Team II restated its conclusion: "Scripture is a contextually located function of disembodied cultural authority that enables mediation, clarification, and repair through its membership. Scripture mediates community and transcendent Other and prompts possible action."[30]

Team III reached this conclusion:[31] "Scripture is that which generates ineradicable problems and compels its readers to labor for clarification and repair." After class discussion and more work, Team III restated its conclusion: "Scripture is something that generates ineradicable problems for some group of individuals and then compels them, when they retell the event of having experienced these problems, to clarify the event by way of a practice

---

27. Combining my notes with those of Reuben Shank, a graduate student in the course.

28. Members: Jill Clare and Ellie Okwei.

29. Members: Nathan Hershberger and David Barr.

30. Team II added: "The concept of membership entails an in-group and out-group differentiated by the authority to which they subscribe. Individuals and groups that adopt a given authority are in fact enacting the same Scripture: although Scripture always has a specific temporal and geographic context, it may also be identified with that which appears elsewhere or in another manner." The team identified different species of Scripture: (1) Relational Scripture (interactive procedures such as debates, oral readings, performance); (2) Socializing Scripture (ritual stitches between the micro and macro realm of social organization, such as the concept of hajj or pilgrimage. All Scripture is social but not all forms are socializing); (3) Cognitive Scripture (memes such as "Do unto others as you would have them do unto you"); (4) Embodied Scripture (coding concepts through bodily engagements such as circumcision, a nun's habit, or a Tibetan student rocking back and forth during memorization); (5) Scripturalism (the organic process by which variants of Scripture are sustained, grown, and evolved beyond the control of any single human or organization).

31. Members: Dustin Hamby and Maryam Ashraf.

of interpretation and to repair these problems as they are encountered in a given context."[32]

Teaching Scripture and Teaching Reasoning: Students of "What Is Scripture?" read "Scripture" as referring to more than the set of texts that includes the Bible, the Qur'an, and so forth. The data for their laboratory work came from accounts of the way such texts were employed by Muslims, Christians, Jews, and Buddhists in various cultural and historical contexts. But the goal of the laboratory work was to mine the data for evidence of how these texts were received by those for whom they were "Scripture": through what practices and performances the texts were received, with what consequences for those who received them, and how the texts were perceived as signs of certain processes or understandings or modes of being. One team observed that what various peoples name "Scripture" serves to mediate their collective relation to that which is Other or transcendent. Another team observed that Scripture draws a distinction between those who recognize its authority and those who did not, where claims of authority might be shared by other communities. A third team observed that Scripture is associated with reparative processes. Understood soteriologically or pragmatically, Scripture *introduces* something problematic into the lives of those who receive it, compelling them to narrate stories of trials or suffering and to respond to the stories by seeking sources of repair.

These were sophisticated results from an advanced graduate course related to SR. The other SR courses I describe in this chapter focus more on the textuality of Scripture and the way textual meanings draw traditions and people together as well as apart. But all these courses concern reasoning as well as textuality. Even if the topic of reasoning is not raised explicitly, courses in TR and SR engage students and teachers in processes of interpretation and reflection that interrupt patterns of epistemology, ontology, and practical reasoning that are more typical of the modern university classroom. Chapter 5 offers more extended reflections on the reasoning parts of

---

32. Reuben Shank evaluated the reports: "The first team moved beyond a two-sided concept of scriptural authority... to Scripture as a context-specific function of a communal authority that empowers members to engage in various modalities of repair.... Scripture as social authority is no longer anonymous but one that enables members of the community to respond fruitfully to problems of all sorts. The second team discovered the action or practical conduct that follows upon the relation between a community and the Other.... Semiotics helped identify Scripture as the event wherein a relation between a community and its Transcendent led to the development of a fruitful practice. For the third team, pragmatics sharpens the 'ineradicable' character of 'scripture-related' problems.... Semiotics clarifies the conditions of communal response to some unavoidable problem.... In short, each team approaches a basic formula: xSyz which reads simply 'Scripture is that x which if z then y.'"

SR teaching: a review of reasons for bringing SR into the classroom and of the patterns of reasoning that tend to get stimulated by the SR classroom.

CHAPTER 5

What Is (Really) Going on in the SR Classroom?[1]

SR as Training in "Knowing Enough"

SR IS A FAMILY of practices. Like yoga, these practices have consequences for cognition, consciousness, spirit, emotion, understanding. Like rituals of worship and religious study, the practices have consequences for a range of relations: between person and person, text and interpretation, tradition and practice, persons and God. Like university as well as inter-congregational text study, the practices have consequences for the way individuals perceive different text-traditions and for the way different text-communities engage with one another. Observing thousands of SR study sessions over twenty-five years, I have observed many consequences of sustained SR practice, most of which—by far—are good consequences in the eyes of practitioners and of facilitator-scholars of SR. There is no predicting which consequences will characterize the practices of which group. But there are recurrent tendencies to be observed. The question is: who can observe them, using what tools of observation? The answer I offer throughout this book is: not just any observer and not just any tools.

The patterns and consequences of SR are largely invisible to disciplines of inquiry governed by two-valued conditions of truth or falsity, which means to most of the disciplines of inquiry promoted today by the dominant academic guilds in the humanities and social sciences. These patterns and consequences *can* be observed through disciplines informed by three- or

---

1. My thanks to Megan Helbling for assistance and editorial help on this chapter.

multi-valued conditions of truth. These include quantum logics, three-valued (non-Saussurean) semiotics, pragmatics, fuzzy logics (and comparable logics of relation or of vagueness), and related models of performative meaning. Readers may be unfamiliar with these latter disciplines, but this is not because they are odd or unscientific. It is because dominant guilds in the humanities and social sciences retain outmoded (in most cases, pre-twentieth-century) logics of inquiry, many of which are largely unchanged since Aristotle and certainly since Newton. Among such guilds I include those that claim to be highly critical of "scientistic" approaches but that, perhaps unwittingly, assume that scientific inquiry need be two-valued.

Employing several types of multi-valued inquiry, I have been able to draw formal models of patterns of SR reasoning and of SR relations. Over hundreds of SR sessions over the years, I have practiced ways of facilitating SR sessions that might, each time, nurture patterns of SR reasoning around the table; and I have learned ways of correlating a given model of SR with a given pattern of SR. Through this process, I have compiled a set of functional models, each of which serves as a rule of thumb for facilitating a given type of SR session. Extending this work, my hope is to identify ways of measuring the potential implications of a given pattern of SR for even the slightest observable changes in the way participants interpret the force of scriptural verses and in the way they engage those who interpret Scripture differently. In the last section of this chapter, I summarize in non-technical terms what I hope SR scholars might gain from such measurements. In the next section, I introduce what I consider the single most powerful effect of SR among religious practitioners: engaging "unknowing" as a positive activity of knowing.

I assume that, accustomed to the academy's primarily two-valued models of inquiry, readers might misinterpret my claims about unknowing as if they represented a choice for only one pole of the contrast pairs knowing/unknowing, apophasis/kataphasis, positive/negative accounts of reason, rationalist/anti-rationalist philosophies, or scientific/humanistic inquiries. Preferring uncertainty in the short run to misinterpretation in the longer run, I explore ways of bringing conventional, two-valued assumptions out of hiding, contrasting them with multi-valued logics, and only then reintroducing patterns of SR reasoning as patterns best identified through multi-valued inquiries. The result may seem hard to follow, but that is only because it is unfamiliar, and it is unfamiliar only because the dominant guilds have, wittingly or not, kept it that way. SR practice does not challenge the usefulness of two-valued logics. It challenges only the dominant guilds' efforts to over-extend the use of such logics beyond their proper domains and, thereby, to keep multi-valued alternatives out of view. I expect that SR reasonings will be valued, and valued for the right reasons, by academics and non-academics who simply happen, like members of many folk societies, to think about everyday things in multi-valued ways.

I hope general readers will not skip the technical pages to follow but will, instead, try to skim through them to glance at the differences between either/or (two-valued) models of inquiry and models that recognize the rationality of multi-valued claims. Examples of the latter are: "The evidence for this claim is incomplete, but there is reason for me to trust it until clearer counter-evidence emerges," or "She loves him" (understood as a claim about her reasonableness, having weighed the evidence), or "538 predicts that it is 83 percent likely that X will win."

ON UNKNOWING

One reason I respect and like religion is that religions recognize that significant aspects of their central truths and gifts are unknown *and* that to say something is unknown does not imply that it is out of reach. Religions tend to narrate events of direct encounter between human beings and what is unknown, so that the unknown is unknown to everyday cognition but not unknown in every possible way. In chapter 1, I refer to a tendency of religious practitioners to turn toward "the hearth"—their source of ultimate values and meaning—comparable in some ways to what Appleby calls the sacred. When I refer to the hearth of a religion, I am not making any claim about what religion or a religion really is. Instead, I am offering an operational (pragmatic) claim. Let me illustrate what I mean. Over twenty-five years and literally thousands of sessions of SR study, I am accustomed to seeing certain things happen somewhat regularly in the environments of Scriptural Reasoning and teaching. After all this time, I still cannot say for sure what I am seeing. But I can forecast well enough that, when I see a certain activity in an SR circle, I can form a testable hypothesis about what will happen next, either in the short or somewhat longer term. Offering such an hypothesis illustrates what I mean by offering an operational claim about religion. It is not a claim about what really is out there in the world or what really is the essence of something. It is a claim only about a proven utility: that attributing a certain, named characteristic to a given activity has enabled a research team (many times over) to anticipate that some other unseen activity will soon be visible to members of the research team.

This operational approach is doubly useful. For one, it respects the unknowable dimension of religion, while also serving the needs and conditions of a given project of research. An operational claim is offered only with respect to the assumptions and questions of the inquirers; its results are judged true or false to the degree that they enable inquirers to forecast, evaluate, or act as they hope to in relation to the subject of inquiry. This means that the results of inquiry cannot be generalized beyond the interests of the inquirers, except to the degree that additional researchers come to share these interests.

I adopt a comparable, operational approach to the study of SR. Offering claims that are verifiable but not ontological, I pursue an *operational approach to knowing that parallels the method of Formational SR*. SR engages its participants in processes that retain a degree of unpredictability, because each moment of reading or debate has the capacity to alter the direction of group study, even if in subtle ways. We cannot, therefore, privilege any single account of "what SR is": each session of SR practice has the capacity to alter what we mean by SR, even if in slight ways. Some readers may be uncomfortable with this degree of indeterminacy, but others may agree that knowledge and indeterminacy make happy bedfellows for scientists who explore the tiniest dimensions of the natural world (subatomic particles) as well as for religionists accustomed to disciplined practices of meditation and prayer.[2] Both understand Pascal's Wager; both appreciate the power of probabilistic reasoning as a measure of knowledge appropriate to our creaturely world; and both are comfortable with knowing in the face of the unknowable: what we might call "knowledge enough." I believe many children are comfortable with this kind of knowing, as are explorers, creative thinkers, poets, and, as I imagine them, practitioners of folk religions for whom "knowing God or the gods" is a matter of deep relationship rather than of clear vision.

In these terms, my primary account of SR is epistemological: SR as training in Knowing Enough. We may say that SR offers refresher courses in knowing enough for those who once encountered the sacred with surprise or even shock but who have since grown accustomed to domesticated forms of religious life. Or we may say that SR offers reassurance for those whose traditions suffer great change: when a tradition that once offered conceptual and linguistic coherence now seems beset by disorder and incoherence. SR offers reassurance, because it may renew practitioners' trust in the elemental words of their scriptural canons, apart from traditions of instruction that have, for the moment, lost their vitality. Or, in the open-ended liberal arts classroom, we may say that SR offers surprising lessons in "knowing in the face of unknowing" for students less familiar with religious traditions, who assumed that religious knowledge was always of the conceptually coherent

---

2. For a complementary essay, see O'Hara, "The Sentiment that Invites Us to Pray."

type, but who now discover the mysterious and polyvalent dimension of sacred Scriptures.

Here are brief clarifications of this epistemological account. Around the SR table, participants are free to read scriptural verses in terms of tradition-based learning, but traditional commentaries are not themselves on the table as subjects of group study. I therefore caution against practicing formational SR too often! Formational SR helps practitioners rediscover how far their scriptural canons may stretch, but it is unwise to over-learn this lesson, since, if over-stretched, the canons may lose their power to guide everyday life. I therefore recommend something like TR as an exercise for more regular use: scriptural study accompanied by traditional commentaries. TR encourages study across difference, but among different individuals or denominations within a single scriptural tradition.

SR is an effective learning tool in the liberal arts classroom, but there too it should be employed prudently. SR study can be meaningful for both traditional and non-traditional students, but excessive SR study could appear to relativize the tradition-specific contexts of performative meaning. Students should regard the time of formational SR study as if it were set-apart from the rest of class time, like a kind of in-class yoga of scriptural study. Another classroom challenge is to protect the dignity of the traditions or non-traditions represented in class while, at the same time, inviting students to comment freely. My preferred method is to draw class attention to individual words and verses rather than to larger textual units. Most students consider this a novel approach that stimulates them to read Scripture in surprising ways: relying, for example, more on their direct observations and sense of language and less on their longer-term habits of belief. Students report that they do not typically associate this approach with either the classroom or religion: this is something new and unexpected. In my observation, the students have entered an environment of probabilistic knowing or "knowing in the context of unknowing."

SR training in "knowing enough" is training beyond the limits of Hellenic accounts of the "unknown" as the "nonfinite." SR offers direct contact with the unknown. What can this mean? I shall approach this question through an informal distinction between the predominant Hellenic sense of the infinite (*apeiron*) as chaotic and the predominant biblical and Qur'anic sense of the infinite as a primary characteristic of God the Creator. My account is informal, because I am not drawing technical distinctions or examining borderline cases. Plato serves as prototype: denying infinity to the Demiurge (god), because the infinite (*to apeiron*) is formless: that which can be ascribed to the material substratum but never to what has or gives form. The infinite, says Socrates in the *Philebus,* denies form and thus knowledge. For

Plato as for Anaxagoras, the origin of the universe is formless (*to apeiron*), but out of the unformed the demiurge brought form and fashioned the cosmos. To exist in this cosmos is to be formed, and to know is to know form or what is formed. But what of a God who is unknown and whose infinity is a source of all creation and all knowledge? The movement of SR reasoning is a movement from known to unknown and to new discoveries within the unknown. It is highly unlikely that such a movement can be comprehended within the frame of Hellenic understandings of the known and the unknown. The Neo-Platonist Plotinus intimated God's infinity, but explicit philosophic claims about divine infinity emerged only from Jewish, Christian, and Muslim accounts of God.

An epistemology appropriate to SR may be drawn out of both classic and contemporary Abrahamic philosophic sources, starting with Augustine. Augustine, the Christian Platonist, entitled a chapter of his *City of God*, "Against Those Who Assert that Things that are Infinite Cannot Be Comprehended by the Knowledge of God":

> Far be it . . . from us to doubt that all number is known to Him whose understanding, according to the Psalmist, is infinite. The infinity of number . . . is yet not incomprehensible by Him whose understanding is infinite. And thus, if everything which is comprehended is defined or made finite by the comprehension of him who knows it, then all infinity is in some ineffable way made finite to God . . . Wherefore, if the infinity of numbers cannot be infinite to the knowledge of God, by which it is comprehended, what are we poor creatures that we should presume to fix limits to His knowledge, and say that unless the same temporal thing be repeated by the same periodic revolutions, God cannot either foreknow His creatures that He may make them, or know them when He has made them?[3]

After adopting the Platonic axiom that finite form is the measure of knowing, Augustine then introduces into the axiom a scripturally grounded distinction between human and divine knowing: finite form is the human measure of knowing, but God's understanding is infinite. It is God who makes what is infinite finite for us so that we might know it. Note the implication Augustine draws out in *Trin.*: "God, although Incomprehensible, is Ever to be Sought." In these terms, the unknowing recognized by religion is not skepticism but a call to recognize the limits of finite knowing and an invitation to another dimension of knowing. Is this other-knowing independent of the created world? Augustine continues:

3. Augustine, *Civ.* XII.18.

> [T]he prophet Isaiah testifies that the Lord God can be found when He is sought. . .: "Seek the Lord; and as soon as you have found Him, call upon Him: and when He has drawn near to you, let the wicked man forsake his ways, and the unrighteous man his thoughts." If . . . when sought, He can be found, why is it said, Seek ye His face evermore? Is He perhaps to be sought even when found . . .?[4]

Human knowing is by way of what humans know, creaturely knowledge. But this knowledge invites the knower to a different relation to the author of what we know: a mode of knowing mediated through the failures of creaturely knowledge. Augustine continues:

> [T]hings incomprehensible must so be investigated that no one may think he has found nothing when he has been able to find how incomprehensible that is which he was seeking.. . . For it is both sought in order that it may be found more sweetly and found in order that it may be sought more eagerly. The words of Wisdom in the book of Ecclesiasticus may be taken in this meaning: "They who eat me shall still be hungry, and they who drink me shall still be thirsty. For they eat and drink because they find; and they still continue seeking because they are hungry and thirsty."[5]

My account of unknowing and infinity is offered in dialogue with Jewish and Muslim as well as Christian philosophic theologians whose approaches can be brought into fruitful dialogue with Augustine. My account draws on biblical and rabbinic use of certain Hebrew roots: *amar v'ayehi*, God "spoke and it was." Aboriginal creating is '*MR*, a form of the verb "to speak." Rabbinic sages make use of a parallel verbal root, *DBR*, to introduce a verbal noun form that reifies the creating-speaking: if *DBR* is translated "to speak," then *dibbur* translates as "that which is spoken" or also "spoken thing." Another step takes us to *davar*, "thing." Without venturing a scholarly claim, I like to refer to "creatures" (literally *briyut*, from the *hapax legomenon br'*, "to create") as *dibburot* or "spoken words" understood as creatures or "spoken things." I retranslate the terms as present participles: "speaking-words" understood as "speaking-things": referring, not to things that speak, but to things whose being is identical to their being continuously spoken by their creator. In such terms, created things and revealed words display parallel streams of divine speech, and I imagine the two streams as united in their beginning (the divine speaker) and in their ending (worldly

---

4. Augustine, *Trin.* XV.2.2.
5. Augustine, *Trin.* XV.2.2.

actions) and as displaying separation only in the meantime, space-time of this world. This picture complements my account of SR from the perspective of infinity and unknowing.

My long-time colleague Basit Koshul offers complementary readings of Muhammed Iqbal's Qur'anic account. Koshul writes that, in his critique of the classical ontological and cosmological arguments, Iqbal rethinks "the dualistic categories of cause/effect, designer/designed and ideal/real. In their stead we approach the divine by interpreting experience as a symbol of a reality that is fundamentally relational in character: 'the First and the Last, the visible and the invisible.'"[6] Iqbal observes that the classical cosmological argument "begins with a distinction between cause and effect, but the way that it unfolds displays a movement from the finite to the infinite," asking us "to conceive of the universe as a finite effect proceeding from an infinite uncaused first cause." Iqbal criticizes the argument for seeking "to reach the infinite by merely negating the finite. But the infinite reached by contradicting the finite is a false infinite. . . . The true infinite does not exclude the finite; it embraces the finite without effacing its finitude."[7]

For Koshul, Iqbal's Qur'anic account of the infinite complements Augustine's biblical account.[8] I would add that it also complements the account of Hasdai Crescas, the early modern Jewish philosopher who offered a major critique of Maimonides' Aristotelian understanding of infinity. Crescas criticizes Aristotle's argument against the existence of an infinite body as circular reasoning, since "it is just this limitation that we seek to establish. One who asserts the existence of an infinite body denies the assumed definition."[9] Crescas then criticizes Aristotle's related claims about the infinite, for example: that the infinite cannot be composite because, if so, its elements must be infinite (Crescas counters that the non-existence of infinite elements is assumed rather than demonstrated); that the existence of infinite elements is impossible because infinity cannot be conceived (Crescas counters that this is to assume without demonstration that what exists must be conceivable); and that an infinite body could not possibly exist (Crescas counters that this is to assume without demonstration that bodies are necessarily limited).

---

6. Koshul, "Muhammad Iqbal's Reconstruction."
7. Iqbal, *Reconstruction*, 23.
8. For a related, SR approach see Faizi, "Averroes on the Relationship between Philosophy and Scripture"; see Yazicioglu, "Redefining."
9. Crescas, *Or Adonai*, 15. For a complementary approach, see Fenton, "Hasdai Crescas."

BEYOND WHAT THE INDIVIDUAL KNOWS

When we refer to knowing, who do we assume is the subject who knows? On the preceding pages, I have, consistent with current conventions in the philosophy of religion, written as if the subject could be an individual human being or God. For the rest of this chapter, I will, against the conventions, write as if a social group and a language system could also act as subjects of knowing. I will not attribute to a group or system the kind of consciousness or cognitive intentionality we associate with individual human beings or other animals. This will be another kind of knowing and agency, but an actual worldly agency, nonetheless. It is the kind of agency I attribute to successful SR groups that, over time, become agents of the reasoning dimension of SR. I claim that, while individuals are essential rational agents within SR groups, the reasoning we call SR is irreducible to any collection of these agents' individual contributions. Readers may prefer more conventional claims: that, for example, what I call a group's agency is a metaphor for the collective effect of individual claims offered around the SR table. But I shall respect the lesson Peirce thinks he learns from Galileo: that, of two hypotheses, the *simpler* is to be preferred, meaning "the more facile and natural, the one that instinct suggests."[10] My account of group reasoning is more natural to my observations of hundreds of SR sessions than are efforts to attribute the R in SR to a collection of discrete elements (such as individual reasonings). I should add, however, that my account is categorical and taxonomic rather than explanatory: an effort to place SR in the appropriate category of types of human activity, rather than to promote some single *explanation* of the SR phenomenon.

The preceding account of knowing enough introduces terms for moving from a model of strictly individuated agency to one that includes non-individuated agency. In the next section, I illustrate some of these terms. My goal is heuristic rather than constative, introducing ways of thinking about and modeling non-individuated agency without arguing that readers ought to adopt these:

1. *Knowing as participating rather than grasping: in Neoplatonic theology.*
   A familiar trope in Neoplatonic philosophy and theology, knowledge through participation is a helpful way to think about non-individuated knowing.[11] So, for example, Augustine:

---

10. Peirce, "A Neglected Argument for the Reality of God," (1908) CP 6.477.

11. For complementary explorations in SR and Christian theology, see the work of Tom Greggs, for example, *Barth, Origen*, 66, 83, 87, 113. For complementary studies in SR, semiotics, Augustine, and Platonic traditions, see Ticciati, *Apophaticism*.

> Now the death of the *soul* is ungodliness, and the death of the body is corruptibility, through which comes also a departure of the *soul* from the body. For as the *soul* dies when God leaves it, so the body dies when the *soul* leaves it; whereby the former becomes foolish, the latter lifeless. For the *soul* is raised up again by repentance, and the renewing of life is begun in the body still mortal by *faith*, by which men *believe* in Him who justifies the ungodly; and it is increased and strengthened by good habits from day to day, as the inner man is renewed more and more. But the body, being as it were the outward man, the longer this life lasts is so much the more corrupted, either by age or by disease, or by various afflictions, until it come to that last affliction which all call death. And its resurrection is delayed until the end; when also our justification itself shall be perfected ineffably. For then we shall be like Him, for we shall see Him as He is .....[12]

In Jonathan Teubner's reading, *Trin.* offers a two-leveled account of participation. On one level, humans are sinners whose access to God requires the prior preparation of *deprecari,* to "weep and implore" God again and again to draw the supplicant out of the pitiful state of sin and then to pray (*precari*) with all confidence once having received "the free gratuitous pledge of health through the one and only saviour and enlightener .... Here *deprecari* signifies a prayer for mercy or pardon, for something to be taken away, and *precari* ... a kind of prayer or supplication for something to be given." Teubner concludes that "participation is, for Augustine, surprisingly caught between *deprecari* and *precari*, rather than some supernatural extension beyond *precari*."[13]

In Augustine's terms, participation requires the soul's death and resurrection through repentance and through "good habits from day to day." For the body, there is no such participation "until it come to that last affliction which all call death. And its resurrection is delayed until the end." In that end, "we shall be like Him, for we shall see Him as He is." In this way participation becomes identification so that the individual's distinct identity enters that of God. In the prototypical rabbinic account, the analogue to participation is not identification but intimate relation, through which the human individual or community walks hand in hand with God. In the Augustinian or rabbinic account, participating in the divine life is knowing enough, as God wills.

12. Augustine, *Trin.*, IV.4.5.
13. Teubner, *Prayer*, 93–94.

2. *Knowing as participating in rather than grasping: in faith.*

As noted in chapter 3, prophecy is about the unseen, since it is about the future, which we do not see clearly.[14] To have faith in the prophet's words is to trust in something about which we have no control; it is a matter of relationship, not vision, and relationships involve dispositions, like fearing/not fearing, accepting/not accepting. One can have stronger or weaker faith, and that is why the truths of faith are informed by a logic of probability: if you see something unclearly, you have knowledge of it to some degree or probability. This is Pascal's Wager: to trust and act on what you do not fully see; this is knowing enough.

3. *Knowing as participating in rather than grasping: in a logic of relations.*

Peirce's logic of relations introduces a formal model of knowing through participation: aRb (where a and b participate in a relation R), to be distinguished from a=b/a≠b (where a is/is not equivalent to b), and from a=μb (where the equivalence is mediated by some constant μ). Here R is a three-part relation that stands independently of any set of members. If, therefore, I offer a model of my knowing x, iKx, I do not appear as the subject of knowing (I know x) but as a participant with x of the knowing relation K. Comparably, if I love y, I appear as participant with y of the love relation L, iLy. In these terms, participating in the relation of Knowing (or Loving or Having) is knowing (/ loving/having) enough: a, b, c . . . i are finite, but there is no knowing the limit of K or L or H. . . .

4. *Knowing as participating in rather than grasping: in non-binary semiosis*

Peirce's triadic model of signification offers an epistemic analogue to his logic of relations. Any sign may be modeled as S-O-I: a Sign that refers to its Object with respect to (according to the rule of) its Interpretant. There are many kinds of sign, defined as an activity of signification or as what stimulates such activity. Peirce characterizes a Symbol, for example, as a signification that refers to its *object* by virtue of some implicit law that causes the symbol to be *interpreted* as referring to that object. A symbol thereby *influences* the way its interpretant attributes meaning to it. Modeled in Peirce's logic of relations, a Symbol appears either as S=sIo (where sign and meaning/object are brought into the Interpretive relation) or (in my reading) as a three-dimensional relation xSyz. These relations can be diagrammed in three-dimensional Cartesian coordinates:

---

14. Chapter 3, 64.

WHAT IS (REALLY) GOING ON IN THE SR CLASSROOM? 123

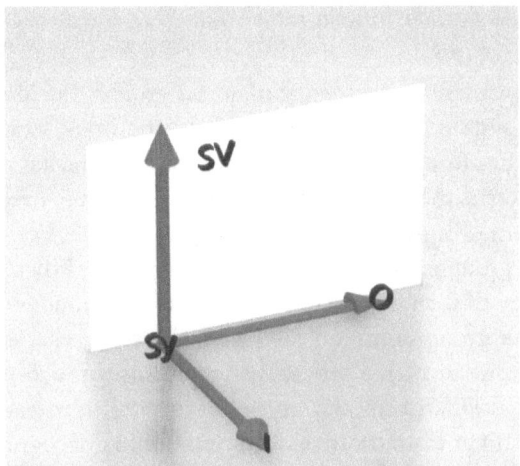

Here, the Relation is that Symbol (at the null coordinate) whose coordinates/vectors are: Sign-Vehicle (that which stimulates someone/thing to participate in the Symbol), Interpretant (patterns of possible relations that legislate how the addressee responds to the Sign-Vehicle), Object. I refer to an addressee, but this designation refers vaguely to a role in the process rather than to a space-time specific individual. The Symbol gives rise to a potentially indefinite process of sending and receiving signs in space-time.[15] Modeling an individual addressee's participation in the Symbol shows how an individual may retain identity within the process, while, at the same time, how the process exceeds any individual's grasp or conceptualization. The individual participates in the chain of transmission but cannot control it without interrupting the semiosis. Participation in a semiotic chain is knowing enough, playing one's role as individual in the process of signification.

5. *Knowing as participating in rather than grasping: in ecosystems.*

As noted in chapter 3,[16] individuals do not live in isolation but inhabit ecosystems, complex and variously integrated contexts of activity. When highly integrated, these contexts display features we might associate with collective individualities, in which case we say that individuals participate in ecosystems and networks. When minimally integrated, these contexts may appear haphazard and unpredictable, environments where individuals participate in few relationships, exposed to chance encounters, some of them dangerous.

15. Cf. Ricoeur's account of how "the symbol gives rise to thought" (Ricoeur, *Symbolism*, 347–57).

16. Chapter 3, 56.

6. *Knowing as participating in rather than grasping: in social groups and language systems.*

When considering the agency of social groups, the idiom is neither a neural system and its cognitions, nor the brain, nor any effort to derive logics from the history of reflections on mental processes. The agency here is the language of a given social group. I regard language as a system of signs that have a variety of meanings or consequences for some group or community of language users. I therefore associate the agency of such a group with the triadic semiotic process through which the group communicates and shares its characteristics over time. I think of such a process as the means through which a group remembers differences and unities according to measures of space-time that differ from those of cognition. I think of cognitive activities, for example, as tending to measure time with respect to certain disjunctions: inner vs. outer time, time vs. space, time as measure of difference vs. time as succession of qualities. I think of societal agency as operating, independently of such disjunctions, with respect to a series of temporalities, each specific to a societal task or communicative goal. Societies may measure events by calendrical or other language-specific cycles (such as commemorations of religious or national events); they may measure change and thus time according to linear sequences of events that are unpredictable in detail but anticipated in type (such as events of political succession or of seasonal migrations) or unpredictable in type but retained in literary memory (such as climate-induced migrations or certain wars); and they may measure time according to sequences of change in language form (changes in grammar or vocabulary) or in the character of other social institutions and practices.

As agents of change, I think of languages, themselves, as operating through the idiom of relations: primarily social relations but also relations of more formal and less visible kinds (such as phonemes, sense qualities, predicates and subjects of possible judgments, modes of reflection, logics of science, models of possible worlds). I therefore think of social groups and languages as different but complementary agents of activity, each adopting the other as idiom of action. In these terms, knowing enough characterizes the participation of individuals in social groups and language systems.

7. *Knowing as participating in rather than grasping: inquiry.*

As noted in Chapter 3, inquiry refers to a practice of reasoning whose goal is to influence patterns of thinking or of reasoning itself. To join an inquiry is therefore to participate in activities that extend beyond the individual reasoner's control, including consequences of the individual's engagement with others in the world.[17]

8. *Knowing as participating in rather than grasping: pragmatic inquiry and pragmatism.*

As noted in chapter 3, pragmatism seeks to correct several errant tendencies in modern academic inquiry, including tendencies to limit one's academic inquiry to the work of a specialized guild, without: (a) evaluating the contribution of that guild's work to societal repair; (b) testing the contribution of one's inquiry to repairing whatever problematic situations may have prompted it; (c) examining the societal setting of these problematic situations. For Peirce, the discipline of philosophy has primary responsibility for monitoring and repairing such academic errors; the persistence of these errors is a sign of philosophy's failing to fulfill this responsibility. The goal of pragmatism is therefore to influence changes in philosophic inquiry, but with broader implications for the academy's engagement with the societal world.

A PRAGMATIC MUSEMENT ON SOCIETAL DYSFUNCTION AND REPARATIVE INQUIRY

In his early writings, Peirce associated pragmatism with Alexander Bain's doctrine of "doubt and belief": that rational inquiry arises in response to specific doubts and is completed once those doubts are answered and replaced by new or refined beliefs. Peirce gradually reframed "doubt and belief" as a doctrine of habit change: the goal of pragmatic inquiry is to identify and recommend ways of repairing the dysfunctional habits that underlie failed practices.[18] In these terms, pragmatic inquiry entails knowing enough in the sense that knowing is conditioned by its reparative stimulus and goal and is proven only to the degree that it fulfills its goal.

---

17. In the terms of chapter 3, cognitive activities, from sensation to rarified reflection, are products of human engagement with others in the natural and social worlds.

18. In his later writings, Peirce presents pragmatism as a method of evaluating context-specific truth-conditions, rather than as a general account of rational inquiry. Peirce recognizes that some forms of inquiry such as mathematics may yield products that are neither true nor false but something other, such as beautiful or not. Other inquiries may produce recommendations for action that are neither true nor false but something other, such as strong, weak, or probable. The results of reparative inquiry may be true or false (if the repair is successful or not) or a third value such as helpful or not, questionable, and so on.

Peirce spent relatively little time exploring the implications of pragmatic inquiry for societal repair. Stimulated by suggestions in Dewey's commentaries, I offer here a pragmatic musement on societal dysfunction/suffering and reparative inquiry. My goal is not to introduce any empirical claim but to imagine what a society might look like if it were created by pragmatists: a thought experiment through which readers might evaluate the possible consequences of taking pragmatism seriously.[19] I describe only one aspect of this society: the way its institutions, including the academy, are organized to serve as instruments of any one of five levels of pragmatic repair.

Level 1: Human beings in the flesh, guided by everyday habits of behavior

On a first level, we see only the activities of flesh-and-blood individuals within a given society, and we read their actions as displaying the effects of behavioral habits. We assume that individuals may suffer either bodily wounds or other kinds of dysfunction in their everyday practices, that they may offer public signs of such suffering, and that these signs may stimulate other members of the society to take notice and come to their aid. For example, a child might stub her toe and cry. Her mother may hear and come to her aid. Perhaps the mother decides that soap and water and a Band-Aid are called for, but nothing more, and perhaps this works. For the sake of the thought experiment, we would stipulate in this case that the daughter's habits of everyday practice are interrupted by her injury and that her mother's habits of reparative practice enable the child to return to everyday activities. *According to our model of pragmatic inquiry, interrupted habits function within the social order as dual signs: indicative signs (constative or locutionary) of some degree of social dysfunction and imperative signs (performative or illocutionary) of the need for some manner and degree of repair.* On this first level of analysis, we should not try to identify which habits are interrupted and which reparative actions are called for. *We need only stipulate that relations of dysfunction and repair are immanent in the social order and that our analysis pertains to only one set of effects: evidence that, within the social order, some actions/non-actions are read, dually, as indicative signs of interrupted habits and imperative signs of a need for repair.*

---

19. This thought experiment serves the function Peirce assigned to a pragmatically reconceived metaphysics: not a portrait of the world but a means of pre-testing a logic of repair by imagining what a portion of the world might look like if it were constructed strictly according to this logic.

Level 2: First-level service institutions

Imagine, this time, that the mother's remedy fails to stop her daughter's bleeding, and the mother takes her daughter to the hospital or doctor. We will use the term "first-level service institutions" for all social services provided to help flesh-and-blood human beings repair interrupted habits that they are unable to repair on their own: in addition to medical practices, we may think of all public works, police, military, houses of worship (when providing religious services beyond those performed by individuals or families at home), and so on. These institutions are guided by their own habits of reparative inquiry (to attend to failed, everyday efforts) and action (to test and apply recommendations for correcting these failures).

Level 3: Second-level service institutions, the university and other research institutions

Imagine, this time, that doctors are unable to stop this poor child's bleeding, and other hospitals fail as well. We may say that, in this case, first level service institutions proved incapable of repairing an interruption in everyday habits. Let us stipulate that this interruption in second-level habits of repair stimulates the work of a second-level service institution, such as a research hospital. Analogous services are provided by institutes of engineering, business, law, architecture, nursing, criminology, diplomacy, religion and theology (including seminaries), and so on. Second-level reparative inquiry completes its work by recommending habit changes in first-level institutions of repair: for example, introducing better diagnostic and reparative technologies. The success/failure of this second-level inquiry is evaluated by specialists from both first- and second-level institutions. For Peirce, second-level reparative inquiry is science, in the Aristotelian sense of disciplined inquiry. Peirce classifies the natural and social sciences as "special sciences" (*idioscopy*), because they include axioms and beliefs that are not shared by the society at large. Like Aristotle, Peirce argues that scientific inquiry would be circular if its premises were themselves products of the inquiry. It is philosophy's task to disclose such premises, but only in response to dysfunction within a given community of scientific inquiry.

Level 4: Third-level service institutions: schools of philosophy!

I add an exclamation mark, because contemporary departments of philosophy have drifted far away from how Peirce envisioned their reparative function. In his 1902–1903 classification of the sciences, Peirce defined philosophy as *coenoscopy*, a discipline for "examining what is common (or everyday)" in human experience. Peirce identified logic as philosophy's prototypical work (supported by phenomenology and metaphysics). He offered pragmatism and semiotics as instruments for repairing what he took to be modern philosophy's dysfunctional practice of logic. Peirce's new model includes reflection on both *logica utens,* or the immanent logic of everyday practice (which I identify with the semiotic study of everyday habits), and *logica docens,* or normative logic. I identify the latter with the logic of reparative inquiry, whose form is adjusted to meet the needs of each context-specific project of reparative inquiry. The service work of immanent logic is to examine interrupted habits. The service work of normative logic is to diagram testable, context-specific rules for repairing those habits.

In these terms, the goal of Peirce's pragmatism is not to replace philosophy but to correct modern philosophy's decreased attention to the reparative dimension of academic inquiry: philosophy's responsibility is to nurture logical models of reparative reasoning, diagnostic instruments for evaluating each discipline's capacities to attend to society's service institutions, and recommendations for enhancing these capacities. Philosophers cannot perform such work without participating directly in the disciplines they examine, which implies that philosophy cannot be undertaken only within the confines of a self-contained discipline or department. Another implication is that individual philosophers would have time and capacity to participate in only one or two research disciplines, for example, sociology and statistics, physics and mathematics, ethics and politics.

There are at least three ways in which philosophy may fail to fulfill its service: (1) If it seeks to explicate the assumptions of science without evidence of dysfunction in a given science (in which case, its efforts become foundationalist); (2) If it denies its responsibility to serve the sciences in this manner; (3) And if, in the effort to repair dysfunctions in science, it lacks resources to explicate scientific assumptions. Peirce offers his pragmatism to repair each of these failings: to criticize the binary logics that encourage failure #1, to introduce an imperative to counter failure #2, and to explicate the normative logic that should repair failure #3.[20]

20. The pragmatist Richard Rorty famously took to the streets in his later years to draw attention to what he considered unrepaired societal injustices. Rorty's work on the streets illustrates several levels of our model of reparative inquiry. By joining protests on behalf of victims of unresponsive social institutions, he drew attention to failures of second-level service institutions. Less directly, he also impugned failed efforts by academicians to take account of their social responsibilities. One aspect of his work on the streets is, however, inconsistent with the division of labor outlined in our model. Even if philosophy's work is ultimately in service to everyday life, our model limits

Level 5: Fourth-level service: pragmatism

For Peirce, pragmatism is a method of self-repair for modern philosophy. If so, pragmatism's immanent logic would also include the dysfunctional habits of philosophic inquiry that pragmatism seeks to repair. Pragmatism's normative logic would propose testable rules for repairing these habits. Peirce identified philosophy's dysfunctional habits with "Cartesianism" and "nominalism," and his critique of these is a resource for the critique of "binarism" that helped fuel the project of Scriptural Reasoning. But what did he consider pragmatism's normative logic? On one level, the answer is obvious: the method of pragmatism is a norm for repairing modern philosophy's errant habits. On another level, however, this answer leaves open the questions of what norm of inquiry warrants the pragmatic method and of what logic guides repairs of pragmatism as needed. I have sought to answer these questions through three decades of research, and the results play a central role in my account of the contribution pragmatism makes to SR and that reasoning out of Scripture makes to pragmatism. Because the arguments are long and technical, I will offer only an outline of my conclusions with added explanations. My broadest conclusions are: (a) Since pragmatism is a reparative inquiry, its normative logic must, as in Aristotle's practical syllogism, presuppose an imperative to repair; (b) Since the pragmatist is also a modern philosopher, pragmatic inquiry must include conflicting habits: tendencies toward abstraction and tendencies toward embodied practice; (c) Pragmatic inquiry emerges first as a means of repairing the ill effects of a pragmatic philosopher's conflicting habits. If so, pragmatic repair is self-repair, but the self-repair is not final; conflicting habits remain the condition of a pragmatist's life in this world (the pragmatist's *semper reformanda*); (d) An individual's pragmatic inquiry derives from an activity of societal (or group) self-repair, whose immanent logic is conflictual and whose normative logic is reparative; (e) The normative logic must include an imperative to repair. Within Peirce's work, there are allusions to such an imperative, but he does not identify the imperative as such. In the following sections, I describe the allusions and propose a way to identify their occluded referent.

---

philosophy's service to that of monitoring its colleagues' work in the academy. As a human being, Rorty belonged as much on the street as any member of society, but, there, his voice did not merit any privileged attention.

Level 6: Fifth-level service: repairing pragmatism

In 1877–1878, Peirce introduced his pragmatism to correct errors in his 1867–1868 critique of Cartesianism. In 1905–1906, he reintroduced his pragmatism, renamed pragmaticism, to correct errors in his peers' efforts to practice pragmatic inquiry: "Being struck by the absence of any serious attempt on the part of the very zealous promoters of the pragmatist movement to support any argument for the truth of their principles . . ., I resolved to set forth the reasons that . . . there is one, and but one, line of scientific investigation that is capable of satisfactorily ascertaining whether, and in what sense, the principle of pragmatism is true or false."[21] Peirce's effort to display these reasons (what he called his "proof" of pragmatism) generated his most exciting and mind-opening writings, but, restless as Augustine,[22] he pushed his effort ever further. A few fine Peirce scholars have sought to complete the proof within the terms of Peirce's formal studies. I find their work convincing within these terms, but I also find that these terms are not fully adequate to the task. Like Peirce, they presume that this proof would be thoroughly formal. Their presumption has merit, since, like Peirce, they successfully demonstrate how to conduct formal reasoning as a non-binary, diagrammatic performance that could potentially reenact its object (technically, its dynamical object), rather produce a copy of it (technically, an iconic and thus binary copy). But they—and Peirce—overlook two essential features of pragmatism: that its proof must include an imperative to repair (without which there is no irresistible motive to choose the pragmatic approach over others) and that this imperative includes a ceaseless drive to self-repair that complements an irresolvable inner conflict between conventional and reparative habits of inquiry.[23]

On inner conflict: A reparative activity like pragmatism must include conflicting habits: in the case of pragmatism, both reparative habits of

---

21. *Peirce MS* 296, 1–2. Roberts identifies this manuscript as drafts of an unpublished article from 1906–1907: Roberts, "An Introduction," 124.

22. See chapter 3, 71–73, where I speculate about the "restlessness" Augustine describes in *Conf.*

23. Like Peirce in "A Neglected Argument," or Kant in the Second Critique (his argument for the categorical imperative), these Peirce scholars may read their effort as exerting the force of an ontological argument. Or like Peirce's and Thomas Reid's studies of common sense, they may read their effort as laying bare their indubitable beliefs and inferences. All such readings anticipate the pragmatic imperative (its performative form and its indubitability for those who receive it), but they fail, nonetheless, to warrant their modality *as* an imperative to repair. Similarly, Peirce's proofs demonstrate *how* to repair modern philosophy's binarism, but they do not display *why*. On Kant, see Goodson, "Kant and the Nature of Doctrine."

reasoning and the dysfunctional habits these are meant to repair: for example, foundationalism and intuitionism. How, then can pragmatism or any other reparative activity succeed? Peirce answered that question through a thought experiment. Imagine, he said, that reparative reasoning is a dialogue between two kinds of reasoning: B-reasonings, which guide our everyday needs (like figuring out how to avoid traffic or how to pass a law test) but also require regular correction; and A-reasonings, which are rarely useful for everyday needs but serve as infallible guides for repairing other reasonings. Peirce proposes that, if our thinking worked this way, then, when any B-reasoning fails, we would correct it by way of other B-reasonings; and, if we exhausted the series of our available B-reasonings, then, rather than lose hope, we would trust our A-reasonings to guide us in seeking new ways to think about the problem we face. In Peirce's terms, A-reasonings function as indubitable beliefs, suggesting that such beliefs are only conditionally indubitable, since they may, on rare occasions, fail.[24]

My speculation about levels of service institution extends Peirce's thought experiment: when one level of B-reasonings fails to repair a given dysfunction, the problem is referred to the next level, whose practices first appear as A-reasonings, previously unknown on the previous level. Functioning as B-reasonings on their level, these A-reasonings are consulted as possible resources for generating new methods of repair. The process continues up to the level we now consider: repairing dysfunctional practices of pragmatism. In Peirce's naturalist account, pragmatism rests on indubitable beliefs, whose characteristics he seeks to identify through formal proofs. Recall, however, his conflicting habits, of which his drive for formal proof exhibits one and his drive to repair exhibits another. Pragmatic reasoning requires persistent inner conflict and the reparative activity that accompanies the conflict. The efforts of Peirce and his disciples to prove pragmatism extend rather than resolve this inner dialectic. In my reading, to complete the proof of pragmatism is not to complete it literally but to identify the indubitable beliefs and acritical inferences that serve as ultimate interpretants of *both* sides of the conflict. Peirce and his disciples perform this work only for the formal, diagrammatic side of the conflict, but not for the reparative side, whose ultimate interpretant I call the pragmatic imperative. To pursue only the former is to occlude the conflict, veiling the indubitable ground of

---

24. Peirce acknowledges that "when I say *indubitable*, I mean ... indubitable today for me," adding that "proof does not consist in giving superfluous and superpossible certainty to that which nobody ever did or ever will doubt, but in removing doubts which do, or at least might at some time, arise" (Peirce, "Regenerated Logic," [1896] CP 3.432). Here, Peirce sets limits to his Scotch Common Sensism (see Peirce, "Issues of Pragmaticism," [1905] CP 5.438–63).

the imperative to repair. To occlude is not, however, to dissolve. Undisclosed signs of the conflict will remain: what I call the undisclosed allusions embedded in Peirce's writings.[25]

Four allusions: Here are elements of Peirce's writings that I read as allusions to additional, unnamed sources of the pragmatic imperative.

> 1. In his *1893 reflections on Religion and Science,* Peirce writes that religion is "in each individual . . ., a sort of sentiment . . ., a deep recognition of something in the circumambient all. . . . But religion cannot reside in its totality in a single individual. Like every species of reality, it is essentially a social, a public affair."[26] Against positivists and rationalists, Peirce argues that religion derives from sources deeper than individual religion. Religion is not about mere belief but "is a life," and, like all lived practices, it is articulated through a *vernacular* vocabulary. Peirce's mature understanding of the vernacular belongs to his "critical common sensism" and underlies this claim from his 1905 credo: "'God' is a vernacular word, and like all such words, but more than almost any, is *vague*."[27] John Smith writes,
>
>> Peirce had much to say about vagueness, but he returned ever and again to the same points: insofar as a concept, sign, [or] representation is vague, to that extent the principle of contradiction does not apply to it. . . . Any proposition is either true or false when its identity has been determined. . ., but the condition does not hold insofar as these constituents remain vague. The second consideration about vagueness is that a vague sign is one which reserves for some other sign or experience the task of completing the determination.[28]
>
> Any definition of a vague term is a context-specific determination of it. The meaning of "God" is therefore disclosed only through conditional propositions that describe the behavior that would follow from our employing that term. To know "God" is, as suggested by the

---

25. For interested general readers, here is a summary of what I find convincing in these proofs: They demonstrate the inadequacy of modern efforts to define truth-functionality as necessarily two-valued (framed within the limits of two-valued Cartesian coordinates). They identify classes of rational, empirical claims that are served by multi-valued truth conditions: including observations of quantum phenomena, tri-relational claims, value judgments, religious beliefs, and claims about the objects of religious beliefs.

26. Peirce, "A Religion of Science," (1893) CP 6.429.

27. Peirce, "Answers to Questions Concerning My Belief in God," (1906) CP 6.494.

28. Smith, *Purpose*, 175.

Hebrew biblical term for "knowledge" (*yidiah*), to act in relation to the object of that term. Because the term belongs to the publicly shared vernacular, to know "God" is therefore to enact some publicly shared set of behaviors in the world.

2. Peirce's most significant theo-philosophical treatise, "A Neglected Argument for the Reality of God," makes surprising use of the vernacular term, *God*. As neatly summarized by Smith, "A Neglected Argument" attempts to do justice to both experience and reasoning by "providing rational grounds for holding that the deliverances of direct perception are trustworthy."[29] Continuing an early theme, Peirce suggests that reasoning about "God" begins with "musement, . . . a kind of 'pure play' of the mind which, on the one hand, is guided by the object of contemplation, and, on the other, progresses in accordance with the 'attentive observation' of the muser and the direction which his internal conversation assumes."[30] The object of musement is the world of experience, but referred to its ultimate categories: three universes, in fact, which Peirce calls the universes of mere ideas, of brute facts, and of the signs that connect objects from all universes together. Observing variety, then homogeneity and, finally, the singular fact of *growth* common to all universes, the muser enters "certain lines of reflection which will inevitably suggest the hypothesis of God's reality,"[31] which is God's presence, not as brute fact, but as *ens necessarium*, "the ultimate, purposive ground of each universe."[32]

The description of musement constitutes Peirce's "Humble Argument," a species of reasoning about God that arises only out of indubitable and precritical inferences that cannot be anticipated by any formal argument. The Neglected Argument, per se, is a "commentary on the Humble Argument and asserts that the latter represents the results of the same attunement between reality and the human mind which makes all science possible."[33] Peirce's highly significant conclusion is that the hypothesis about God's reality derives from the same kind of precritical reflection that underlies scientific method: the Neglected Argument gives rise to a third argument, which "consists in the development of those principles of logic according to which the humble argument is the first stage of a scientific inquiry that produces,

---

29. Smith, *Purpose*, 177.
30. Smith, *Purpose*, 179–80.
31. Peirce, "A Neglected Argument," CP 6.465.
32. Peirce, "A Neglected Argument," CP 6.465.
33. Smith, *Purpose*, 181.

not merely scientific belief, which is always provisional, but also a living, practical belief, logically justified in crossing the Rubicon with all the freightage of eternity."[34]

The principles of logic are deduction, induction, and abduction. Peirce's notion of abduction is of great significance in his accounts of God and of scientific reasonings. Already in his early critique of Descartes, Peirce argued that modern philosophy failed to discriminate two distinct elements of cognition: the impression (indexical sign) *that* something is *there* and an intuition (iconic sign) of *what* characteristics that something may have. Peirce argued that, by assimilating these two functions, modern logic recognized only two of the irreducibly three elements of scientific practice. A modern logician like John Stuart Mill recognized only the two activities he called deduction (necessary reasoning from universal principles) and induction (a deterministic account of the empirical observations that generate universal principles). Consistent with Kant's assertion that "existence is not a predicate," Peirce replaced the modern account of induction with distinct accounts of *abduction* (probable reasoning that predicates certain characteristics of something that exists in the world) and a chastened notion of induction (probable reasoning that tests the claims of abduction against empirical evidence). Peirce characterized abduction as the exclusive source of creativity in scientific reasoning: the process of proposing which characteristics, already available in consciousness/language, could be predicated of what is encountered in the world.

In Smith's terms, Peirce's goal is not to reduce religious thinking to scientific thinking, but to show philosophers and scientists that the hypothesis of God's reality is trustworthy because it belongs to the same class of abductive inferences that includes the abductive stage of scientific inquiry.[35] Scientists may mistrust the hypothesis because it remains more obscure than those adopted in scientific explanations. Unlike scientific hypotheses, however, this hypothesis has a "commanding influence over the whole conduct of life of its believers."[36] The pragmatic meaning of the hypothesis is therefore explicit in the concrete rules of conduct that it determines, while the pragmatic meaning of scientific hypotheses is usually undeveloped.

3. In "A Prolegomena to an Apology for Pragmaticism," Peirce proposed his Existential Graphs: a "system of diagrammatization by means of

---

34. Peirce, "A Neglected Argument," CP 6.485.
35. Smith, *Purpose*, 181–82.
36. Peirce, "A Neglected Argument," CP 6.490.

which any course of thought can be represented with exactitude."[37] A diagram is a sign that "is predominantly an icon of relations" (CP 4.418), introducing "*characteristics* of objects that are not already given" but are "logically possible" and "belong to the process of thinking" (CP 4.531). Rather than *refer* to their objects semantically, the Graphs re-enact/re-create their objects. Fittingly, albeit surprisingly, Peirce characterizes graphing as a collaborative activity of writing "scripture," as in "scribing a graph." He names the two collaborators the *graphist* and the *interpreter*. Scripture is a dialogic activity: "we are to imagine that two parties (they may be two bodies of persons, two persons, or two mental attitudes or states of one person) collaborate in composing [an assertion] . . . and in operating upon it so as to develop [an argument]" (CP 4.552). The graphist scribes the graph; the interpreter introduces "such erasures and assertions of the graph" as are consistent with the conventions of graphing and with the interpreter's purposes. In another part of the essay, Peirce characterizes the process of diagraming as a representation of the process of creating and transforming worlds (such as those universes of experience described above) or habits:

> In order to fix our ideas, *we may imagine that there are two persons one of whom, called the grapheus, creates the universe* by the continuous development of his [or her] idea of it, every interval of time in the process adding some fact to the universe. . . . *The other of the two persons concerned (called the graphist) is occupied during the process of creation in making successive modifications . . . of the entire graph. There must be an interpreter, since the graph, like every sign founded on convention, only has the sort of being that it has if it is interpreted.* (CP 4.552)

In sum, Peirce imagines the process of creating a graph as both interpreting and replicating the process of creating whatever world the graph graphs.

4. In an 1893 article, "Evolutionary Love," Peirce introduced his doctrine of "Christian Love." In Smith's words,

> [Peirce's] theory of evolutionary love has two sides. . . . Peirce's Johannine theme that "God is Love" in opposition to the "Gospel of Greed" [and]. . . a conception of evolutionary development which is distinct from both pure chance and mechanical necessity. . . . Against the philosophy of unqualified individual

---

37. Peirce, "Prolegomena to an Apology for Pragmaticism," (1906) CP 4.530.

self-assertion ... he set the law of love or Gospel of Christ, which says that we are to sacrifice our own perfection to that of our neighbor, and to merge our individuality in sympathy with persons around us.[38]

Peirce applies his notion of Christian love to reclassifying Darwinian conceptions of evolution, arguing that the Darwinian conception represents only one of three modes of evolutionary development. With respect to the universe of qualities (see above), evolutionary development or growth is *Tychastic* or "evolution by fortuitous variation." With respect to the universe of forces, it is *Anancastic* or "evolution by mechanical necessity." With respect to the universe of relations, it is *Agapistic* or "evolution by creative love," for example "the adoption of certain mental tendencies ... by an immediate attraction for the idea itself ... [through] the power of sympathy."[39]

Interpreting the four allusions: I interpret these allusions as contributing to a single, undisclosed set of indexical signs whose collective referent is Peirce's pragmatic imperative. At the center, in the Apology, is the formal work Peirce sought to employ exclusively for his proofs of pragmatism. Surprisingly, it is in this mathematical-logical treatise that Peirce summons the images of divine creation (as dialogue between grapheus and graphist) and of divine revelation (as dialogue between the graphist and interpreter). Why did Peirce choose to introduce his formal construction through these biblical allusions? I ask a complementary question of his comparably unusual Neglected Argument. In this case, where the explicit topic is a proof for the reality of God, Peirce suggests that musement on three universes of experience will uncover the etiology of three elemental forms of rational inference (deduction, induction, abduction). Why did Peirce choose to conclude his ontological argument with an account of elemental logical forms? I do not know why in either case. But I find that, if these two remarkable essays are read together as a theo-philosophic exchange, the resulting dialogue introduces a pragmatic apology for Peirce's religious faith as a condition/interpretant of his nonbinary system of diagrammatic reasoning. Peirce appears to vindicate his faith in the creator and revealer God by way of the process of nonbinary reasoning that is the fruit of this faith: without this faith, there is no binding condition for practicing nonbinary reasoning, which, we learn, is the kind of probabilistic reasoning that requires trust/faith for its adoption. Why would Peirce

---

38. Smith, *Purpose*, 168.
39. Peirce, "Evolutionary Love," (1893) CP 6.307.

require such a binding condition? He answers this question explicitly throughout his career: there is otherwise no binding condition for disciplined scientific reasoning about the actual world (and the universes of actual experience). Binary inferences are inadequate engines of empirical and experimental science. The surprising implication is that the condition for this discipline is faith, or prior relation to the God of creation or revelation. The complementary implication is that the formal logic and practice of empirical science is the ontological *cum* pragmatic *proof* of this faith. As argued in the Neglected Argument, abduction is tested/proven only in its empirical consequences. By way of allusion, this faith is abductive: perhaps it is the prototype for all abduction, just as the name "God" is the prototypically vague term, where what is vague is tested/proven through its empirical determinations.[40]

If one grants my account of this theo-philosophic exchange, only one item would remain to complete a search for Peirce's pragmatic imperative. Intimated in Peirce's 1892–1893 essays on religion,[41] this is Peirce's relation to God as Redeemer and not only as the Creator and Revealer subtly named in the two 1905–1906 essays. "Belief in the law of love is Christian faith."[42] Peirce may try to assimilate the Johannine notion to his philosophic formalism, characterizing love, at times, as a strictly attractive force and, in this 1893 essay, as an evolutionary principle.[43] Nonetheless, I read "law" as an allusion to the pragmatic imperative, as in his claim that "It is absurd to say that religion is belief," since it is a life, as in the church's precept about the Way of Life, which is love,[44] and which runs counter to the nineteenth century's Social Darwinism as a "Gospel of Greed."[45] To sacrifice oneself for the neighbor is to act on a certain law of life rather than on mere belief; in other words, it is a commandment, and I take that to be an imperative.

---

40. For a compelling study of abduction, theology, and SR, see Quash, *Found Theology*. For a complementary essay, see Leigh, "Energetics."

41. Peirce's 1893 Monist series: "Evolutionary Love," CP 6.287–317; "Mind and Matter," CP 6.272–86; "Man's Glassy Essence," CP 6.238–71; and "The Law of Mind," CP 6.102–62.

42. Peirce, "A Religion of Science," CP 6.441.

43. "Everybody can see that the statement of St. John is the formula of an evolutionary philosophy, which teaches that growth comes only from love, from I will not say self-*sacrifice*, but from the ardent impulse to fulfill another's highest impulse" (Peirce, "Evolutionary Love," CP 6.289).

44. Peirce, "A Religion of Science," CP 6.439–41.

45. Peirce, "Evolutionary Love," CP 6.294.

My argument for this third allusion is a reparative rather than plain-sense reading of Peirce. To warrant the consequentialist dimension of pragmatism, Peirce appeals overtly to Jesus' words: "Pragmatism is nothing but a corollary to Jesus' injunction 'That ye may know them by their fruit.'"[46] We therefore have evidence that Peirce appeals to Scripture on behalf of his pragmatism. Since Jesus's words concern prophecies, we also have evidence that Peirce's consequentialism concerns testing claims about what is unseen, like the triadic relations of semiosis and of love that one could diagram in Peirce's Existential (Gamma) Graphs.[47] My corrective is simply to uncover scriptural sources for the reparative dimension of pragmatism. I do this because Peirce's drive to prove pragmatism is warranted only if extended to the indubitable beliefs that guide pragmatism's reparative as well as diagrammatic dimensions. Despite Peirce's occasional, naturalist efforts to identify neighbor-love with a cosmic law, I cannot locate any indubitable ground of Peirce's reparative drive other than neighbor-love as a law of the gospel and thus a scriptural imperative. It makes sense to read Peirce's cosmic claims as offered with respect to this imperative as interpretant. But, considering Peirce's analyses of abduction, indubitable belief, and the vague term "God," it does not make sense to read his cosmic claims as introducing notions of love independently of this interpretant.[48]

What, then, does this extensive study of Peirce's proofs of pragmatism tell us about the reasoning in SR? In this chapter's concluding pages, I sketch nineteen dimensions of SR-reasoning that become most visible when this reasoning is examined in the light of Peirce's proofs. I hope readers may see how this reasoning shares at least the following features with a pragmatism that serves the philosophy of science and identifies the ultimate object of scientific inquiry as God's created world and ultimate Interpretant as God's creating, commanding and redeeming word:[49]

---

46. Peirce, "Search for a Method," (1893) CP 5.402n2

47. See Peirce, "Existential Graphs," (1903) CP 4.409–13, and "An Improvement on the Gamma Graphs," (1906) CP 4.573–84.

48. That is, of this *type* of interpretant; I find no other token of this type than his reading of the Gospel of Love.

49. Where such claims remain within the limits of knowing enough.

DIMENSIONS OF SR REASONING SEEN IN THE LIGHT OF PEIRCE'S PROOF OF PRAGMATISM

1. *My overall conclusion is that SR is a type of knowing enough, and the models of knowing enough derived from Peirce will help explain how SR reasoning may in fact work.*

2. *Knowing enough is neither knowing nothing nor knowing too much.* SR works, first, because it inhibits tendencies of religionists to assume that religion must know all, which in our terms is knowing too much. SR works, second, because it inhibits the modern critique of pursuing too much, which is to pursue too little: to assume that, to temper its pretensions, religion must be removed from public attention or that religious mysteries must be identified with what cannot be spoken.

3. *SR has a capacity for knowing enough, because it has a capacity for neither of these two extreme alternatives,* and this is because it has the capacity for non-binary reasoning and may, in fact, function as a significant source of it.

4. *SR calls members of each participating religious tradition to bring their religious hearths with them to the table of Formational SR.* That is the most obvious surprise of SR: that each participant's religious values are brought to the table, made public. There is therefore a protection against too little. But the success of SR is to maintain warmth rather than heat across the participating hearths: SR carries protections against too much.

5. *SR knows little about religion,* somewhat the opposite of those who may claim to know with certainty that religion is something that should not appear in public and of those who know with humbler certainty that religion merits a place in the public eye when it serves or even is a source of what is universal for humanity. SR knows only modestly about each religion represented in an SR circle: only what is displayed in participants' comments on scriptural texts. In this sense, SR knows only enough about religion and each religion to keep the discussion going.

6. *Like pragmatic reasoning, Scriptural Reasoning is functional/operational.* SR reasoning is neither objective nor subjective; its goals do not include uncovering the "true" meanings of scriptural words or encouraging participants to clarify what they truly believe or what they consider the "truths" of a given canonical tradition. SR's goals are indefinite and shaped ad hoc by the dispositions of its participants. In these terms,

SR reasoning maintains the sort of mystery and unpredictability some associate with the sacred.

7. *After the fact, SR reasoning appears to have gone somewhere*: perhaps in the sense that Abraham went off and found himself in a place that God would show him, or perhaps the way the Holy Spirit goes where it will, while to those who meet it this becomes *a defining place*. In this way, SR participants tend most often to report that SR's study taught them something new and surprising.

8. *According to the consequentialist dimension of pragmatism, what is real but unseen is known through its fruit. SR displays a comparable consequentialism*:[50] Understanding follows the practice of SR rather than preceding it, like the angels who declare before God's commanding voice, "We do first, and then we understand."[51] In Augustine's words: "[T]hings incomprehensible must be so investigated that no one may think that he has found nothing when he has been able to find how incomprehensible that is which he was seeking. . . . For it is both sought in order that it may be found more sweetly and found in order that it may be sought more eagerly."[52]

9. *SR nurtures knowing beyond the limits of what individual participants know.* SR participants often report two things: that they experience great individual freedom in SR's practice of text reading and that no individual controls the reasoning that moved around the SR circle. The simplest explanation is that the agent of SR reasoning is a *we*, neither an I nor a discreet set of I's.

10. *SR knowing is knowing through participation.* Individual readers participate in what, after the fact, appears to have been a group's reasoning. And the group appears to have participated in some form of interaction among a multiple set of texts and text traditions.

11. *SR knowing is knowing through trust and thus faith.* To participate in the reasoning of SR, each reader must jump in, trusting the few rules of SR and coming gradually to trust the other participants.

---

50. *Unknowing and consequentialism*: Peirce's prohibition of proof by self-evidence implies that "proving" a formulation is a temporally extended, inductive process. In most cases, further evidence will be available in a yet more distant future. In the long run of experience, the proof of something will be fully known. But we will need to act on such proof in the meantime before it is fully known. For that reason, proving becomes an activity of knowing enough, of acting on only the likelihood that something has been sufficiently proven.

51. *naaseh v'nishmah* (Heb.), Exod 24:7: see chapter 1, 2.

52. *Trin.* XV.2.2.

12. *In SR, knowing is relational.* The Hebrew term for knowing, *yidiah*, comes closest: as in "Adam *knew* Eve" or also "They *knew* that they were naked," and "The human has become one of us, *knowing* good and evil." In each case, knowing is a species of intense relation: they saw/experienced their nakedness and its significance; they gained intimate familiarity with moral distinctions; and they shared sexual intimacy. As noted earlier, Peirce offers a logical model for this kind of knowing: *aRb* (where a and b participate in the Relation) to be distinguished from *a=b* (where identity is a two rather than three-part relation). Discouraging objective *or* subjective knowing, SR encourages a tri-relational type of knowing, where I read a verse of Scripture to mean X and you read it to mean Y, but where we understand each reading as xRi (it is x with respect to my way of reading) and yRy (and it is y with respect to your way of reading).[53]

13. *SR knowing is social and linguistic.* In SR, participants gain knowledge through their participation in a sociolinguistic activity. What individuals claim to know about a verse or about other participants' beliefs is conditioned by factors over which individuals have limited control. The individuals' knowing is thus no more than knowing enough. If my SR colleague says, "they knew they were naked simply because they had no clothes (!)," I might counter that "they knew this because they were embarrassed." But I might not have perceived that my colleague's comment was an ironic response to another colleague or that "had no clothes" meant something other than I assumed. My knowledge claims are limited, because the flow of interpersonal relations in SR is never fully transparent to me and because the horizon of grammatical forms and linguistic meanings exceeds my comprehension.[54]

14. *SR knowing is a form of inquiry that extends beyond any participant's familiar ways of knowing.*[55] This inquiry serves many goals. Whatever

---

53. See chapter 2, 51.

54. As noted in chapter 3, SR enables its participants to speak from the heart and express their individuality freely. The power of SR is to nurture such individuality while also nurturing a movement of non-individuated reasoning that belongs to an SR group as a whole. In chapter 6, I offer semiotic models of SR as language-based and society-based.

55. In my observation, participants allow themselves to join processes of scriptural reading and interpretation whose directions they cannot predict. The processes are in this sense non-finite, since they are not limited by any participant's definition of what is traditionally required. Some participants retain prior associations of Scripture with words associated with One who is infinite. For these participants, the result is a somewhat new experience of integrating "religious study" with a non-finite social activity. Here, I search for words that reflect the liminal character of the experience of SR for

their expertise in a set of text traditions, participants cannot anticipate how a group's questions about reception history, social events, intergroup encounters and competing expertise may transform what it means to study a text's meaning. As hearth-to-hearth engagement, SR introduces participants to unexpected relations with previously unfamiliar texts and traditions and new interpersonal engagements across religious borders.

15. *SR knowing is a form of reparative inquiry.* One goal of SR is hermeneutical repair. A typical SR practice is to ask, after reading a verse aloud, "what does anyone find challenging or problematic in that verse?" The problem is not within the verse *per se* or within a participant's mind; it is in-between, in the relation between text and reader/community of readers.[56] This does not mean that the text is adjusted to fit the community or the community adjusted to fit the text, but that a text deemed problematic is a sign of something problematic in the readers' society/ies. Called by the text to "read" their social narratives more deeply, readers are called by these narratives to explore the text even more deeply, and the engagement continues, deep to deep. For SR, scripture's problematic words function as dual signs: of some trouble festering in the reader's societal world and of some source of repair yet undisclosed to the society.

David Ford's reparative study of Ephesians offers a helpful illustration. As noted in Chapter 2, Ford argues that the plain sense of Ephesians appears to offer a realized eschatology from which it is a short step to supersessionism.[57] He seeks alternative readings of Ephesians that might repair this negative potential. One alternative, for example, is recommended by what Ford calls Ephesians' ethic of non-coercive communication: speaking the truth in love (4.15) with all humility and gentleness (4.2). Ford's lesson is that, without bypassing the words of Ephesians, alternative readings could repair the words' capacity to do ill.

16. *The reparative activity of SR may include the following features:*

---

participants in long-term SR groups. For some, SR exceeds their prior definitions of either traditionally "religious" study or extra-religious study. It remains an "in-between" thing because it is not yet fully defined. Its haziness may allow participants to experiment with something new without breaking their conventional sense of what either their religiosity or their secularism allows. After the SR session, they may return to their conventional practices with some modestly new expectations.

56. I paraphrase my characterization, in chapter 2, of SR's reparative reasoning as reasoning deep to deep: the depth of Scripture and the depth of a reader's society.

57. Chapter 2, 33–44.

WHAT IS (REALLY) GOING ON IN THE SR CLASSROOM? 143

a. *A response to hermeneutical dysfunction: training in polyvalence.* SR helps repair interreligious tension and conflict by offering training in non-binary practices of reading and interpreting sacred texts. A first step in the training is pragmatic: to associate the sacrality of Scripture with its *relation* to its devotees, especially its function as behavioral authority and guide. A second step is to observe differences between monovalent and polyvalent readings of the plain sense of Scripture: devotees' tendencies to attribute one or many possible meanings to words and verses. A third step is to observe the binary course of thought/reasoning that tends to accompany monovalent readings and the non-binary course that often accompanies polyvalent readings. A fourth step is to learn and test SR's working assumption: that monovalent reading and binary thinking accompany occasions of interreligious tension and conflict. A final step is to experience SR study as an environment for introducing monovalent readers and binary thinkers into practices of polyvalent reading and non-binary thinking. Over time, long-term SR participants learn to facilitate this kind of SR study.[58]

b. *A response to societal dysfunction.* Note, for example, my account of SR study in Cape Town, designed to address serious social tensions among the more traditional Jewish, Muslim and Dutch reform communities.[59] Chapter 4 illustrates classroom teaching on SR and social change.[60] Chapter 6 further addresses SR as a response to interreligious tension and conflict.

c. *A response to inadequacies in academic inquiry.* Earlier in this chapter, I characterize pragmatism as an effort to correct modern philosophy when it fails to fulfill its social responsibility, which is to correct the academy when it shirks its responsibility to help repair society's service institutions when they fail to address conditions of human suffering. SR shares in pragmatism's corrective effort, as well as in one of pragmatism's methods of repair: correcting academic (including philosophic) tendencies to binary reasoning.[61] Each chapter of this book addresses some consequence of

---

58. For further discussion of training in polyvalence, see chapter 1 on vagueness and polyvalence (29–31), chapter 2 on plain sense and interpretive reading (25–26), and chapter 4 on classroom training (86–94).

59. Chapter 1, 9–11.

60. See chapter 4, "How to Teach SR and Service Learning" (97–100) and "How to Apply SR to Peace and Conflict Studies" (101–4).

61. Below, 164–67.

binary reasoning in the modern academy.⁶² SR's response is not to promote scriptural study in all disciplines (!), but to promote non-binary practices of reasoning, for which FSR serves as a source of training: what we may label *SR reasoning as socialization in non-binary reasoning*.⁶³ As noted in chapter 3, SR has the potential to engage human beings in their depths, countering "positivist efforts to mend human relations . . . [according to] the belief, for example, that matters of the heart or soul are not those on the basis of which we can make publicly verifiable claims or launch publicly significant projects of societal repair."⁶⁴

d. *A response to inadequacies in pragmatic inquiry.* Pragmatism itself needs periodic repair. Here, SR's academic role is of utmost significance, since SR offers an otherwise inevident way of completing Peirce's proof of pragmatism by disclosing the scriptural sources of pragmatism's imperative to repair. While Peirce only alludes to Christian love as his pragmatic imperative, SR identifies this imperative as the indubitable foundation of each Abrahamic tradition's imperative to repair suffering and to foster love of neighbor. If, in one canonical tradition, the imperative appears as a doctrine of Christ's love, it appears in the other two as a command both to love God and to love one's neighbors as oneself. Embedded in the Tanakh, the command is identified in popular imagination with such verses as "You shall love the Lord your God with all you heart" and "Love your neighbor as yourself" (Deut. 6:5 and Lev. 19:18). The Muslim interreligious statement, "A Common Word Between Us," offers this Qur'anic parallel:

Of God's Unity, God says in the Holy Qur'an: *Say: He is God, the One! God, the Self-Sufficient Besought of all! (Al-Ikhlas* 112:1–2). Of the necessity of love for God, God says in the Holy Qur'an: *So invoke the Name of thy Lord and devote thyself to Him with a complete devotion (Al-Muzzammil* 73:8). Of the necessity of love for the neighbour, the Prophet Muhammad (صلى الله عليه وسلم)

---

62. In chapter 1 (5), I note that academic disciplines fail to nurture non-individualistic modes of teaching and learning in the humanities. In chapter 2 (26) I note that SR seeks to temper the modern tendency to press individual thinkers to overcome their creatureliness.

63. As noted in chapter 2 (29–32) SR reasoning provides instruction in three-part relations: for example, relations among the plain sense + the intention of scripture + the activity of a community of readers.

64. Chapter 3, 55.

said:[65] *"None of you has faith until you love for your neighbour what you love for yourself."*[66]

Does this imperative extend to action beyond the bounds of one's canonical community? SR's commission is to act on the assumption that it does. In this way, SR offers scriptural proofs of its own pragmatic maxim. As for an analogue to Peirce's formal proofs, I read the reasoning that emerges around an SR circle as a sociolinguistic process of diagramming the non-binary logic of SR. Here, I understand Peirce's formal reasoning as *diagrammatic reasoning*. As noted earlier in this chapter, Peirce defines "diagram" as a sign that "is predominantly an icon of relations" (4.418), introducing "*characteristics* of objects that are not already given" but are "logically possible" and "belong to the process of thinking" (4.531). An Existential Graph is not a discrete diagram/icon, but a "system of diagrammatization by means of which any course of thought can be represented with exactitude" (4.530). In other words, it is the graphist's *activity* of scribing some series of icons (the graphist's *scripture*) that reenacts the "course of thought" that is the object of the graph. Around the SR circle, analogously, each participant's reading/interpretation of a given verse constitutes an icon and thus diagram of a *relation between participant and verse*. Another reader offers another icon, but SR reasoning is not constituted by some discrete series of icons. Most often appearing only after five or six sessions of a new SR group, the reasoning of SR emerges as a course of thought specific to this group at that time. In retrospect, the group may recall that such a course of thought first appeared after certain questions and responses about some verses introduced some set of more general tropes and themes, which led to a further series of questions and responses about the relation of those tropes and themes to the original verses. The SR reasoning may appear to have emerged during this latter series, as a more intensely directional *line* of comments moved from participant to participant, engaging many voices around the table, speaking out of many approaches to text and religion, voicing many opinions, but moving in an increasingly discernable direction or small set of directions—before discussion turned elsewhere, without conclusion or mark. Characterized within Peirce's vocabulary, the SR reasoning or course of thought *was represented, at that time*, through the *way* that the latter line of comments moved from one to the next,

---

65. From the Hadith, *Sahih Muslim* 1:72.

66. *A Common Word*. For related commentary, see Ali Aref Nayed, *Vatican Engagements*. Amb. Nayed has been a long-term member of the SSR Board and SR convener.

each comment a discrete icon. I want to say that this *movement* constituted a process of diagrammatization, which process *represented* the group's SR-reasoning *with exactitude.*

Stimulated by Peirce's Existential Graphs, I have elsewhere composed a set of semiotic diagrams of SR as reparative reasoning. For specialists, I offer a larger sample in the final pages of chapter 6. For general readers, I offer one sample diagram of SR as pragmatic inquiry: illustrating that it is possible to map the logic of SR just as one would map the logic of other kinds of reparative inquiry:

Reparative SR: $(S_1 \rightarrow O_e | I_e) \rightarrow (I_e) \rightarrow \Sigma\, S\, (S_1 \rightarrow O_r | I_p)$, where O_e=problematic interpretation; I_e=problematic interpretant; I_p=pragmatic/reparative interpretant; O_r=repaired interpretation.

(Here, the pragmatic Interpretant names conditions of dysfunction with respect to which a sign vehicle, such as a scriptural verse, refers *both* to failed rules of relation *and* to rules of repair. *To repair an interpretant is to direct a community to reread it as determining some symbol to mean X*—here, a reparative rule—*where it previously meant Y*—here, a failed rule.)

17. *SR inquiry reflects conflicting habits, goals and contexts of inquiry.* This is another way that SR reasoning parallels pragmatic reasoning.[67] If the parallel is close, then SR might be served by conflicting tendencies toward reparative vs. diagrammatic inquiry—renaming the latter "iconizing inquiry" to fit the context of a non-philosophic practice. I think the parallel is indeed close, since SR is served by desires to repair/heal and by desires to clarify meaning (which is equivalent to bringing the unknown to light and, thus, to graph or scribe). While they may become complements, these desires also compete, as I observe in the competing goals that animate SR's founders and current teachers as well as in the process of SR-reasoning as I formalize it.[68] When SR practice is dysfunctional, it appears to serve only one of the desires or to serve them in a conflictual way. I infer that, when SR works well, the

67. On SR and inquiry, see Rashkover, "Scriptural Reasoning." See also Adams, "Making Deep Reasonings Public."

68. Successful SR is animated by a range of competing desires, including desires to promote academic/scientific vs. religious/tradition-based inquiry, or the plain sense vs. the interpretive sense, or one tradition/denomination vs. another. But some competing desires weaken SR: including desires to promote objective vs. subjective inquiry, or Scripture's universal vs. particular meanings. Such competitions are articulated in binary terms for which there are no mediating thirds. SR's work is not to mediate such binaries, but to repair them through a process of inquiry I introduced earlier, in the discussion of "deep to deep" reparative inquiry: above, item #15 and throughout chapter 2.

two are contributing in dynamical but adequately harmonious ways. I cannot tell you, however, by what means the two are engaged this way, except to redescribe how we institute and facilitate Formational SR. The lesson is that the "means" of integrating SR's foundational desires is by way of *Scripture* and that, to enter this way, one follows the rules/practices of FSR. How to know one is following well? "By their fruit": checking the many signs of successful and unsuccessful SR as reported, for example, in this book, always returning to the actual practice to see for sure (or sure enough). For SR, Scripture *in* SR is the third with respect to which, alone, SR's competing desires yield what we hope.

18. *SR reasoning is a critical revelatory reasoning.* In his proof of pragmatism, Peirce sought to trace projects of rational inquiry back to the indubitable beliefs they presuppose. SR reasoning complements Peirce's effort by examining scripturally grounded indubitable beliefs and uncovering among them scriptural sources of the pragmatic imperative. SR reasoning demonstrates, moreover, how practices of rational inquiry may emerge out of practices of reading Scripture as signs of a scriptural community's indubitable beliefs.[69]

Abrahamic traditions tend to apply cognates of the English term "revealed" to the text canons whose words are read as signs of such beliefs. In classical rabbinic tradition, preferred terms are *mattan Torah* (the giving of Torah) and *dibburot hashem* (God's spoken words). Classical Qur'anic tradition has comparable preferences: for example, *wahi* (guidance) and *qur'an* (recitation). SR studies the kinds of reasoning that emerge as readers receive and discuss the products of these speakings/revelations. I label SR's activity "critical," because SR's interpersonal and interreligious setting allows participants to experiment—temporarily—with a broader range of readings than they are accustomed to, without trespassing on traditional rules of behavior.

19. *SR reasoning diagrams the possibility of Hearth-to-Hearth engagement.*

I devote chapter 6 entirely to SR's contribution to the theory and practice of Hearth-to-Hearth Peacebuilding (H2H). In this section, I introduce H2H more broadly as an application of all the dimensions

---

69. Or, in Peirce's terms, how these practices may *grow* out of SR-like practices of reading Scripture across differences. In the "Neglected Argument," Peirce recommends musing on the "phenomenon of growth" in each universe of experience. In other writings, he redefines "generalization" as "the growth of ideas": a worldly, social process through which ideas "spread" to additional courses of thought and additional populations. I mention this because Peirce's account helps explain *how* reasoning could grow out of scriptural reading: patterns of relation implicit in SR reading gradually extend to and merge with other patterns, including additional dimensions of reflection.

of SR reasoning introduced above to the work of reducing conflict among participants from competing value traditions. H2H does not introduce adversaries into circles of scriptural study. Its relation to SR is essential, but indirect. H2H trains its architects and facilitators in FSR and trains at least the architects in what I label SR logic. To identify this logic, an H2H team first diagrams dominant patterns of SR reasoning observed within an experienced circle of scriptural reasoners. In other words, the team diagrams what I have earlier named an SR group's process of diagrammatization. To accomplish this, the team first shares in an extended series of FSR sessions. Secondly, the team retreats to choose an instrument for diagramming, for example, semiotics or whatever formal system they prefer. Thirdly, members of the team experiment with ways of scribing SR's course of thought within this system. The fourth step concludes the process: the team reads and debates samples of what they have scribed, sharing comments around the table in ways that are analogous to FSR (without the Scripture), until one or two distinct courses of thought emerge around the table. I apply the term "SR logic" to these courses of thought understood as processes of diagramming what will serve as the elemental patterns of H2H. Team members will try to scribe the processes. *What they scribe will serve as useful reminders of the team's SR logic, but the logic is a process of diagrammatization that the team must reenact each time it meets to construct and perform programs of H2H.* The team's FSR remains the indirect source of this process, and that source includes the scriptural canons they read across differences.

Readers may find concrete illustrations of H2H programs in chapter 6. I will conclude this section by noting ways that H2H embodies illustrative dimensions of SR reasoning:

a. *Critical revelatory reasoning*: As defined in chapter 1, a "hearth" refers to what is most valued in a religious group's beliefs and practices. I define hearths loosely as dimensions of life that members of a religion turn to in times of crisis in the hope of drawing nearer to their deepest values and identities.[70] H2H extends a notion of hearth to what is most valued in any value-centered group's beliefs and practices. In Peirce's terms, what is most valued tends to be informed by a group's indubitable beliefs. SR identifies scriptural canons as signs of certain religious groups' indubitable beliefs, displayed through what these groups consider processes of revelation or divine speech. Architects of H2H assume that

---

70. Chapter 1, 21–24.

each value-centered group identifies unique elements of material culture as signs of shared indubitable beliefs and that the group's value-centered reasonings emerge out of activities of interpreting and debating these signs.

b. *A reparative response to societal dysfunction:* This is definitional.

c. *A reparative response to hermeneutical dysfunction:* H2H focuses on conflictual and non-conflictual ways that stakeholders read signs of their indubitable beliefs.

d. *Knowing that is relational, social, linguistic, participatory, non-binary:* H2H employs diagnostic tools that examine stakeholder groups' practices of communicating value judgments as indicators of probable near-future behavior toward other groups. The work is therefore social and linguistic. H2H offers methods of remediation that engage stakeholders as participatory co-agents.

e. *H2H nurtures knowing beyond the limits of what individual participants and stakeholders know. H2H knowing is knowing enough.* Methods of H2H are designed by SR-trained architects (who do not, therefore, know too little); but, in all processes of remediation, stakeholders are equal partners with H2H architects/agents (who do not, therefore, know too much).

CHAPTER 6

Hearth-To-Hearth Interreligious Peace Building

AFTER FOUR CHAPTERS OF intense discussion of SR in the classroom and in contemporary academic thinking, chapter 6 returns to the theme introduced in chapter 1: SR as an approach to peacebuilding.[1] This is the dimension of SR that gets most public attention and for good reason, since religion-related violence is increasing globally. This chapter offers three arguments about religion-related violent conflict: (i) At the present time, governmental and civic agencies dedicated to conflict resolution fail to identify any successful method for diagnosing the contribution of religion/religious behavior to such conflict or to its resolution; (ii) SR introduces models of reasoning and practice that may repair this failure; (iii) One such model, "Hearth to Hearth Peace Building" (H2H), is now ready for field tests in regions of conflict. The chapter offers three additional arguments about how to employ SR: (a) Formational SR (FSR) is *not* an appropriate instrument for peacebuilding in settings of violent conflict; (b) The Logic of SR (SRL) *is*, however, a vital resource for peacebuilding in settings of religion-related violent conflict, and SRL is obtained by constructing logical diagrams of the elemental patterns of SR reasoning displayed in FSR; (c) H2H is an application of SRL to the setting of religion-related violent conflict. I introduce general features of H2H by applying SRL to a general model of such conflict. *For practical use, analysts must reframe H2H (or comparable instruments) with respect to the conditions and objectives of location-specific peacebuilding activities and in dialogue with stakeholders to the conflict.*

1. My thanks to Devan Keesling for assistance and editorial help on Chapter 6.

I divide the chapter into two sections. In section I, "Religion and Violence," I offer general claims about why governmental and civic agencies have failed to identify and address religion's role in violent conflict. I compose section I for a general audience. In section II, "H2H Peacebuilding and the Logic of SR," I offer more technical claims about the potential peacebuilding contributions of SRL and H2H. In the process, I offer concluding accounts of why FSR may succeed and of how and why SR reasoning may contribute to peacebuilding. I compose section II for a somewhat more specialized audience.

I. RELIGION AND VIOLENCE

Religion is Dangerous. Recent studies suggest that religion is indeed a significant factor in armed conflict around the world. According to a 2014 Pew Research report, "the share of countries with a high or very high level of social hostilities involving religions reached a six-year peak in 2012. A third of the 198 counties and territories included in the study had high religious hostilities in 2012, up from 20% as of mid-2007. Religious hostilities increased in every major region of the world except the Americas."[2] These conflicts were driven by a broad range of factors, but interreligious animosities and violence played as significant role. In fact, of thirty-five significant armed conflict reported in 2013, the top two factors were matters of identity (twenty-one conflicts) and matters of religion (twenty-one conflicts).[3]

I interpret such reports as evidence that what I call "religion" is dangerous to humankind. But I add that there is nonetheless a solution to religion-related violence, and that what I am calling "religion" is a primary source of

---

2. The following contrast illustrates a stark difference between institutes that do or do not recognize religion-related conflict as meriting distinctive attention by diplomats and foreign policy analysts. (1) On the one hand, the International Peace Research Institute reported: "Since the end of the Cold War, armed conflicts around the world have declined substantially," UCDP/PRIO. (2) On the other hand, Pew Research has documented a steady rise in religion-related violent conflict.

3. According to a 2014 Pew report, "the share of countries with a high or very high level of social hostilities involving religion reached a six-year peak in 2012. A third (33%) of the 198 countries and territories included in the study had high religious hostilities in 2012, up from 29% in 2011 and 20% as of mid-2007. Religious hostilities increased in every major region of the world except the Americas." "Global Peace" as measured by the Global Peace Index (GPI) has been steadily deteriorating over the last seven years, with 111 countries deteriorating and fifty-one improving. Conflict has been driven by a broad range of factors, but interreligious animosity and violence has played a significant role.

a solution. In the following section, I offer a six-point argument to support this interpretation. Before I start, however, let me clarify something.

One lesson I learned from twenty-five years of SR practice is that *our behavior as possible contributors to peace building will be demonstrably improved if we adopted the following, operational models for collecting data about what I will call "indigenous religious value judgements."* The data will be speeches, sermons, teachings and, in some cases, informal presentations by leaders and teachers of groups participating in a given conflict. Guided by our operational categories of "religious values," researchers will cull that data for evidence of "religious value judgements," from which researchers would base their diagnoses of a given religious group's contributions to conflict as well as its possible contributions to conflict resolution. My argument is that researchers would indeed "impose" certain stipulated definitions of religious values, but the validity of these definitions would be measured only by the success or failure of the diagnoses that they stimulate. Once a given conflict-specific study is concluded, the stipulated definitions are retired. Even if a set of diagnoses prove fruitful, the specific claims offered about the "religion" and "values" of a particular group are no longer useful. Any subsequent study will rely on new operational definitions. If, case after case, this diagnostic approach proves unfruitful, then, this way of formulating operational definitions will itself be set aside.[4] Here is my argument:

Proposition #1: Religion has always been dangerous because each religion has traditionally housed a means of granting individual human beings direct access to the deepest values of a given society.

Here, I use the term *values* to refer to a means of direct access to the rules of behavior that hold a society together and that therefore bind members of a society together. Think, for example of the values cherished by a Christian denomination: perhaps they carry names like love, agape, compassion, care for neighbor, living Christ-like. Or think of values cherished by a Jewish denomination: perhaps they carry names like loving-kindness,

---

4. Some social scientists today are suspicious of claims about another society's "values," fearing that such claims may misrepresent a society's indigenous practices. I do not, however, seek to identify "what is really going on" in another society or "what values really are" in general. I offer frameworks whose validity is measured strictly by the relative strength or weakness of their contribution to some finite task of repair or problem-solving. In this case, there are two problems to solve: the fact that most cases of religion-related violent conflict escape current efforts at repair and the fact that no agency involved in conflict resolution appears to make use of successfully field-tested tools for diagnosing and repairing such conflicts. I do not know what religion is or values are. But I have evidence that, by examining a certain class of judgments by members of stakeholder groups in religion-related violent conflicts, responsible agents may be able to plan more successful peacebuilding strategies.

teaching, Torah. Or think of values cherished by a Muslim denomination: perhaps they carry names like compassion, charity, zakat, tawhid, the oneness and unity of God. When I refer to "values," I do not refer only to words like these, but, beyond words, to all the detailed habits of behavior that we may at least imagine lie behind them. When I refer to "granting humans direct access," I mean offering individual leaders or sages the capacity to perceive, comprehend, and thereby manage and change a society's defining rules of behavior.

My operational argument is that, if religion can be said to offer access to such deep values, then it could be said to offer mere human beings (perhaps one or two prophets, or perhaps all members of a society) the power to influence and modify the very order and fabric of their societies. Should leaders arise who are not moved by a spirit of goodness or holiness, then religious knowledge could grant them the power to influence a social order for ill. Or, should leaders arise who have good intentions but limited understanding, then their unintended errors could influence the social order for ill as well. If such leaders had charisma, they could teach and excite members of a social group to throw their energies into actions that, little by little, could undo the fabric of a social and moral order. That is why religion is dangerous: it uncovers knowledge that could possibly be used for ill.

Proposition #2: Religion is even more dangerous now, today.

There are many reasons why, but I believe the strongest and deepest reason is that modern Western civilization has for centuries tried its hardest to undo the power of religions in our lives. The nineteenth-century sociologist Max Weber and the twentieth-century sociologist Peter Berger and others have labeled this effort the "secularization hypothesis": the belief that, as society advances in modernity, religion retreats. According to this belief, intellectual and scientific developments have undermined the supernatural and superstitious ideas on which religion relies for its legitimacy. Therefore, religion becomes more and more "hollow," until a loss of active membership forces each religion into obscurity. But why would the modern effort to weaken religion make religion more dangerous? The opposite should be the case! Here is my five-step response:

   a. *Religion did not go away*. It was pushed away from the power centers of Western civilization but remained quite strong on the outskirts and even stronger around the rest of the world. Currently 84 percent of the world's population identifies as "religious."

   b. *There has been a draining of brainpower and cultural energy away from the great religions of the West.*

c. *That draining away took place not only in the West but also in the Third World nations colonized for 300 years by Western powers, who consciously tried and succeeded to reduce religious influence in those nations.*

d. *After 300 years of colonialism, religion remains strong in the passion of its followers both East and West, but religion also remains underdeveloped through centuries of interrupted education and refinement. That is a very dangerous mix: when, on the one hand, religious passions are reawakened after the fall of colonialism, while, on the other hand, religious education was suppressed and retarded through those very centuries of colonialism.*

e. *My conclusion is that, when religious learning is underdeveloped, then members of religious groups behave badly when confronted by new challenges. They behave badly, not because their religious traditions lack the needed wisdoms, but because they are severely under-educated in those wisdoms. Lacking traditional wisdom, they react to events out of unrefined human passion, however much they do so in the name of their religion.*

Proposition #3: There are three reasons why the world's great powers have failed to resolve religion-related wars and violent conflict:

a. *The Western foreign affairs community, including the United Nations, has only recently taken official note of the global increase in specifically religion-related violent conflict.* As late as 2006, the UN annual report claimed that "the world is becoming less war-prone. . . . The number of international conflicts has been falling since the mid-1970s, the most sustained decline in three centuries."[5] The reason for this cheery claim is that the UN report did not include religion-related violent conflict that appeared to be non-state-supported, even, we should add, if the state support was there but indirect and through third parties. Earlier, I cited a 2014 Pew report indicating that, from 2007 to 2014, what it called "religious hostilities" climbed to an all-time high. And before 2007? Our evidence is that, except for studies of state-sponsored restrictions on religion, survey data did not attend to the topic of religion-related conflicts at all before 2006. And how could that be? Neither Western diplomats nor their professors back in the major foreign affairs graduate schools considered "religion" a distinct category of human experience and behavior. What some of us now

---

5. "Miniatlas of Human Security," in *Human Security Index*.

call "religion-related" conflict was previously buried under the categories of political, social, or economic factors. In *The Mighty and the Almighty*, former Secretary of State Madeleine Albright offers a vivid illustration. She acknowledges that, as US ambassador to the United Nations and Secretary of State, she and other Western international leaders held the conventional view of foreign policy specialists: that religion is not an appropriate subject for analysis or discussion. Then she had a change of heart, discovering that the secularist paradigm is no longer adequate; understanding international affairs today requires an understanding of religion.[6]

b. *Each analyst or policymaker tends to examine religion-related conflict from the perspective of only one analytic discipline that they also privilege as most important. But religion-related conflict is of a kind that can be diagnosed and healed only by a coordinated assemblage of all the major kinds of analysts and agencies. Because this has not yet been attempted, no single case of conflict has been resolved.* The source of this argument is Jerry White, former Deputy Assistant Secretary of State, who oversaw a Department of State working group that addressed religion-related conflict. Mr. White came to this argument after visiting major sites of conflict around the world, observing the role of religion in the field, and observing the failure of American or British or UN agencies to respond effectively to this kind of conflict. He saw three kinds of institutions working hard to respond to religion-related conflict: governmental agencies like the State Department, religious and interreligious institutions, and a variety of civil society agencies including universities, peace building NGOs, medical teams, and so forth. He observed that, through the sponsorship of these institutions, thousands of agencies do good work in the field, caring for victims and, in some cases, negotiating reductions in degrees of religion-related violence. But he also observed that none of these institutions has succeeded in stopping any case of ongoing religion-related conflict. And why not? As noted above, White argues that to observe religion-specific conditions of conflict, analysts would have to assemble evidence from all dimensions of a given conflict, examined through all available engines of observation, interpreted through transdisciplinary practices of analysis. But no such coordinated effort has been undertaken. In the meantime, government officials see a political strife and seek to solve it politically; interfaith councils see a lack of understanding across religions and seeks to teach religion more clearly; economists

---

6. Albright, *The Mighty*, 8–11.

see an economic crisis; military analysts see the need for a balance of power. And none of these efforts succeeds.

c. *Despite the diminishment in state power in many parts of the world, the most influential Western governments remain strongest agents of response to conflicts. But Western foreign policy leaders and researchers have inherited a centuries-old assumption that the careful study of religion is not requisite for foreign policy research, policymaking, or negotiation.* For Jerry White's three years at the State Department, I served as his academic consultant on religion and conflict. Through those years, I witnessed firsthand how resistant department heads, ambassadors, and hundreds of foreign service officers were to taking religion seriously as a necessary subject for strategic study. Things are better now than they were twenty years ago, before academic scholars and peace building researchers began writing volumes about the importance of religion in international affairs. Nonetheless, the career diplomats who articulate our foreign policy are the products of generations of learning to ignore religion.

The results are disastrous. I will provide only one illustration from what I saw at the Department of State just a year after the fall of Qaddafi, at the end of the US and its allies' bombing efforts. I observed the reception of a briefing from the Libyan diplomat Amb. Aref Nayed, who sought to update Department of State and congressional leaders about the extremely dangerous situation across North Africa. Libya had no effective political infrastructure. Power was divided among several tribes, and the traditional and most respected Sunni Muslim leaders—the Ulema—were ignored by the Western powers. The real problem was that Western powers, both diplomatic and military, overlooked the traditional religious leadership because they were traditionally neither activists nor militarized. In the initial months and years after the bombing stopped, American and British diplomats began to favor the more radical Muslim Brotherhood leaders and militias, apparently because they had for years lobbied Congress as well as the British Home Office, because they offered the West influence among what appeared to be the emergent Muslim power base in North Africa, and because they came ready-made with sophisticated weapons, thereby relieving the West of the financial and logistical burden of arming what they considered friendly forces in Libya. Amb. Nayed warned that militant Islamicists from outside Libya would take advantage of the power vacuum and enter the country to achieve political and religious advantage. The briefing included an urgent request for on-the-ground peacekeepers, or at least military support, for the traditional leaders who would need time to nurture a central government.

The briefing concluded that, without support from West, the Islamicists would not succeed, and the traditional religious leaders would win political and military support from most of the Libyan population, 85 percent of which retains bonds of respect and affection for the traditional Ulema. The briefing warned that, if the West continued its apparent support for the Muslim Brotherhood forces, the most likely result would be protracted civil war.

The briefing convinced Jerry White, but it did not convince top decision-makers, including those in Congress who would have to pay for the relatively modest costs of providing the requested peacekeeping resources. In my observation, it was difficult for US diplomats to comprehend the differences among different Muslim groups in Libya, especially differences between Muslim leaders who represented centuries old Libyan values and Islamicist leaders whose values emerged primarily outside of Libya. During the two years that followed that unsuccessful briefing, almost all the briefing's warnings came true. *My final claim addresses why I argue that, despite these failures, there are indeed potentially effective avenues to religion-related peacebuilding.*

Proposition #4: *Religion-related peacebuilding requires a somewhat new concept of peacebuilding.*

The concept is only "somewhat new," because it is commonplace within many folk communities. It is nonetheless "new," because modern thinkers have tended to strip this commonplace wisdom away in favor of a few abstract principles that are useful only in certain situations. I shall begin by oversimplifying my claims so that you might see them more clearly. Then I will present them with subtler details.

In simplified terms, my claim is that the failed efforts to interrupt religion-related violent conflicts have all displayed the following assumptions of modern diplomacy over the past 200 years: that the defining sources of conflict and resolution are nation-states rather than extra-state actors that operate across state borders; that analysts can identify the causes of major conflicts and that there are only a few identifiable causes (efforts by groups to achieve power, social influence, and control of land and wealth); that religious groups participate in such conflicts for the same reasons; and that there is therefore no need for analysts to identify religion-specific reasons for their political behavior. Readers will not be surprised that, having claimed that these are failed assumptions, I proceed to argue that what I call the "new concept" of peacebuilding addresses the uniqueness of religious behavior and of the scientific disciplines needed to examine it. Readers may, however, be surprised by my next claim: that, when trained in strictly modern methods of analysis, students of politics and conflict may literally lose the capacity to "see" the phenomena of religious behavior. The new concept introduces guidelines for recovering that capacity. Here is a sample:

   a. *First, do not study "religion" as a general type of human experience.* Study only specific religions. More specifically, study how groups involved in conflict practice their local variety of a given religion. To do this, listen to group members describing their religions in their own terms: what language they use to describe it, what narratives, what rituals, what rules of behavior, including religion-based rules of economic, political, and individual or psychological behavior. This listening introduces a language, a way of speaking about the group's deepest values, which shape all aspects of their behavior in a given conflict.

   b. *Then, re-examine reports you collected about a religious group to see how the group's religious vocabulary displays its deepest values and how those values inform the group's deep-seated rules of economic, political, and social behavior.* Identify the study of religion with a study of the way a specific group's deepest values coordinate the group's economic, political, and societal behavior. That is what was missing in analyses of conflict up till now: attention to the values that coordinate all aspects of a group's activity; what we call "religion" refers to the languages and practices through which most local non-Western groups coordinate their values.

   c. *In this way, you may add one element to the prevailing, modern approach to diplomacy: studies of how each group involved in a conflict identifies its own deepest values and of how those values coordinate the group's economic, political, and social behaviors.* To perform this type of value study, analysts will need to acquire several skills and subjects of study that are not currently included in the curricula of leading programs in politics and foreign affairs. These additional skills and subjects are gathered here under the name "Hearth to Hearth Peacebuilding" (H2H).

Introducing Hearth-to-Hearth Peacebuilding (H2H)

The goal of H2H is modest: to serve as a field-testable contribution to repairing religion-related violent conflict. Its intended contributions are one degree more specific and modest: to introduce models for diagnosing religion-specific sources of such conflict and for identifying religion-specific resources for conflict resolution. More specifically, still, H2H adopts a single framework for conflict diagnosis and remediation. The framework is defined as clearly as possible so that its successes and failures will give clear evidence of what to avoid and what to seek when building better models in the future. In this section, I identify this framework and comment on its potential strengths and limits.

The H2H framework is strictly operational. To reiterate what I explained earlier, the H2H framework is not intended to mirror anything in the world. It is not a framework for clarifying what conflict, values, religion, and peace "really are." It is a framework strictly for shaping the cognitive activity of analysts and the planning and field activity of peacebuilders. Readers familiar with Immanuel Kant might draw an analogy here and say that, in Kantian terms, this is comparable to a moral framework for instructing human behavior rather than an epistemological framework for identifying elements of the world in which we behave.

H2H focuses on language-based analyses of small group behavioral proclivities. It focuses on language for several reasons: because language is overt and relatively easy to observe; because speech by group members displays identifiable indices of group behavioral tendencies and of notable changes in such tendencies; because SR is a language-based practice and twenty-five years of SR practice has lent us testable hypotheses about what changes in language behavior may correlate with what probable changes in behavioral proclivities.

H2H language study focuses on speech and writing (teachings, speeches, sermons, essays) by teachers or what we call "agents of socialization" in small religious or "value-centered" groups.[7] *Within this speech and writing, H2H focuses on certain verbal "indices" or symptoms that correlate reasonably well with testable signs of group behavioral tendencies. Drawing on literatures of semiotics and linguistic pragmatics, we* (the H2H research team) *employ the term "indices" as pointing to certain actions or habits of action in the world. Such indices do not also display semantic properties: that is, they indicate the*

---

7. Because our operational study of religion is value-based, our study of religious groups is simultaneously a study of what we call value-centered groups. We have discovered that our diagnostic methods apply equally to groups that describe themselves as religious and as non-religious but that display intensely value-centered judgments: for example, Sea Shepherds (a radical environmentalist group in the USA) or Marxist-like groups. When we array the results of our studies on a single axis, most religious-group results occupy one side of the axis, with some of the non-religious groups among them, while other non-religious groups occupy the other side of the axis along with self-described humanistic religious groups. We conclude that all these groups may be successfully analyzed and compared within the terms of our value-based system of measurement.

fact of movement or change, but no definite information about who or what moves or changes.

We find it useful to apply the label *"value term"* to verbal indices of group behavioral tendencies. Value terms are introduced within the languages spoken by a given group and defined through indigenous usage. *We define the term "value" operationally, as referring to a set of behavioral "preferences" (or patterns, rules, habits, or tendencies) within a given group, on the evidence of indigenous accounts as elicited for the sake of specific H2H endeavors.*[8]

At its current stage of development, H2H introduces a nine-point scale of testable correlations between certain changes in value-term usage and certain probable changes in values. As indicated in table 1 changes in value-term usage are measured as changes in what we currently label *"linguistic flexibility,"* which refers to technical measures of the likelihood that speakers-and-listeners will assign or tolerate any one of nine degrees of change in the character of value-term usage.

Table 1: Linguistic Flexibility Measurements for a Sample of Ten Value-Centered Groups (classified according to the 9-pt. VPA Scale (where 1=excessive inflexibility, 8+ = excessive flexibility)[9]

Group Name	Description	Low	High	Range	Average Score
ISIS	Radical Islamist	1	2	1	1.1818
Westboro Baptist Church	Fundamentalist Baptist	1	2	1	1.2857
Sea Shepherds	Radical Environmentalist	1	3	2	1.6429
Liberal Judaism	Liberal Judaism	1	8	7	3.2340
John Piper	Conservative Evangelical	1	5	4	3.4000
Dorothy Day	Progressive Catholic	2	5	3	3.7647
Rabbinic Judaism	Rabbinic Judaism	4	4	0	4.0000
Bahai	Pacifists	1	6	5	4.5227

8. My work on values is influenced by Max Kadushin, my teacher at the Jewish Theological Seminary in the 1970s. See Kadushin, *Rabbinic Mind*; Kadushin, *Worship and Ethics*; and Ochs, ed., *Understanding*. I also draw on Vanessa Ochs's studies of what she has named "Jewish Sensibilities." See V. Ochs, "Ten Jewish Sensibilities" and V. Ochs, "The Jewish Sensibilities."

9. As illustrated in figures 1 and 2, below, the table compares results of manual and computational VPA analyses of from fifty-eight to 774 documents representing hortatory speeches and writings from a range of religious and value-centered groups.

| Integral Yoga | American Yoga community | 1 | 8 | 7 | 4.8980 |
| Mehr Baba | Indian Guru | 2 | 9 | 7 | 5.3909 |

H2H measurements apply to speech and behavior in any "value-centered" group, by which we mean any group whose members tend to recognize and respect the behavioral implications of value terms as they appear in the "value judgments" offered by recognized group teachers and leaders. We identify "value judgments" as elements in speech that assert of something "in the world" (independent of the speech itself) that it is the subject of a given value: which means that a given range of behaviors is recommended in relation to this subject.

"Religious groups" are characterized as value-centered groups that practice and display an exceptional degree of reflection on group values. Such speech can be observed in statements and teachings by group leaders and teachers, in literatures held in high esteem by group members (such as scriptural commentaries), in liturgical texts and commentaries maintained by the group, in individual and small group practices that make use of such texts, and in institutions dedicated to education in such values.

The diagnostic methods of H2H apply indistinguishably to what we label "*religious groups,*" and "*value-centered groups*" in general. H2H analysts have discovered that, when measuring group speech patterns according to our nine-point scale, they can place any given value-centered group along a continuum of measurements and that religious groups (identified through indigenous reports) may be placed along the same continuum. I will spare readers more technical details, except to note that these measurements address a range of parameters, including frequency of value judgments per unit of speech and what we label linguistic rigidity/flexibility. According to the evidence we have gathered over the past five years, such religious groups tend to fall on one side of the continuum, but there are occasional exceptions where a value-centered group appears on the "religious group side," while a religious group appears toward the other side. Such similarities and differences among religious and other value-centered groups are not of concern to us. Having located operational measures of religious group behavior, we are now beginning to extend our analyses to groups whose measurements approximate those of religious groups.

"Religious value terms" and "religious values" are measured in the same way any value terms and values are measured. We classify such terms and values as "religious" *when* indigenous groups recommend such a

classification.¹⁰ This means that, operationally, H2H examines religious value terms only as they appear in active religious value judgments (as defined above) and measures them according to the nine-point scale of rigidity/flexibility. H2H identifies religious values as a religious group's behavioral preferences. While the value terms are defined indigenously, H2H identifies behavioral preferences eclectically, guided by both indigenous classifications and by analysts' observations. Such preferences need not, therefore, be associated with specifically "religious" or "other" kinds of behavioral preference. For H2H, behavior such as religion-specific ritual, is a worldly activity with visible signs and symptoms that can be observed by out-group as well as in group measures, such as walking, embracing, pushing away, and so on. To be sure, there are classes of behavior that analysts might not recognize without some training in indigenous classifications. For the most part, H2H analysts assume that those classifications are disclosed through indigenous religious value terms, so that once the terms are identified, they may be associated with observable behaviors—or with sets of sub-classifications of terms with associated observable behaviors.

Value Predicate Analysis (VPA) is a central instrument of H2H diagnostics. H2H generates an expanding repertoire of diagnostic and analytic tools, of which the current prototype is the following level ("A") of VPA:¹¹ examining the pragmatics (performative behavior) of value judgments in speeches and other oral and written teachings by the leaders and teachers of small or modest sized religious groups (or other value-centered groups). Level A employs the following operational definitions. As noted above, "value terms" refer to verbal indices of "values," defined as sets of group behavioral preferences; "value judgments" refer to spoken or written assertions that predicate some value of something "in the world" (things that listeners could observe in the world, such as a given person, event, or group). Such value judgments are distinguished from judgments that predicate some value of another value (we currently label these "doctrinal judgments"). Value terms are examined only if they appear in the predicates of such value

---

10. A demanding reader might ask, "But how do you choose to label a given indigenous classification as 'religious?'" That is a good question but not one we fret about given the strictly functional goal of our work. We use common sense; we gather information eclectically; and we refine our classifications based on new evidence. Practically speaking, most cases we examine are small groups that identify themselves as some sect or variety of what academics tend to call the world's major religions, most of them Abrahamic or Asian. On the statistical margins are groups that self-identify in other ways and that some scholars might label as "religious" or as "ideological" or "philosophic" groups.

11. There are currently several levels of VPA diagnostics. I describe here the one that we have most thoroughly refined and tested ("Level A").

judgments; this excludes value terms that appear as the subjects of spoken or written judgments or as members of lists of value terms. Level A examines the range of meanings that group members tend to associate with a given value term as it appears in the predicate of a value judgment offered at a given time and place. VPA analysts establish "baseline" ranges of meaning within a given group over a given time period (such as three to six months). The focal work of Level A is to evaluate changes in range of meanings at given times and, where possible, to collect evidence about significant events taking place in the group at approximately these times. These changes are measured quantitatively and classified according to the current, nine-point H2H scale of linguistic flexibility, from "1" ("least flexible") to "9" ("most flexible"). Drawing on past evidence, new information, and continually refined analytic models, H2H diagnosticians correlate VPA measurements with probable group tendencies to behave in certain ways in relation to other groups. As illustrated in Figures 1 and 2, diagnosticians currently associate lower numbers in the scale with tendencies to pre-set patterns of behavior that do not change or adjust to changing behaviors of other groups. The middle range of numbers is associated with behaviors typical of most established religious groups in relatively non-conflictual relations. Level A analysts label this behavior "bureaucratic," meaning that such groups relate to other groups according to established institutional norms in a given society, rather than according to religion-specific tendencies (which tend to be observed only within the non-public behavior of group members with one another). The higher range of numbers is associated with a diminishment of predictable patterns of relations to other groups; extreme numbers (toward 9) are associated with the potential dissolution of group identity. Numbers in-between these three primary sets (sets of low, middle, high numbers) are associated with a somewhat greater proclivity to interactive engagement with other groups.

Figure 1: Illustrating Linguistic Inflexibility, ISIS.[12]

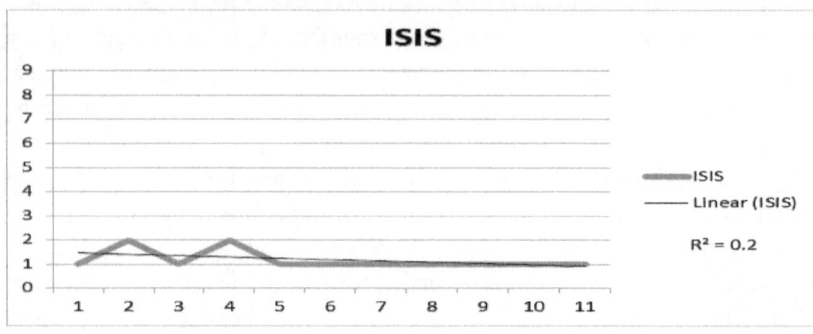

Figure 2: Illustrating Balanced Linguistic Flexibility, Dorothy Day.[13]

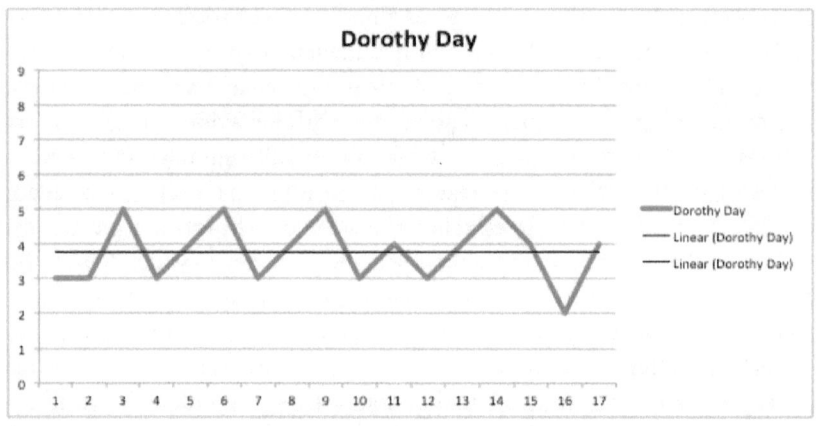

12. Figure 1 graphs a sample of 11 documents (x-axis) from the ISIS publication *Dabiq*, with VPA measurements (y-axis) of 1 (nine documents) and 2 (two documents). The measurements display nearly maximal linguistic inflexibility, suggesting extreme resistance to change and extreme unresponsiveness to changes in the behavior of other groups.

13. Figure 2 graphs a sample of seventeen documents (x-axis) from Dorothy Day's contributions to *The Catholic Worker*, with VPA measurements (y-axis) between 3 and 5. The measurements display balanced linguistic flexibility, suggesting that her activist community would adapt well to changing environmental conditions (social and other).

Figure 3: Illustrating Unusually High Linguistic Flexibility, Mehr Baba.[14]

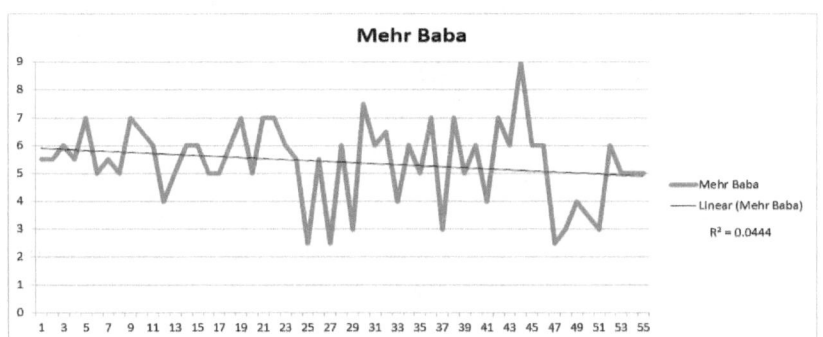

Diagnosing the dangerous side of religion: These days, many governments are paying extraordinary amounts of money for "large data" diagnoses—such as "sentiment analysis"—of potential, "terrorist" tendencies among certain groups. Reviewing what is available in the public domain, our team judged that some of the diagnostic techniques appear credible, and some appear to be adopted for the sake of earning money and little else. We hypothesized that some governments seek this information for apparently legitimate reasons, but that some may seek it as a means of publicizing evidence that would justify military actions planned long before the search for evidence. H2H analysts have found that it is in fact not very difficult to identify linguistic markers of tendencies to extreme violence: marker #1 on the nine-point H2H scale.[15] This identification is less difficult, for one, because efforts to identify such groups usually call for a single contrast between potentials for "imminent violent behavior" and for "anything else." It is less difficult, moreover, because there is a range of corroborating linguistic evidence in addition to the Level A numbers.[16]

---

14. Figure 3 graphs a sample of fifty-five documents (x-axis) from the Hindu guru's hortatory writings, with VPA measurements (y-axis) varying between 3 and 9. The measurements display an unusually high linguistic flexibility, suggesting that his disciples would interpret his words in highly individuated ways and that any society of such disciples would rarely participate in concerted action.

15. Our data suggests that groups displaying VPA of 1 (and sometimes 2) are fully committed to lines of concerted action. Some of these groups are non-violent, but all groups planning or engaged in violent action display VPA of 1 (or between 1 and 2).

16. We are currently refining and field testing three additional markers of linguistic flexibility/inflexibility: Level B measures value-to-value judgments; Level C measures categories of narrative style; Level D measures what we call "meta-values," which appear to signal ways of changing or reorganizing relations among sets of values.

There is reason to ask why government and academic researchers tend to focus only on such "terrorist" markers. What are the practical goals of such a focus? Aside from the questionable goals I alluded to above, one may assume the answer is "to get early warning of potential attacks and to recommend protective strategies." This answer makes sense, but only for a limited number of situations: where the results of the diagnosis are timely (therefore excluding cases where the results appear to serve the purported "long-term" purposes of either testing the diagnostic methods themselves or purportedly "keeping long-term tabs on a given group"), where purported terrorist activity would be of demonstrably significant threat to identifiable populations, and where the results of the diagnosis were directly received by agencies authorized to take protective action and capable of performing that action in measured and effective ways (ways that would not potentially cause greater loss of life or societal disruption than the purported terrorist activity itself). Even in such situations, there is reason to ask how such measured, protective action could take place without more refined measures of the manner and degree of probable terrorist activity and of the behavioral tendencies of groups potentially endangered by this activity, potentially indifferent to it, potentially supportive of it, and potentially motivated and capable of resisting or repelling it. H2H addresses these latter questions.

H2H diagnostics apply comparably to potential religious group contributions to violent conflict or to its resolution. The diagnostics are strictly operational, which is to say that H2H analysts make no claims about the intrinsic character of any group they study. They claim only that reading certain linguistic markers in a certain way generates certain field-testable expectations about a group's probable behavioral tendencies towards other groups in the near term. Such expectations are meaningful to the degree that they generate corresponding field-testable expectations about best practices for engaging a given group. H2H analysts are currently testing the following correlations between the nine-point range of linguistic markers and a corresponding range of best practices for engagement.[17]

---

17. See Ochs et al., "Value Predicate Analysis." The research and writing team included Nauman Faizi, Jonathan Teubner, and Zain Moulvi, along with analyst/translators Essam Fahim, Ilma Qureshi, Sara Aziz, Zoya Mirza, and thirty undergraduate research interns and managers Gates Young, Jinhee Lee, Mubashir Khizar, Cheryl Leow, Paola Pinzon Hernandez, and others.

II. H2H PEACEBUILDING AND THE LOGIC OF SR

H2H is analogous in several ways to FSR, but it is not identical. It is informed by the logic of SR (SRL), but not by SR's literal practice and setting. SR is study across difference in a setting of unsettled peacetime (peacetime with underlying potential to conflict); H2H is deliberation across difference in a setting of non-peace. On the following pages, I first outline the primary characteristics of H2H. I then explore how each of these characteristics is anticipated in the practice of FSR, albeit in a different idiom. I discuss differences as well, concluding that FSR provides the optimal training for facilitators of H2H, although H2H does not itself entail small group study of scriptural sources. I then explore how SRL serves as the logic of H2H as well as of Scriptural Reasoning: diagramming elemental characteristics of FSR and transporting them from the context of scriptural study across differences to the context of efforts to repair religion-related violent conflict.

Peace applications of Formational SR: As described in detail in Chapters 1, 2, and 5, Formational SR is the prototypical point of entry into any manner of SR practice or SR reasoning. From several perspectives, it is intrinsically a practice of "peace." Through twenty-five years and some 6000+ sessions, it has a proven record of enabling religious practitioners to engage one another, without rancor, in heart-to-heart studies of one another's sacred texts. In over 90 percent of such sessions, practitioners—from highly orthodox to liberal—have entered with uncertainty or tension about the process and then decided to return, typically for six to eight or more sessions. They engage in a practice whose goal is not to resolve violent conflict but to inhibit interpersonal and intergroup tensions that might arise from perceived conflicts of values, beliefs, commandments. We could call this a practice of peace (*shalom*) in the sense of wholeness (*shlemut*): where believers from different revealed traditions are able to stand before one another without veiling or hiding their deepest and deeply contrasting beliefs (where, before one another, they can open their Scriptures *wholeheartedly*) and without shielding themselves from hearing the heartfelt voices of other Scriptures.

FSR therefore displays the wholeness (*shlemut*) of differing believers and beliefs sharing the same table and same moment of time without loss of difference. Beyond enabling these different human beings to share a common space and time, FSR may also be said to enable different religious languages to interact: for phonemes and graphemes, grammars and syntax, vocabularies and values, modes of thinking, and patterns of performance to interact through the speech and dialogue of the SR participants, along with their arguments, reasonings, and discoveries. Individual participants may eventually become aware of these interactions and react to them, but we may assume that the initial consequences affect subliminal habits of thinking, speaking, and hearing before any habit-change becomes a topic for individual reflection and comment.

What are the characteristics of SR practice? As illustrated in chapter 2, a sketch of the elemental characteristics of FSR may be drawn from the practices of both TR and SR: TR illustrating how scriptural reasoners engage the plain sense of verses drawn from specific canons; SR illustrating how reasoners engage movements of interpretation across the canons. Revisiting my sketches from chapter 2, I will briefly summarize the features of TR I observed in Steven Fraade's study of rabbinic midrash and the features of SR I observed in an issue of the *Journal of Scriptural Reasoning*. I will recharacterize each feature in terms of the pragmatic semiotic introduced in chapters 3 and 5.

Primary Characteristics of TR as Tradition-Specific Commentary

In chapter 2, I observed the following features of TR-like study in Steven Fraade's account of the midrash collection *Sifre Devarim* (*Sifre Deuteronomy*). I summarize them here as features of TR that reappear as features of the canon-specific dimension of scriptural study in SR:

1. "Ancient scriptural commentaries... are always about the text as a whole." Such commentaries are, therefore "not simply a series of declarative assertions about the meaning of words in the text but an attempt to *effect* a relationship between that text overall and those for whom it is 'Scripture.'"[18]

2. *Atomization: the commentaries divide each verse in order to explicate its parts.*[19] Addressing Deuteronomy 32:7, for example, the *Sifre* isolates the base-text, "Remember the days of old" and scribes alongside it a series of different rabbinic readings of the plain sense, such as, "[God said to them:] Take heed of what I did to the earliest generations."

---

18. Fraade, *From Tradition*, 13–14. As sources of his notion of double-dialogue, Fraade cites, among others, McGann, *Social Values*, esp. 19–31; and Fish, *Doing What Comes Naturally*, esp. 57–67; with ultimate sources in John Searle, J. L. Austin, and Mikhail Bakhtin.

19. Fraade, *From Tradition*, 26, where he adds this account of how Sifre achieves its "refiguring of the biblical text of Deuteronomy in relation to the event of revelation." The commentary "lift[s] . . . scriptural verses from other scriptural contexts" and refigures them "in the newly created context of commentary to Deuteronomy."

3. *Double-dialogue*: Commentaries are "systematic series of explanations or interpretations"[20] that atomize base-texts into successive subunits, attaching interpretive comments to each sub-unit. Thus, the *Sifre* returns, "sooner or later," to add new comments on the same sub-unit: a dialogue between base-text and interpreters that redoubles itself with each new reading of the base-text.[21]

4. *Commentaries that are doubly dialogic are interactive and (to varying degrees) relationally binding.* As students of the *Sifre* "work through the commentary, the commentary works through them."[22] These students are therefore *bound* to Scripture as unending source of new information about itself in relation to them.

5. *Commentaries that are doubly dialogic engage Scripture as vague but made definite through the time and relational context of interpretation. Scripture's meaning therefore varies with respect to variations in context.* Even with respect to a given context, relations between text and meaning are not formulaic; the interpretive relation between Scripture and commentator must be renewed on each occasion of interpretation.[23]

6. *Commentaries that are doubly dialogic identify Scripture as multivocal.* Fraade observes "that the most elementary reader of early rabbinic midrash would recognize that on virtually every 'page' of the tannaitic midrashim . . . we find multiple interpretations of single scriptural words or phrases."[24]

7. *Commentaries that are doubly dialogic tend to display self-reference.*[25] Acknowledging their status *as* commentary, these commentaries signal that their words are not literal windows to divine intention or to *the* meaning of Scripture. Fraade comments that the *Sifre* "portrays the broader class of rabbinic authors *as* among the *objects* of its commentary."[26]

---

20. Fraade cites *Webster*'s definition.
21. Fraade, *From Tradition*, 14.
22. Fraade, *From Tradition*, 14.
23. Fraade, *From Tradition*, 14.
24. Fraade, "Response," 342. Fraade comments on his treatment of *Sifre Devarim Ha' azinu*, pis. 306, to Deut. 32:1 where he counts "thirteen interpretations of the first two or three words of the verse." Citing Fraade, *From Tradition*, 123–62.
25. Below, I diagram a commentary's self-reference as conditioned by its pragmatic interpretant and Meta-I.
26. Fraade, *From Tradition*, 27.

Primary Characteristics of SR as Scriptural Study Across Difference

In Chapter 2, I observed the following features of SR study in "Healing Words: The Song of Songs and the Path of Love," an issue of *The Journal of Scriptural Reasoning* (JSR):

1. *Reading from Affliction to Healing.* General Editor Willie Young observes: "Intertextual reading repairs scripture so as to repair and heal communities. As this pattern emerges, we may begin to see how the brokenness of scripture is not a change in God, but rather leads to a change within us."[27] Young illustrates several features of this pattern of reading, which I label "*hermeneutical healing.*"

2. *Sensitivity to multiple levels of meaning (polysemy).*

3. *Respect for the plain sense of a scriptural text (or its elementary narrative or assertion). The reader returns to the plain sense after each "deeper" level reading.*

4. *Trust that, on deeper levels of reading, scriptural texts will address specific afflictions within the reading community.*

5. *Hopes that such readings also open pathways toward healing these afflictions.*

6. *Textual Affliction:* But patterns of hermeneutical healing may also introduce instruments of affliction into scriptural commentary, since a reader's sensitivity to the afflictions of a given reading community may, in some cases, include sensitivity to communal values that may, knowingly or unknowingly, prove to be sources of suffering for others. Readings are also potential sources of affliction.

7. *Integrating fragments into new wholes:* For Goshen-Gottstein, rabbinic commentaries imitate the Song's integrative performance by collecting disparate fragments from the Song and reintegrating them in ways that display otherwise inevident instructions for healing. This process of hermeneutical healing trains the rabbis' readers to attend to human suffering the way the rabbis' commentaries attend to afflictions in the scriptural text.

8. *Uncovering divine attributes of love:* In Safi's reading of Sufi accounts of divine love, "God takes on a range of humanizing attributes. . ., including characteristics most often associated with human love. As God

---

27. Chapter 2, 46, citing Young, "The Song of Songs."

takes on these attributes, the beloved is brought more intimately into God's presence."

9. *In sum, difference is not source of affliction for SR*: the co-presence of difference is SR's source of joy. In Young's words, "I will let love speak for itself, as the authors and respondents think with their scriptures and traditions, and with one another."[28]

Constructing SRL Diagrams of TR/SR Practice

There are several reasons why it is important to construct models of each element of this diagram of SRL: (a) The effort to construct a well-formed model is one way to test the rationality of the logic and, thereby, of the practice it models. Here "rationality" does *not* imply a reductive or binarist character; because, (b) SR demonstrates that it is possible to *reason* coherently from out of sources that the modern academy deems anti-rational or at least extra-rational. We claim that the modern academy's critique is a symptom of the binarism implicit in its own models of rationality and that both SR and post-Newtonian experimental sciences employ non-binarist standards of reason. To construct a coherent model of SR is one way to test the rationality of these standards; (c) The model illustrates one of the non-binarist features of SR: that its reasoning is both context-relative *and* potentially generalizable. "Context-relative" does not mean "utterly contingent"; it simply means not context-independent and, therefore, not overgeneralized. A model displays generalizable features, and it displays marks of the original conditions that prompted its construction. *A model is not a representation of "the way something is"; it is, instead, an instrument built to serve some worldly purpose.* To say that it has generalizable features is to say that other reasoners may have occasion to employ these features for other purposes; (d) *Models are transportable rules of rationality.* A model provides a means through which a given practice of reasoning may be transported from one context to another. A model is like a menu written for the sake of someone else's eating pleasure, not *reading* pleasure; (e) To see if SR can be moved from its original Abrahamic context to other contexts, we need to formalize SR, that is, to reduce its rules *per experimentum* to a transportable form, a menu. This semiotic system is *only one way* to diagram SRL.

(1) *SR/TR may be diagrammed as processes of sign interpretation (semiosis), where (a) a Sign Vehicle refers to its (b) Object with respect to (c) conditions/rules of signification provided by its Interpretant.*

28. Young, "Song of Songs."

Formula 1: S→O|

> For example, according to the midrashic practices (Interpretant) of the Sifre, "Remember the days of old (*olam*)" (Deut. 32:7) refers to "Take heed of what I did to the earliest generations."[29] *Elements of this semiosis may be examined both individually (as atomized) and with respect to their relation to the entire process.*
>
>   a. The relations of a sign vehicle to its objects may be identified (atomized) as *Icons, Indices* and *Symbols.*

Formula 1.1 S= (S_{ic}, S_{in}, S_{sy})

>   b. An icon refers to a *rheme*, or possible characterization of something somewhere. A rheme is always an Immediate Object (IO), which means the *sense* of some sign.

Formula 1.1.a: S_{ic} → —

> Drawing on the previous illustration, "[divine action toward] the previous generations" is a rheme, characterizing what could possibly happen.
>
>   c. An index refers to an existent, or something somewhere. An existent is always a Dynamical Object (DO), which means *the referent* of some sign.

Formula 1.1.b: S_{in} → •|E_{in}

> Drawing on the previous illustration, "what I did" serves as index of an event in Israel's sacred history: God's punishing the Generation of the Flood.[30]
>
>   d. A symbol refers to some rule of relation (or "rule") according to which something somewhere could be characterized in some manner, that is, some rheme might be predicated of some object. A rule may be IO.

Formula 1.1.c: S_{sy} → — •|I_{sy}

> Drawing on the previous illustration, any midrashic statement operates as Symbol: for example,
>
> > *Remember the days of old:* [God said to them:] Take heed of what I did to the earliest generations: what I did to the people of the

---

29. Chapter 2, 50, referring to Deuteronomy 32:7.
30. Chapter 2, 49.

generation of the Flood, and what I did to the people of the generation of the Dispersion [Tower of Babel].³¹

The entire sequence brings (a) a sign-vehicle ("Remember . . .") into relation with (b) its probable dynamical object ("What I did to these generations"), (c) with respect to the rabbinic practice of midrash as interpretant. For the intended Israelite/Jewish reader, the rule of relation (aCb) is an imperative that links disobedience and probable punishment in a manner that would most likely influence the reader's (or reading community's) future behavior.

    e. As introduced in 1.1.c, the Object of a symbol includes DO (referents) and IO (senses).

Formula 1.1.d: $O_{sy} = (DO, IO)$.

In the preceding example, "What I did" functions as DO; "[divine action toward] the previous generations" functions as IO.

(2) *A symbol may be atomized, in which case any element of a symbol may also be read as a symbol, including icons, indices, and possible interpretants functioning now as symbols.*

Formula 2: $S_{sy} = (- + \bullet + |I_{sy}|)$.

As illustrated in the preceding items, the Symbol illustrating 1.1.c is atomized into the icon and index, illustrating 1.1.b and 1.1.a.

    a. Symbols may be read monovalently when their interpretant assigns them only one possible meaning.³²

Formula 2.1: $S_{mv} \to O_{mv}|I_{sy}$, where $O = - \bullet$ and where $O_{mv} \text{ V} \sim O_{mv}$.

For example: Fraade reads the Dead Sea Scroll *pesharim* as prototypically monovalent readings of Tanakh:

> And God told Habakkuk to write down the things that are going to come upon the last generation, but the fulfillment of the end-time he did not make known him. And when it says, "So that he can run who reads it" (Hab. 2:2), the interpretation of it concerns the Teacher of Righteous, to whom God made known all the mysteries of the words of His prophets.³³

---

31. Fraade, *From Tradition*, 75, citing *Sifre Devarim par. 310*.

32. There are sub-cases for which the monovalence applies only to rheme or only to index.

33. 1QpHab 7.1–5, citing translation in Horgan, *Pesharim*.

Fraade comments that the Scriptures, "understood to communicate God's salvific plan for history, were thought to be veiled in mysterious language whose meaning had not been disclosed to the prophets and their contemporaries but only to the Teacher of Righteousness. He in turn, it is presumed, dictated them in the form of *pesher* commentaries to his sectarian followers."[34]

    b. Symbols may be read polyvalently when their interpretant assigns them more than one possible meaning (reference to meaning is not strictly limited by the law of excluded middle).

Formula 2.2: $S_{sy} \to \Sigma\ (O|I_{sy}$, where $\sim (O\ V \sim O))$.

To illustrate: the *Sifre* offers multiple readings of every base-text, for example, "'Moses said the Lord came from Sinai. He shone upon them from Seir'" (Deut. 33:2); "[this tells us] that Moses began not with the needs of Israel but with the praise of God." Another interpretation: "When the Holy One Blessed be He revealed himself in order to give the Torah to Israel, he did not speak to them in one language, but in four languages."[35] Another interpretation: When the Holy One . . . revealed Himself to give the Torah to Israel, He revealed Himself not to Israel alone but to all the nations."[36] And more!

(3) There are several dimensions of Interpretant.

    a. The interpretant as "mind" includes the sum of all possible value predicates in some sign system that includes such symbols as sign vehicles.

Formula 3.1: $|I_{mi} = \Sigma\ S \to -|I$

My teacher, the scholar of rabbinic midrash Max Kadushin, sought to identify elements of what he called "the rabbinic mind," depicted as a network of elements, each one a polyvalent symbol, named by the rabbinic sages' biblically derived terms for sacred values: such as "God's Justice"(*middat hadin*), "God's Mercy" (*middat harachamim*),

---

34. Fraade, *From Tradition*, 3–4. As illustration, Fraade cites 1QpHab 9.3–12:
[When it says,] "on account of human bloodshed and violence done to the land, the city, and all its inhabitants" (Hab. 2:8b). The interpretation of it concerns a [W]icked Priest whom—because of wrong done to the Teacher of Righteousness and his partisans—God gave into the hand of his enemies to humble him with disease for annihilation in despair, because he had acted wickedly against His chosen ones."

35. The midrash associates Sinai with Hebrew, Seir with Roman language, Mount Paran with Arabic and so on. Cited in Fraade, *From Tradition*, 30.

36. The Sifre alludes to Psalm 138:4, "All the kings of the earth shall praise You O Lord, for they heard the words you spoke."

"Acts of Loving-kindness" (*gemilut hasadim*) and "God's Spoken-Word" (*dibbur*).[37] For Kadushin, the symbols function as *vague (under-determined) rules of behavior* whose characteristics are displayed in the actions they determine, including *acts of rabbinic scriptural interpretation and of rabbinically inspired acts of value-driven behavior in the future*. Restated in my formal vocabulary, Kadushin sought (a) to identify these interpretive acts with the individual homiletic (*haggadic*) *midrashim* that the rabbinic sages redacted into midrash collections (such as the *Mekhilta* or *Sifre*); (b) to diagram individual scriptural interpretations as what he called "haggadic statements," whose predicates are biblically derived sacred values and whose subjects are worldly habits of action that illustrate these values; and (c) to help repair contemporary Judaism by reintroducing the sages' sacred values as inspiring behavioral models for contemporary Jewish youth. Take, for example, this midrash in the *Mekhilta*:

> "Moses took the bones of Joseph with him" (Exod. 13:19). This proclaims the wisdom and the piety of Moses. For all Israel were busy with the booty, while Moses busied himself with the duty (*mitzvah*) of looking after the bones of Joseph. Of him, Scripture says, "The wise in heart takes on duties" (Prov. 10:8).[38]

Kadushin diagrams the midrash as a haggadic statement that Moses performed acts of Loving-kindness (*gemilut hasadim*) and that these were also acts of *Mitsvah* (observing divinely commanded duties).[39]

In the terms of pragmatic semiotics, Kadushin's rabbinic mind displays the sum of all possible objects of classical rabbinic values. This is a network of real possibilities, not actualities. Kadushin's depictions of the rabbinic mind are also observations about real possibilities. Stimulated by literary and historical studies of the rabbinic period but not reducible to them, his observations are *abductions* about the network of *rhemes* (*Formulae 1.1.a,b*) that may have constituted the sages' palette of named behavioral values *and that could serve as a normative resource for Jewish behavior today*.

b. The Interpretant as "language system" includes the sum of all rules of relation (aRb) available in that system.

Formula 3.2: $|IL = \Sigma aRb \,|I$

37. Kadushin, *The Rabbinic Mind*.
38. *Mekilta*, 176.
39. Kadushin, *A Conceptual Approach*, 220–21. For recent work in pragmatism and rabbinic Judaism, see Hashkes, *Rabbinic Discourse*; and Schiffman, "Pragmatism."

To illustrate: As *mind*, the "rabbinic mind" refers to a network of *rhemes*, or possible predicates of rabbinic (or rabbinically inspired) value judgments; as *language*, it refers to the conceivable set of value judgments that *could be enacted in a community of* rabbinic (or rabbinically inspired) actors. In Formula 3.2, "R" represents a rheme, such as loving-kindness, when enacted as predicate; "a" represents the resulting value judgment, such as "Caring for the dead is an act of loving-kindness," and "b" represents the worldly context of this judgment: for example, the textual setting of Moses' carrying Joseph's bones, or the contemporary setting of someone's caring for someone's funeral arrangements.

c. The Interpretant as "community of interpreters" names the societal actors and relations with respect to which a sign vehicle refers to its possible objects.

Formula 3.3: $|I_c = \Sigma|I_c$ [Here, the interpretant functions as a "communal interpretant," I_c.]

Continuing the preceding discussion: the communal interpretant I_c would refer to the community of interpreters and actors who adopt a model of the rabbinic mind as a source of behavioral instruction.

d. The Interpretant as "pragmatic condition" names conditions of error/disruption ("a problematic situation"), with respect to which a sign vehicle refers *both* to failed rules of relation in some system *and* to urgent efforts to locate reparative rules according to which the conditions of suffering/disruption could be repaired.

Formula 3.4: $|I_p = \Sigma e$ [Where e=error/problematic situation]

I speculate, for example, that Kadushin read the secular behavior of young Jews in the mid-twentieth century as symptoms of a crisis in contemporary Jewish value systems. If so, he may have identified the behavior as signs, on the one hand, of modern Judaism's failed models and methods of instruction in lived Jewish values and, on the other hand, of contemporary Judaism's responsibility to rediscover sources of repair within the classic rabbinic teachings. In semiotic terms, the failed models represent problematic interpretants of Jewish value judgments; Kadushin offered his account of the rabbinic mind as a reparative or pragmatic interpretant (I_p). To repair an interpretant is to direct a community to reread it as determining some symbol (such as a set of Jewish values) to refer to X (for Kadushin, these were inspiring values such as *Gemilut Hasadim*) rather than Y (for Kadushin, these

HEARTH-TO-HEARTH INTERRELIGIOUS PEACE BUILDING   177

were outmoded or errant versions of rabbinic beliefs that he believed discouraged Jewish youth).

Formula 3.4r (Formula for repair): $(S_1 \to O_e) \to (S_1 \to O_e | I_e) \to (|I_e) \to \Sigma (S_1 \to O_r | I_r)$ $|I_p$, where O_e = problematic behavior as referent/object of problematic judgment $S_1 \to O_e$; I_e =problematic interpretant; O_r =repaired behavior as referent of interpretation; I_r = repaired interpretant. For Kadushin, O_e = errant behavior by Jewish youth; I_e = errant representations of Jewish values; $\Sigma (S_1 \to O_r | I_r)$ $|I_p) $ = his account of the rabbinic mind as pragmatic interpretant ($|I_p$) that introduces conditions of potential repair ($|I_r$).

> Formula 3.4r suggests how the pragmatic interpretant ($|I_p$) introduces conditions for self-reference. The formula: (1) Diagrams errant behavior as the referent of errant value judgments, $S_1 \to O_e$, indicating that these judgments customarily veil or ignore their interpretant: in other words, these judgments lack self-reference. (2) Introduces the pragmatic interpretant as condition for identifying the problematic interpretant ($|I_e$) that conditions the errant value judgments $(S_1 \to O_e | I_e)$. In this way, the pragmatic interpretant is a source of abductions that bring problematic interpretants (habits of value judgment) to probable self-reference. (3) Introduces the pragmatic interpretant, secondly, as condition for repairing the problematic interpretants, to be tested by the judgments and behaviors they generate. Non-errant behaviors (O_r) would serve as probable signs of non-problematic value judgments ($S_1 \to O_r$) and, thereby, of non-problematic interpretants ($|I_r$). (4) Thereby diagrams repaired judgments as conditioned explicitly by their interpretants $(S_1 \to O_r | I_r)$. *Referring both to their objects (repaired behavior) and their interpretants, the repaired processes of judgment include self-reference.* These processes are therefore relational (aRb, where R=$|I_r$), unlike the errant judgments whose interpretants are veiled. As noted earlier, Fraade characterizes rabbinic midrash as bearing this kind of self-reference. He examines the "double dialogue" of the *Sifre*, as it collects a series of different readings of biblical base-texts from Deuteronomy, returning sooner or later to add new comments on the same base-text.[40] The double-dialogue displays self-reference by marking each rabbinic reading *as* a rabbinic reading by a given sage $(S_1 \to O_r | I_r)$, rather than as an independent, constative account of the object of that reading $S_1 \to O_r$, where O_r v ~O_r.
>
> (4) For SRL, there are several dimensions of text-reading that correspond to these dimensions of Interpretant.

---

40. See here 50, 175.

a. Texts may be diagrammed as collections of sign-vehicles, functioning primarily as symbols (that can be atomized as well into icons and indices). These collections may be read as ordered or non-ordered, as aggregated or as atomized into any kinds of element (letter, word verse, pericope, book, and so on) depending on the operative interpretants.

Formula 4.1: $T = \Sigma\, S_{sy} = (S_1, S_2, \ldots S_n)$

Illustration: Thus, the biblical stich, "In the beginning of God's creating heaven and earth...," may be read as a symbol and atomized into icons such as "God's creating heaven and earth" and indices such as "earth" (when read as cosmic object of the term "earth").

b. Texts may be interpreted as collections of linguistic objects, since any symbol may also be read as the object of another sign.

Formula 4.2: $T = \Sigma\, (S_{sy} = - \bullet) = (S_{sy1} = - \bullet 1,\ S_{sy2} = - \bullet 2, \ldots S_{syn} = - \bullet n)$

Illustration: According to the rabbinic midrash, *Genesis Rabbah*, "'In the beginning' (*b'reishit*) names the principle of life" (treating 'Beginning' (*reishit*) as that according to (or "within") within which "all is created"). According to 2.2: 'In the beginning' may be atomized and read as indexical sign of a reified object, in this case a principle.

c. Texts may be interpreted as interpretants and as collections of interpretants, in so far as any symbol may be read as defining the rule of mind and language according to which another sign is interpreted.

Formula 4.3: $T = \Sigma\, (S_{sy} = |I) = (S_{sy} = |\, I_1,\ S_{sy} = |I_2 \ldots S_{sy} = I_n)$

Illustration: According to the medieval commentator Rashi's summary of rabbinic readings, Genesis teaches in its plain sense that light was created first, not heaven and earth, since the opening word, "In the beginning of" is grammatically in a construct form, referring to the beginning of God's creating . . ., when he created light. Here, a grammatical reading of the first word serves as interpretant of Rashi's reading.

d. Texts may be interpreted as collections of propositions or truth claims. Here, a set of words constitutes a symbol only when the immediate object of that set is a proposition.

Formula 4.4: $T = \Sigma\, (S_{sy} \to - \bullet |I_c) = (S_{y1} \to - \bullet,\ S_{sy2} \to - \bullet, \ldots S_n \to - \bullet)$

Illustration: This approach is illustrated by any reading of the first chapter of Genesis as containing a series of self-evident truth claims, such as, "First God created heaven and earth. The earth was unformed." And so on. While I argue that such interpretants are often misguided, the semiotic option remains a feature of SRL.

    e. Texts may be read monovalently when their interpretant assigns each symbol in a text only one possible meaning.

Formula 4.5: $T = S_T \rightarrow O_T | I_c$, where $O = -\bullet$ and where $O_T \vee \sim O_T$.

    For illustration see 2.1 above.

    f. Texts may be read polyvalently when their interpretant assigns each symbol in a text more than one possible meaning.

Formula 4.6: $T \rightarrow \Sigma\, (O_T | I_y,$ where $\sim (O_T \vee \sim O_T))$.

    For illustration see 2.1 above.

(5) *Strictly for the sake of TR and SR,*[41] *Scripture may be defined semiotically as a Text that, for its communal interpretant, Ic, is (or tends to be) read in the following ways:*

    a. In different contexts, Scripture is read either monovalently or polyvalently:

Formula 5.1: $T_{scr} = (S_T \rightarrow O_T | I_c,$ where $O = -\bullet$ and where $O_T \vee \sim O_T) \vee (S_T \rightarrow \Sigma\, (O_T | I_{cy},$ where $\sim (O_T \vee \sim O_T))$.

This is a first distinguishing mark of Scripture vs. other kinds of texts: in its plain sense, a text of Scripture does not preclude monovalent or polyvalent reading; the choice is determined only by the relation of scriptural text to reading community.

    b. *Scripture includes symbols that are read according to the communal interpretants as symbols of a Meta-Interpretant (Meta-I), which is an interpretant with respect to which all other interpretants of a religious tradition may be lent or denied authority and may be revised and repaired. The Meta-I functions as a pragmatic Interpretant, I_p, with respect to which a community's set of different interpretants (I_{c1-n}) operate in different ways within a single community:*

Formula 5.2: $[(|I_p = \Sigma(|(S_m \rightarrow O_{m1}|I_{c1}], [S_m \rightarrow O_{m2}|I_{c2}, \ldots S_m \rightarrow O_{mn}|I_{cn}]$.

This is a second distinguishing mark of Scripture vs. other kinds of texts. The Meta-I includes symbols that are read according to the communal interpretant (I_c) as symbols of the set of all possible pragmatic

---

41. This a functional/operational definition of practical use for constructing and testing the practices of TR, SR, and H2H; it is not an empirical judgment about the character of Scripture!

interpretants (I_p). The latter are defined by their reparative function: any errant or unclear symbol or text can be repaired if and when it is included in a practice of interpretation guided by an appropriate I_p (one that has successfully repaired such a symbol in the past). A religion itself is served semiotically by the Meta-I with respect to which any I_p can be repaired: this religion-general Meta-I is, in this sense, the I_p for all I_p in the community. *The Meta-I functions as an ultimate condition of self-reference within any set of scriptural interpretations within a community of scriptural readers.* According to *Formula 5.2*, each communal interpretant ($|I_{cn}$) conditions self-reference with respect to itself ($S_m \to O_m |I_{cn}$), but the community of readers may deploy any number of different communal interpretants ($|I_{c1} \wedge |I_{c2} \ldots \wedge |I_{cn}$). However, repairs of all such interpretants are conditioned with respect to the Meta-I, so that the Meta-I serves as ultimate condition of self-reference within the community of scriptural interpretation. In the terms of chapter 5, the Meta-I is therefore the subject of "knowing enough" within such a community. The Meta-I is in this sense ultimately vague, but not infinitely unknowable, since it is known by its fruit in any determinate acts of interpretation and of repair.

6. *Strictly for the sake of TR and SR,*[42] *a Scriptural Religion may be defined semiotically by that unlimited collection of possible symbols whose communal interpretants are lent or denied authority, and may be revised and repaired, by a Meta-Interpretant whose existence is the Dynamic Object of the Religion's Scriptures (or symbols contained in them) and whose effects on communal interpretation constitute the Immediate Object of these Scriptures (or symbols contained in them).* A Scriptural Religion is served by a Commentarial (or interpretive) Literature, comprised of a potentially unlimited set of Commentarial Texts, each of which tends to introduce interpretants that render the meaning of scriptural symbols at least one degree less polyvalent than they may otherwise appear to be. Commentary tends toward monovalence in order to answer questions of some existential urgency to the commentarial community. These interpretants (labeled I_T for "text-specific interpretant") usually belong to a set of communal interpretants whose Meta-I may be associated with some social and hermeneutical moment in the reception history of the Scriptural Religion.

   a. The Meta-I ($|I_p$, defined here as a pragmatic interpretant) is distributed over a set of different communal interpretants (I_c), which

---

42. This a functional/operational definition.

appear in the following formula as the interpretants with respect to which text-specific symbols acquire meaning:

Formula 6.1: $R_{scr} = \Sigma\,(\Sigma S_{scr1} \rightarrow - \bullet|It_1), (\Sigma S_{scr1} \rightarrow - \bullet|It_2), \ldots (\Sigma S_{scf1} \rightarrow - \bullet|I_{tn})$, where $T_x = \Sigma\,(S_{scrx} \rightarrow - \bullet|I_{tx})\,|Ip$. Here, R refers to a religion; R_{scr} to a scripturally based religion (whose Meta-I is disclosed by way of Scripture).

> By way of illustration, Kadushin characterized classical rabbinic Judaism as a scripturally based religion, whose communal interpretants informed different (and potentially contradictory) conditions for interpreting Scripture. On occasions of behavioral and thus hermeneutical crisis, rabbinic communities could appeal to the "rabbinic mind"—conceived, functionally, as a network of rabbinic values—as the scripturally disclosed Meta-I (my term) that introduces probable conditions for identifying and repairing any communal interpretant and, thereby, for communal self-reference.
>
> b. *The reading of Commentarial Texts of a Scriptural Religion may be said, in some sense, to reverse the relation of Meta-I and I_T* in a community's reading of Scripture. Commentarial texts (collections of commentarial symbols, S_{comm}) introduce text-specific interpretants, I_T, according to which Scriptural symbols (S_{scr}) are read in ways that refine or (if one might say) "repair" certain features of those symbols as read according to the communal interpretants (and, by implication, the Meta-I) of Scripture in its plain sense or its *sensus communis*. These features may include apparent polyvalence, vagueness, or contradiction.

Formula 6.2: Given that, within R_{scr}, $(S_{sy1} \rightarrow - \bullet|I_{t1})$ then, within the commentarial community, $(S_{comm} \rightarrow [(S_{scr1} \rightarrow - \bullet|I_c) \rightarrow O_{comm1}]\,|I_t$.

> In Kadushin's vocabulary, acts of midrashic interpretation "concretize" the otherwise under-defined (vague) network of rabbinic values. In my terms, this is to apply a *rheme* (a possible predicate) as actual predicate of a determinate value judgment stimulated by some worldly event.[43]
>
> 7. *Textual Reasoning as a Reparative Response to Conflicts of Interpretation within a Scriptural Religion*

---

43. As illustrated above (176), the worldly event might be someone's caring for someone's funeral arrangements or offering a sermon on the textual setting of Moses' carrying Joseph's bones. The rheme might be "—loving-kindness," and the value judgment might be, "Caring for the dead is an act of loving-kindness."

In the terms of this semiotic, we may define the basic elements of TR, which serves a purportedly single "tradition" of interpretation across the differences that mark a set of sub-communities, denominations, or schools of interpretation within that tradition:

    a. *TR serves a single tradition of interpretation*, informed by a communal interpretant, Ic.

Formula 7.1: $[S \to O | I_c,$ where $| I_c = \Sigma_c]$.

    b. *The work of a TR group is usually stimulated by non-constructive disagreement or potential conflict within a single tradition or community of interpretation.*

Formula 7.2: $[(S_1 \to O_1 | I_c?)$ and $(S_1 \to O_2 | I_c?)$, where O_n V $\sim O_n$, and "?" indicates that it is not yet known if the competing claims share an interpretant.]

    c. *The most frequent cause of potential conflict is competing binarism*: where two or more subgroups of a tradition offer competing, monovalent (either/or) readings of certain symbols, and where these readings raise issues of existential urgency:[44]

Formula 7.3: $(S_{mv} \to O_1 | I_{c1})$ vs $(S_{mv} \to O_2 | I_{c2}$, where *mv* v ~*mv*).

    d. *Repairing Conflicts Between Monovalent Interpretants in TR*

In the terms of SRL, conflicting binarisms are guided by competing, monovalent interpretants. The primary work of TR is to engage participants in shared, intra-religious study, so that, *in effect*, they allow TR's Meta-I to host their study. This Meta-I permits all competing interpretants among the group to operate freely around the table:[45]

Formula 7.4: $|I_p = \Sigma \, (\, [MV1 = S_{mv} \to O_{mv1} | I_{c1}], [M2 = S_{mv} \to O_{mv2} | I_{c2}] \ldots,$ $[MV = S_{mv} \to O_{mvn} | I_{cn}])$.

As a result, competing sub-groups continue to disagree but without interrupting the study. The effect is to reinforce the Meta-I while leaving the sub-group interpretants unchanged in character or strength. *As long as the Meta-I remains in place, the mediate goal of TR is merely quantitative: the longer these sub-groups continue to meet, the more* they will grow accustomed to maintaining relations of shared study at the same time that they maintain their differences. SR scholars observe that, over the long term, shared scriptural study tends to nurture

---

44. See note 32 for an example of binarism that applies to conflict over monovalent readings of symbols (the case in 7.2) as well as conflict over monovalent readings of Hearth-values (*H-Formula 2.5*).

45. See note 52, for a model of text-specific binarism *Formula 8.4T*.

polyvalence. We therefore expect long term TR study to dislodge participants from strictly monovalent and therefore binarist habits of reading.[46]

There are two other categories of TR study: competing polyvalent readings and competing monovalent readings of entire texts or text-canons. I will offer only two comments: (a) the former case is unproblematic, since competing polyvalent readings are contrary (different) but not contradictory (in direct conflict); (b) the latter cases are quite problematic, since participants may tend to delegitimize any of their opponents' readings.

8. *Scriptural Reasoning as a Reparative Response to Conflicts of Interpretation among Scriptural Religions.* The basic elements of SR differ somewhat from those of TR. In SR, unlike TR, subgroups strictly share

---

46. *Tendencies to scriptural polysemy*: There are four reasons why the study of a scripturally based tradition may tend to nurture polyvalent readings. (1) Scripture refers the reader to a source of human and worldly truth, value, and existence that lies beyond the ken of any individual believer or thinker or any group of such individuals. Variously named (God, Lord, Allah, Christ, the One, the Holy, the Creator, Heaven . . .), the reality of this source relativizes all claims to knowledge and, thereby, tends to unsettle any presumption that a singular (monovalent) reading is free of possible error. (2) Scripture introduces standards of worldly measure that originate in and are authorized by this source. Irreducible to finite standards of measure, these divine standards introduce the infinite into everyday life as measure of the good and the true. The infinite stands not only as a negative standard, relativizing all finite judgments and achievements, but also as positive standard, attracting devotees to internalize the infinite as goal and source of their ultimate pursuits. Except for confused followers who are tempted to self-deification, this positive standard tends to erode followers' trust in efforts to identify the true or the good with finite claims—for example, with clear and distinct statements of belief of expressions of "true" feelings or intuitions. As a result, some followers adopt a radical apophaticism, disclaiming any positive assertions about ultimate matters. Others adopt a more measured alternative: with Aquinas, they may make positive use of perfection terms and of analogical reasonings; with Laozi they may make assertions about the wisdom of balance and mean; with the rabbinic sages, they may argue that divine discourses are polyvalent but guide determinate judgments about how best to act in specific occasions of action, where one judgment is appropriate only to one occasion. (3) Scripture introduces its infinite measures as standards of criticism, accompanied, for example, by narratives about human failings. A reader's desire to live up these standards may increase the temptation to read scriptural texts monovalently, assuring oneself of having comprehended Scripture's source. At the same time, reading narratives about human failings makes it difficult for readers not to question their own temptations. (4) Tradition reads Scripture as reading itself. Traditions typically read Scriptures as complex compositions that include heterogeneous genres of discourse, voice, meter, and redaction. The heterogeneity extends to the way individual words and verses are reread in other texts within any unit of Scripture. As a result, every symbol may appear to be read polyvalently within a larger textual unit of Scripture and across a canon. The more a TR group reads together, the greater the inclination to polyvalent reading and the more ingenuity is required to defend monovalent readings.

neither symbols, nor scriptural canon, nor a communal interpretant. Why, then, should they conflict? *Assume, first that there are groups belonging to several different religions (see Formula 8.1) and that there are various genres of disagreement or potential conflict among these groups (see Formula 8.2–5):*

Formula 8.1: Among SR participants are those who claim allegiance to different scriptural religions.

$[R_{scr1} = \Sigma\ (\Sigma\ S_{scr1} \rightarrow \bullet |I_{t1})] \wedge [R_{scr2} = \Sigma\ (\Sigma\ S_{scr2} \rightarrow — \bullet |I_{t2})] \wedge [R_{scrn} = \Sigma\ (\Sigma\ S_{scrn} \rightarrow — \bullet |I_{tn}]$, where $T_x = \Sigma\ (S_{scrx} \rightarrow — \bullet |I_{Tx})\ |I_p$.

Formula 8.2: Conflicts Among Symbol-specific Monovalent Interpretants in SR. $[S_{mv1} \rightarrow O_{mv1} | I_{c1}$, where $mv\ v\ {\sim}mv] \wedge [S_{mv2} \rightarrow O_{mv2} | I_{c2}$, where $mv\ v\ {\sim}mv] \wedge \ldots [S_{mvn} \rightarrow O_{mvn} | I_{cn}$, where $mv\ v\ {\sim}mv\ ]$.

The formula maps an illustrative conflict among three monovalent readings of a given symbol, each reading guided by a different communal interpretant, according to which the symbol and its meaning are defined in a distinct way. Conflicts of this kind may be readily addressed in SR, as they are comparably addressed in TR. Since the conflict is only over certain monovalent symbols, an SR group could readily examine texts and symbols that participants tend to read polyvalently. By accepting the modest, overall rules of SR (permitting one another to freely voice any individual interpretation), participants would have effectively permitted the SR Meta-Interpretant to serve as host to their religion-specific, communal interpretants. As a result, participants will have relativized their communal interpretants, albeit in a safe and limited way.

Formula 8.3: Repairing Conflicts Among Symbol-specific Monovalent Interpretants in SR. $|I_p = \Sigma\ ([MV_1 = S \rightarrow O\ |I], [MV_2 = S \rightarrow O|I], \ldots\ [MV_n = S_{mv} \rightarrow O_{mvn} |I_{cn}]$.

In this formula, "$|I_p$" represents the SR Meta-I, serving as a "pragmatic" or reparative rule. "$I_c \ldots I_n$" represents the various communal interpretants; contributing now to an interreligious practice, definitions will, in a gentle and barely perceivable way, now include each reading offered by participants. Once the SR group grows accustomed to this practice, participants will tend to tolerate open discussions of their monovalent symbols. To relax inner-religious conflict, participants do not need to abandon their conflicting readings of these symbols. They need only tolerate the different readings, by allowing the differences to be voiced without reacting aggressively; this is sufficient to begin to transform contradictory readings into merely contrary or different ones.

Formula 8.4: Repairing Conflicts Among Text-specific Monovalent Interpretants in SR. $[S_{mv1} \to O_{mv1}|I_{c1}$, where mv V~mv] ∧ $[S_{mv2} \to O_{mv2}|I_{c2}$, where mv V~mv] ∧ ... $[S_{mvn} \to O_{mvn}|I_{cn}$, where mv V~mv].

The formula maps an illustrative conflict among 3+ monovalent rules for reading a given text, each rule guided by a different communal interpretant. As in TR, conflicts of this kind are more challenging than conflicts over monovalent symbols, but they may nonetheless be repaired through SR study. The procedure begins with texts that are not defined monovalently, even if this means beginning with extrascriptural texts. This way, the SR group may grow accustomed to working with a shared Meta-Interpretant, even if this work has not yet had any direct effect on each participant's monovalent interpretants [because an interpretant may be defined as a summation of all readings it permits: $I_{cn} = \Sigma\ S_{sy1} \to \bullet|I_{cn}$]. Once the SR group becomes accustomed to the practice, facilitators may invite members to share readings of their monovalent texts, beginning with what appear to be the least controversial pericopes in those texts. Depending on the intensity of the participants' binarist tendencies and the contrasting intensity of emerging friendships within the SR group, participants tend, gradually, to introduce other verses into their interpretations; these may include symbols that they read monovalently. This kind of SR study achieves its goal once participants tolerate open study of all (or most) verses in their monovalent texts. Once again, the goal is not agreement or even a clear move to polyvalent reading; it is simply for participants to voice differences without stimulating aggressive reactions. SR groups may choose to continue their work after meeting this goal. We have observed that, over time, such groups often explore polyvalent readings as well: a sign of significant refinements in the participants' communal interpretants. Such groups may potentially serve as peacebuilders.

Formula 8.5: Conflicts Among Religion-specific Monovalent Interpretants in SR. R_{scr1} ∧ R_{scr2} ∧ ... $R_{scrn,}$ where $T_x = \Sigma\ (S_{scrx} \to - \bullet|I_{Tx})\ |I_p?$, and $(S_1 \to - \bullet, S_2 \to - \bullet ... S_n \to - \bullet)$, and $m = S_x \to - \bullet|$ and m v ~m

The formula maps each religion as a collection of texts and each text as a collection of symbols whose meanings are each monovalent according to the religion's communal interpretant. Formula 8.5 diagrams binarist conflict that has the potential for significant tension or violence.

In most cases, it is best *not* to attempt SR study in such a setting, unless there are significant signs that the groups, or some select members of them, hold weakly to their binarism or seek some alternative. In the latter case, the procedure is similar to that followed in cases of text-specific monovalence, except that SR study should be undertaken with more caution. *A setting of strong binarism raises issues of existential urgency* and may call for H2H Peacebuilding in place of Formational SR.

The Process of H2H Peacebuilding

Addressing settings of tense but nonviolent inter-group engagement, our UVA research team finds it helpful to frame H2H peacebuilding as a four-part process of general modeling, field data collection, field diagnostics, and field recommendations for reparative action. In a current paper introducing this process to peacekeepers,[47] we explain that a testable model of H2H is completed only in the real-time setting of efforts to repair ongoing violent conflict among value-centered groups. Our team's work therefore begins with incomplete models, which we construct by asking how the rules of SRL could be applied to simulated field conditions. We ask readers to envision a region of ongoing, location-specific conflict among several modest-sized religious groups,[48] "stakeholders" to the conflict and to envision several groups of peacekeepers entering the environment. Readers may imagine that the peacekeeping groups are overseen by a Coordinating Team (CT), which includes peacekeeping directors and a team of H2H consultants. We then envision the following four-stage process:

1. *General Modeling*

    As developed in the laboratory, the H2H model is an application of SRL to the likely field setting of religion-related violent conflict. I prefer a form of semiotic analysis, but other formal languages are also suitable. Our research team's current modeling includes applications to natural language processing and to field peacekeeping/peacebuilding strategies, both of which render the model more technical than is appropriate for this book. I will, however, offer a significant sample of the model's primary features. These are semiotic diagrams of: (a) How members of a stakeholder group address the group's *Hearth*, or "center

---

47. Ochs et al., "Value Predicate Analysis."

48. The groups self-identify as religious, each group affirming the sacrality (or "Hearth-like" character) of different sets of privileged values.

of values,"⁴⁹ as Interpretant of their value judgments and the behaviors that follow from them; (b) The Pragmatic Interpretants that mediate tensions or conflict among competing intragroup interpretants (or behavioral tendencies); (c) Several types of inter-group conflict among stakeholder-group Hearths and the judgments that accompany them; and (d) Possible strategies for repairing inter-group conflict, with reference to the possible role of a Meta-Interpretant in such repair. To prepare readers, I will illustrate these diagrams only after introducing the remaining stages of H2H.

2. *Field Data Collection (Semantic Range Analysis)*

The primary data for H2H is language-use by members of each stakeholder group, as examined by members of these or neighboring groups (serving as indigenous researchers). Researchers examine value judgments, displayed in both written and spoken discourse, that predicate what appear to be Hearth-related values of entities, events, or actions in the world. Researchers focus on how group members interpret value judgments offered by agents of socialization in the group: teachers or other respected sources and exemplars of group values. The most useful data identifies value terms or phrases that serve as predicates of the judgments: for example, a set of Urdu-speaking madrasah students may discuss (or debate) teachings that offer value judgments whose predicates include the terms *piyār* ("love," "affection," or "attraction"), *ḥaqīqat* ("truth," "reality," or "being"), *khūbṣūrat* ("beautiful," "lovely," or "admirable"). In this example, researchers ask students to identify what these predicates mean when applied to each of a series of entities or actions in the world.

If group members identify a large set of such value predicates as Hearth-related, then judgments predicated of this set of values may contribute significantly to H2H peacebuilding.⁵⁰ Our field research suggests, for example, that such judgments tend to appear much more often during times of apparent social tension and social change. During such times, group members tend to employ a fewer number of such value terms, and group members tend to define such terms differently than during more ordinary times. In some cases, a group that interprets a term polyvalently during ordinary times may interpret it monovalently in times of tension or change. Another group

---

49. Characterized functionally.

50. I take time to illustrate only some of the reasons why Hearth-related judgments are significant indicators of near-future stakeholder behavior in the context of relation-related violent conflict.

may exhibit a different change: from typical monovalent definition to polyvalence in times of tension or change. Our research has identified nine different types of change in polyvalence in times of social tension, and each type tends to correspond to a distinctive change in a group's behavioral tendencies toward other groups. Our most significant discovery is that the meanings (semantic content) of value predicates are *not* reliable indicators of future group behavior; the only reliable indicators are *changes in the number of meanings a group assigns to most Hearth-values at times of social tension and change.* We call this "change in semantic range," and we label our method of data collection *Semantic Range Analysis*. The results of this analysis may prove significant in helping peacebuilders anticipate changes in inter-group dynamics and facilitate inter-group discourse more effectively.

3. *Field Diagnostics (Linguistic Flexibility Analysis)*

The practical significance of Semantic Range Analysis is disclosed only in *Linguistic Flexibility Analysis*, which identifies field testable observations that correspond to each type of change in the increase/decrease of value-term polyvalence. In this stage of H2H, analysts hypothesize that each type of change corresponds to a class of flexibility/inflexibility in the way group members define value predicates. Flexibility is measured only in the field setting of peacekeeping activities. In real-time, field analysts receive Semantic Range measurements of each of the stakeholder groups' Hearth-related value judgments in a context of conflict. Field analysts recalibrate these measurements in light of immediate field conditions: for example, the real-time proximity of a given group to other groups (where each group displays a given semantic range measurement), along with observations of changing field conditions and of the status and location of peacekeeping groups.

Flexibility is a functional, analytic term that enables us to correlate Semantic Range measurements with potential classes of observable group behaviors and of corresponding peacekeeping recommendations. We define "degree of flexibility" as the tendency of a language group to encourage or discourage polyvalent interpretation. We identify three categories of flexibility: *inflexibility, moderate flexibility,* and *excessive flexibility.* Our field hypothesis is that groups that display a given flexibility will display a corresponding set of three, observable, sociolinguistic traits: Linguistic sensitivity, Interpretive license, and Linguistic response to other groups.

Linguistic sensitivity measures the responsiveness of language-use to changes in the environment. *Moderate linguistic flexibility* corresponds to *moderate linguistic sensitivity*: exhibited whenever speakers adjust their choice of evaluative terms to address changing environmental conditions and whenever readers/listeners adjust their understanding of such terms to fit such conditions. *Linguistic inflexibility* corresponds to *linguistic insensitivity:* the tendency of a group to preserve conventional meanings and syntax despite significant changes in the surrounding social and natural environment. Such language use tends to discourage individual difference and creativity in linguistic choices, encouraging the repetition of conventional speech patterns and semantic usages. *Excessive linguistic insensitivity* is a form of disrupted/dysfunctional language use, where linguistic indifference to environmental changes leads, over time, to an increasing disjunction between semantic expectations and environmental realities. Such insensitivity typically corresponds, as well, to societal efforts to significantly reduce the range of acceptable empirical judgments and value judgments: for example, prohibiting judgments that expand the semantic range of conventional predicates despite individual claims that a given set of conventional meanings no longer corresponds to empirical observation.

Interpretive license measures the degree to which language conventions lend listeners/readers license to interpret the meanings of words and phrases in more than one way. *Moderate linguistic flexibility* corresponds to a *moderate degree of interpretive license*, which typifies Hearth-language use in groups whose semantic choices adjust successfully to changing environmental conditions. *Excessive linguistic inflexibility corresponds to excessive restrictions on reader/listener participation*. In this case, meanings are treated as if self-evident or literal. As in the case of excessive insensitivity, excessive restriction tends to accompany an environment of top-down intervention by political/cultural leaders, who enforce significant political restrictions on individual interpretive license. Such restrictions are associated with rigid societal conventions. These conventions may change radically, but only through the force of what appears to be autocratic decision making, rather than through adjustments to environmental change. *Excessive linguistic flexibility corresponds to excessive interpretive license*, which implies the anarchy of individual choice. We read the excess of license as a symptom of imminent societal breakdown. The strongest policy implication is that groups displaying such linguistic signals may soon fall victim either to inner chaos or to the predatory interests of other groups.

Linguistic responses to other groups: a measure of how a group's language use adjusts to a group's proximity to other groups of various kinds. *Moderate linguistic flexibility* corresponds to a *group's moderate openness to intergroup communication, within the limits of what is deemed necessary to preserving group identity and purpose.* Groups of this kind display neither excessive caution nor excessive desire toward other groups. *Excessive linguistic inflexibility* corresponds to either excessive resistance to intergroup engagement or excessive interest in such engagement. In the former case, inflexibility may appear as *excessive indifference*, which we define as a group's tendencies to avoid contact altogether, tendencies to group self-isolation and non-aggression (except as needed to maintain isolation). Such a group is indifferent to new languages, to the speech of others, and to the meaning of other group speech. In the latter case, inflexibility may appear, to the contrary, as a predatory interest in engagement as a means of absorbing or replacing the lands, goods, and/or populations of other groups. The latter case is *excessive interest in engaging other groups*, including excessive desire for dialogue and/or partnership. Such interest can be symptomatic of a language group's loss of group identity, purpose, or membership. This may be a leading indicator of a group's likelihood of being absorbed into another group (or groups) or of forming a hybrid group with factions from other groups. A group displaying such symptoms may also attract the interests of predatory groups or movements.

4. *Field Recommendations* (*Action Recommendations*)

The goal of this stage of H2H is to offer policy recommendations based on flexibility measurements. In real time, *Action Recommendations* re-evaluate flexibility measurements for the sake of generating a range of recommended peacekeeping actions. The vocabularies and conditions for articulating such recommendations are specific to each peacekeeping institution and, to some degree, each conflict situation. I therefore offer the following policy suggestions strictly for the sake of illustration.

A1: addressing groups that display significant linguistic inflexibility (corresponding to Flexibility of 1–2). Engage such groups with extreme caution. Apply additional modes of CVE analysis in case groups display violent tendencies. (Note that these groups may not necessarily display such violence). Language-based communication with such groups may not be successful. Flexibility of 1 may signal a group's tendency to employ intergroup communication only for the sake of tactical gains.

A2: addressing groups that display moderate flexibility (corresponding to Flexibility of 3–6). Verbal communication with such groups is highly recommended. Expect groups to engage by way of complex bureaucracies.

A3: addressing groups that display either marginal inflexibility or marginally excessive flexibility (corresponding to flexibility of 3 or 5). Certain groups in this range may serve, unexpectedly, as significant conversation partners in peacekeeping. Seek engagement with such groups.

A4: addressing groups that display excessive linguistic flexibility (corresponding to flexibility 7–8+). Such groups display symptoms of potential societal breakdown. Address such groups cautiously, anticipating group fragility.

The Logic of H2H

To conclude Chapter 6, I diagram the overall process of H2H according to the semiotic vocabulary of SRL. My goal is to enable more technically inclined readers to trace elemental patterns of Scriptural Reasoning within my research team's vision of how to conduct H2H peacebuilding in the field. Here, the formulae of SRL are revised to address conditions of conflict among moderate-sized, Hearth-centered groups.

H2H 1: "Hearth" refers to a social group's "center of values," of which religious values are one example among others. "Values" are functionally defined as indigenous names for otherwise inevident ("deep") patterns of socially approved behavior. Agents of socialization in the group (exemplars of approved behaviors) offer exemplary value judgments, whose predicates are preferred names for specific patterns of behavior and whose subjects (indices) identify worldly actions that embody these behaviors. Worldly actions may embody several values. As apprentices, group members seek to imitate these value judgments, learning thereby how and when to practice approved behaviors.

In H2H peacebuilding, *Hearth* replaces *Scripture* as sign, symbol, and interpretant of each stakeholder group's *center of values* and of the work of inter-group peacebuilding. In Formational Scriptural Reasoning (FSR), Scripture is the single focus of shared attention around the SR table; commentary on scriptural verses is the means through which individual participants give voice to their beliefs and value judgments; and the juxtaposition of many such voices is the means through which FSR gives voice to SR reasoning *per se*. At best, this reasoning emerges gradually over many sessions of FSR, as the juxtaposition of voices becomes a directional (yet under-determined) movement of reading and reflection around the table.

The reasoning of SR becomes the context with respect to which potentially conflictual differences around the table become complementary differences and primarily monovalent habits of reading become polyvalent (in a sense that tolerates or welcomes 1-, 2-, 3+ valued readings as appropriate to different verses and contexts of commentary). H2H transforms the terms of FSR by identifying Hearth as the condition of both inter-group difference and the possibility of inter-group engagement. *Conducting Semantic Range and Linguistic Flexibility Analyses, field analysts may identify potential Hearth-groups as those whose Semantic Range averages between 2–6 and whose Linguistic Flexibility is moderate.*[51]

H-Formula 1.1: S_H

Hearths as Sign-Vehicles: Just as a scriptural text is sign-vehicle of any scriptural study as well as of FSR, certain material objects serve as sign-vehicles of a group's Hearth-values. Examples include dugout sailing canoes on Micronesian atoll societies, cattle among traditional east African societies, including the Masai, and legal texts among traditional Muslim and Jewish teachers.

H-Formula 1.2: $S_H \to O_v|$

Group members interpret ("read") these vehicles as signs of values, value-judgments, value-symbols, value-discourse and value-interpretants. Different readings (objects) are determined by different interpretants:

H-Formula 1.3: $S_H \to O_v|I_H$ For example: 1.3.1 $S_H \to -|I_v$ (as sign of value-rheme).

In Micronesia, the canoe might signify "home." Large sailing canoes are families' primary sources of food (deep sea fishing); they are stored inside a family's sleeping hut, where family members sleep beside them. The canoe is thus a sign-vehicle of Hearth-values.

1.3.2 $S_H \to (S_v - \bullet|E_v)\,|I_{ve.}$ (as sign of a value-judgment that applies a *rheme* as actual predicate of a determinate value judgment stimulated by some worldly event).[52]

When seeing a coconut husk float by on the deep sea, the "captain/navigator" of a traditional[53] Micronesian sailing canoe might sing to the spirit Hakur to "lighten our journey and bring us home." I read this

51. See 187–90.

52. See 169, Formula 1.1.a.

53. By traditional, I mean through the 1950's, before Christian and Western values diminished islanders' dedication to local navigational lore and ritual.

singing as bearing such immanent judgments as "We long for home" and "The coconut reminds us of home (of the Spirit who brings us homeward)."

1.3.3 $S_H \to (S_v \to — \bullet |I_{sy}) |I_{vr.}$ (as sign of value-symbol or rule of behavioral relations).

The canoe signifies any of the behavioral patterns that enable captains and their crew to sail great distances and bring sustenance home.

1.3.4 $S_H \to (|I_L = \Sigma aRb |I_c) |I_{vd.}$ (as the group's value-discourse, the sum of all approved value judgments that could possibly be enacted by group members. In the formula, "I_{vd}" refers to an act-specific rule for determinate judgment; "R" refers to a value rheme, "a" to a value judgment that embodies the rheme as predicate, and "b" to the worldly context of this judgment, such as a violent conflict).

Micronesian Hearth-value sign-vehicles, like "canoe," "captain," "Hakur," "outrigger," "navigational lore/instruction," also serve as metonyms for a group's overall value-discourse.

1.3.5 $S_H \to (|I_c = \Sigma |I_c) |I_{vc}$ (as a "community of interpreters" within the group, including the group as a whole: the social actors and relations with respect to which a set of values refers to a set of behaviors).

Our illustrations turn to the field settings of H2H, where stakeholder groups include sub-groups that may offer conflicting calls for action toward outside groups.

H-Formula 1.4a: $(S_H \to (S_v \to — \bullet |I_{sy}) |I_{vr.}) = S_v \to O_v |I_c.$

H-Formula 1.4b: $(S_H \to (|I_L = \Sigma aRb |I_c) |I_{vd.}) = S_v \to O_v |I_{cv}.$

Hearth-related group behavior (including behavior toward other groups) is informed by communal interpretants. H-Formula 1.4a diagrams the value-rule that informs any individual value judgment; 1.4b diagrams a group's overall Hearth-value discourse.

H-Formula 1.5: $(S_v \to O_v |I_c,$ where $O = — \bullet$ and where $(O_v \text{ V} \sim O_v) \text{ v } (S_v \to \Sigma (O_v |I_{cv},$ where $\sim (O_v \text{ V} \sim O_v)).$

In different contexts, Hearth-value symbols are read/applied either monovalently or polyvalently; the choice is determined only by the real-time relation of Hearth-signs to group teachers and members. H2H peacebuilding depends on the capacity of value-centered groups to choose polyvalent Hearth-values, since the primary instrument of H2H is to engage groups habituated to monovalent conversation and facilitate their coming to practice some degree of non-monovalent intra- and inter-group conversation (including debate and negotiation), as informed by each group's Hearth-value discourse. *The defining hypothesis of H2H is that the presence of such discourse enables peacebuilding,* because it increases the probabilities that stakeholders will: (a) commit to the process (since the process enlists each stakeholder's Hearth-values), and (b) gradually consent to the degree of non-monovalent reading that enables negotiations to succeed. These are negotiations that achieve agreement across steep religious (Hearth) as well as material differences, because some degree of polyvalent reading enables stakeholders to expand the capacity of their Hearth values enough to endorse needed material compromises. In this way, agreements may honor rather than compromise stakeholders' deepest values.

H-Formula 1.6e: $I_p = \Sigma e$ (where e=error/problematic situation)

H-Formula 1.6r: $(S_{v1} \rightarrow O_e) \rightarrow (S_{v1} \rightarrow O_e | I_e) \rightarrow (|I_e) \rightarrow \Sigma (S_{v1} \rightarrow O_r | I_r) |I_p$ (where O_e = problematic behavior as referent/object of problematic judgment $S_{v1} \rightarrow O_e$; I_e =problematic interpretant; O_r =repaired behavior as referent of interpretation; I_r = repaired interpretant)

Functioning as pragmatic interpretant, Hearth-value symbols guide the repair of behaviors and thus value-interpretants that the group considers errant. Formulae 1.6 suggest how the pragmatic interpretant ($|I_p$) introduces conditions for self-reference and then repair. The formulae (a) Diagram errant behavior as the objects of errant value judgments, $S_{v1} \rightarrow O_e$, indicating that these judgments may veil their interpretant; (2) Introduce the pragmatic interpretant as condition for identifying the problematic interpretants ($|I_e$) that condition these errors ($S_{v1} \rightarrow O_e | I_e$);[54] (3) Reintroduce the pragmatic interpretant as condition for repairing problematic interpretants, as tested by the judgments/behaviors they generate. Non-errant behaviors (O_r) serve as probable signs of non-problematic value judgments ($S_{v1} \rightarrow O_r$) and interpretants ($|I_r$). Overall, the process is relational (aRb, where $R=|I_r$), unlike errant judgments whose interpretants may be veiled.

H-Formula 1.7: $|I_p = \Sigma [| (S_{v1} \rightarrow O_{v1} | I_{c1}), (S_{v2} \rightarrow O_{v2} | I_{c2}), \ldots (S_{vn} \rightarrow O_{vn} | I_{cn})]$.

This is a second distinguishing mark of Hearth-value symbols: the group's pragmatic interpretants may include symbols of a Meta-Interpretant (Meta-I), diagramed in Formula 1.7 as the interpretant with respect to

---

54. More precisely, the pragmatic interpretant is a source of abductions that bring problematic value-interpretants to probable self-reference

which all other pragmatic interpretants may be revised and repaired. According to the Formula, each communal interpretant ($|I_{cn}$) conditions self-reference ($S_m \to O_m | I_{cn}$), but the community of readers may deploy any number of different communal interpretants ($|I_{c1} \wedge |I_{c2} \ldots \wedge |I_{cn}$), repairs of which are conditioned with respect to the Meta-I. The Meta-I is ultimately vague but not infinitely unknowable, since it is known by its fruit in any determinate acts of repair.

H2H and H1H: Peacebuilding Work Within Individual Value-Centered Groups in a Violent Conflict. An inter-group conflict is a candidate for H2H peacebuilding if its stakeholders are moderate-sized social groups whose members tend to share a value-vocabulary (1.3.3) and a value-discourse (1.3.4) and tend to participate in communities of interpretation within the group (1.3.5). *The following proposals constitute Action Recommendations for on-the-field peacebuilding.*[55] Extrapolating from our work in settings of tension but not violent conflict, our research team models H2H peacebuilding as a two-stage process. In the first stage, peacebuilding teams include and work separately with representatives of individual stakeholder groups. In the second stage, the teams include and work together with representatives of as many stakeholders as possible. In this section, I address the first stage, which I label H1H, since it addresses each Heart-centered group separately.

A Hearth-Value Centered Group. Strictly for the sake of H2H,[56] a value-centered group is defined semiotically by that unlimited collection of possible symbols whose communal interpretants are lent or denied authority, and may be revised and repaired, by a Meta-Interpretant whose existence is the referent (in Peirce's terms, the Dynamic Object) of the Group's Hearth-symbols and whose effects on communal interpretation constitute the sense (in Peirce's terms, the Immediate Object) of these Hearth-symbols. A Hearth-value group embodies its values through the narratives, actions, and memories that deliver its elemental value-judgments. Because they are offered in response to questions of existential urgency, a group's Hearth-related value judgments tend to reduce the polyvalence of Hearth symbols in order to encourage actions that best address the needs of the day. This reduction is most pronounced in times of violent conflict, where stakeholder value judgments tend to display maximal monovalence. H2H draws on the capacity of the same Hearth-values to attract polyvalent readings in less threatening settings. The work of H2H peacebuilders is to attract

55. See 188–92.

56. This a functional/operational definition of practical use for constructing and testing how TR-SR-H2H work; it is not an empirical judgment about the character of religion!

stakeholder representatives to enter such settings within regions of conflict and to engage, there, in non-monovalent debate and negotiation.

Semantic Range Analysis provides quantitative measurements of each stakeholder group's tendencies toward monovalence in the face of threatening conditions. Field diagnosticians employ *Linguistic Flexibility Analysis* to monitor real-time changes in each group's Semantic Range measurements and to anticipate and test how these changes are reflected in each group's *linguistic sensitivity, interpretive license, and modes of response to other groups.*

H1H Peacebuilding: To illustrate best practices for conducting H1H, our research team applies the logic of TR, rather than SRL, to simulated field conditions of violent conflict.

H-Formula 2.1: H1H = Σ [($\Sigma S_{H1} \rightarrow$ —•|Iv$_1$|), ($\Sigma S_{H2} \rightarrow$ —•|Iv$_2$|), ... ($\Sigma S_{Hn} \rightarrow$ —•|I$_{vn}$|)] |I$_p$|. Here, H1H refers to a Hearth-value-centered group, whose pragmatic interpretant is disclosed by way of H-Symbols.

H-Formula 2.2: If, for H1H, ($S_{H1} \rightarrow$ —•|I$_{v1}$|) then, for a value-judgment, ($S_{H1} \rightarrow (S_{v1} \rightarrow$ —•|I$_{v1}$|) I$_{vd}$) = $S_{v1} \rightarrow O_{v1}$|I$_c$|. In the formula, "I$_{vd}$" refers to an act-specific rule for determinate judgment (for which, as noted in 1.3.4, ($S_{v1} \rightarrow O_{v1}$|I$_c$|) =aRb |I$_c$|).

> For example, if a stakeholder group typically assigns three possible meanings to the *rheme* "is trustworthy" (*tells the truth, is your friend, is one of us*), only one meaning may appear in value judgments offered in the context of violent conflict. Applying Formula 2.2 to 1.5 therefore offers a rule for determining Semantic Range:

H-Formula 2.3a: General formula to distinguish monovalent and polyvalent Semantic Range.

[($S_{H1} \rightarrow (S_{v1} \rightarrow$ — •|I$_{v1}$|) I$_{vd}$) =$S_{v1} \rightarrow O_{v1}$|I$_c$|, where O_v v ~ O_v)] v [($S_{H1} \rightarrow (S_{v1} \rightarrow$ — •|I$_{v1}$|) I$_{vd}$) = $S_{v1} \rightarrow O_{v1}$|I$_c$|, where ~ ($O_v$ v~ O_v)].

H-Formula 2.3b: Formula for measuring a sequence of 1–9 classes of Semantic Range.

SR= {a$_n$}$^9_{n=1}$ [($S_{va} \rightarrow$ — •|I$_{v1}$|), ($S_{va+1} \rightarrow$ — •|I$_{v2}$|), ... ($S_{vn} \rightarrow$ — •|I$_{vn}$|)]

> H1H teams meet, for finite periods of time, with representatives of each group's agents of socialization, nurturing conversations about the group's value-vocabulary and value-discourse. One goal is to accustom some group members to speak openly about group values and thereby engage in the peacebuilding process as a value-centered activity. A second goal is to measure the Semantic Range of what appear to be Hearth-Value-Symbols displayed in these conversations. Noting

variations in Semantic Range over time with respect to varying conditions of conflict, diagnosticians conduct Linguistic Flexibility Analyses for each stakeholder group. H1H teams may also note and measure Semantic Range and Linguistic Flexibility within significant subgroups. A third goal is to identify pragmatic interpretants within the group's value discourse. Eventually, the team selects a pragmatic interpretant that may introduce conditions for identifying and, if needed, repairing a range of communal interpretants within the group. A final goal is to accustom the group to the polyvalent value-discourse that is central to H2H peacebuilding. Groups that resist any degree of polyvalent discourse will be unlikely candidates for H2H peacebuilding.

H-Formula 2.4: $(S_{v1} \rightarrow O_{v1}|I_c?)$ and $(S_{v1} \rightarrow Ov_2 \,|I_c?)$, where $O_m V \sim O_m$, and "?" indicates that it is not yet known if the competing claims share an interpretant.

The work of an H1H team is stimulated by non-constructive disagreement or potential conflict within an individual stakeholder group, where intra-group conflict could disrupt any peacebuilding effort. Linguistic Flexibility Analysis helps H1H teams identify subgroups and anticipate degrees of potential conflict among them.

H-Formula 2.5: $(S_m \rightarrow O_1|I_{c1})$ vs $(S_m \rightarrow O_2 \,|I_{c2}$, where $m \lor -m)$.

Intra-group tension/conflict is typically accompanied by competing binarisms: where two or more subgroups offer competing, monovalent readings of Hearth-values, and where these readings raise issues of existential urgency.[57]

---

57. Consider, for example, the urgent issue of messianic claims about the land of Israel. The first Chief Rabbi of Israel, R. Avraham Kook, argued, out of messianic assumptions, that "the congregation of Israel can fulfill its chosenness only in the land of Israel." The ultra-Orthodox scholar, R. Avraham Karelitz, argued, to the contrary, that one cannot reason about what only God knows and that worldly life in the land of Israel is governed by the same religious law that affects life anywhere. Some have pursued this debate in monovalent terms, supported by binary readings of Scriptures. On behalf of competing Orthodox movements, for example, Rav Hayyim Shapira cited Deuteronomy 32:17 ("new ones, who came but lately") as a critique of sacrilegious innovators (read "apostates") like the Zionists; while Rabbi Moses Samuel Glasner read that text on behalf of innovation (read "new discovery"). Rav Shapira read Deuteronomy 11:12 ("a land constantly under the scrutiny of the Eternal") and Numbers 13:32 ("a land that consumes its inhabitants") as warnings that the Zionists' sacrilegious misuse of the land will be punished, while Rav Kook interpreted Deuteronomy 11 to mean that dwelling in the Land of Israel means living with a higher level of divine providence and Numbers 13 to mean that the land's holiness will pollute the sinner as it purifies the righteous. See Ochs, "Meantime."

H-Formula 2.6: $|I_p = \Sigma\ ([M^1 = S_m \to O_{m1} | I_{c1}], [M^2 = S_m \to O_{m2} | I_{c2}] \ldots, [M^n = S_m \to O_{mn} | I_{cn}])$.

Repairing Conflicts Among Monovalent Sub-group Interpretants. According to the logics of TR and SRL, conflicting binarisms are guided by competing, monovalent interpretants. To repair such conflict, H1H engages sub-groups in shared conversation about Hearth-values in the hope that the conversation will be informed by the group's Meta-I. If present, the Meta-Interpretant would enable all competing interpretants within the group to operate freely within the conversation,[58] fostering the degree of non-monovalence that would enable subgroups to voice disagreement without conflict.[59] Another type of intra-group conflict is much more difficult to repair: conflict among competing monovalent readings of a stakeholder group's narratives, memories, and Hearth-related patterns of behavior. Because such readings are offered with veiled interpretants, group members tend to delegitimize any of their opponents' readings. If the interpretants remain veiled despite extended H1H discussion, then H1H will most likely fail. The lesson is that it is, indeed, possible for H1H to fail with a given sub-group or group, in which case it is unlikely that H2H can include this group.

H2H 3: Peacebuilding Work Among Value-Centered Stakeholder Groups in a Violent Conflict. Another type of H2H team includes representatives of each stakeholder group (or of as many stakeholder groups as possible). Such an *inter-group team* meets over an extended period (from three months to

---

58. One challenging type of conflict derives from the groups' shared confusion: they all misread differences among their traditional discourses as signs of contradiction *rather than as signs of the incommensurability of their different, monovalent systems of religious language.* In this case, the purpose of SR is to introduce members of these groups to the experience of shared study across the borders of what they perceive as incommensurable traditions. *If this is a case of Text-specific monovalence (binarism), then:*
Formula 8.1T: $T_1 = \Sigma(S_{sy1} \to \bullet | I_{t1}) = (S_1 \to \bullet, \to S_{s2}, \to \bullet, \ldots S_n \to \bullet)$ vs. $T_1 = \Sigma(S_{sy1} \to \bullet | I_{t2}) = (S_1 \to \bullet, \to S_{s2}, \to \bullet, \ldots S_n \to \bullet)$ vs. $\ldots T_1 = \Sigma(S_{sy1} \to \bullet | I_{tn}) = (S_1 \to \bullet, \to S_{s2}, \ldots S_n \to \bullet)$, where $m = S_{sy} \to \bullet$ and $m\ V \sim m$.
It is challenging to repair conflict involving text-specific monovalent readers, because each group is less accustomed to imagining how to read differently (for example, to imagine how their opponents read) and to tolerate polyvalent readings or different monovalent readings). It requires more artful facilitation to nurture a long-term TR group of this kind. The group may succeed best if it initially suspends study on the texts it reads monovalently and begins with texts that subgroups *do* read polyvalently, even if these are less sacred or authoritative in the tradition.

59. *As long as the Meta-I is present, the mediate goal of H1H is quantitative:* the longer sub-groups continue to meet, the more they will grow accustomed to maintaining relations of shared conversation without veiling their differences. See note 40 on why a scripturally based tradition may nurture polyvalent readings.

a year, or until the process succeeds or fails). The first goal of team meetings is to accustom stakeholder representatives to sharing value-centered comments about a range of topics that may be put on the table, from family and group narratives to diet, literatures, economy and so forth. The goal is not to address contentious issues head-on but to accustom the team to value-related conversation. A second goal is to identify group-specific interpretants (named within indigenous vocabularies) and pragmatic interpretants. As discussion turns to contentious issues, a defining goal of H2H is to encourage polyvalent applications of group value-vocabularies. Another defining goal is to identify whatever may function as a Meta-Interpretant of inter-group discussions and value judgments.

H-Formula 3.1: The setting: stakeholder groups that claim allegiance to different Hearths. $[\mathbf{H_1} = \Sigma\ (\Sigma\ (S_{H1} \rightarrow\ —\ \bullet|I_{v1})] \wedge [\mathbf{H_2} = \Sigma\ (\Sigma\ (S_{H2} \rightarrow\ —\ \bullet|I_{v2})] \wedge [\mathbf{H_3} = \Sigma\ (\Sigma\ (S_{Hn} \rightarrow — \bullet|I_{vn})]$, where $(S_{H1} \rightarrow (S_{v1} \rightarrow\ —\ \bullet|I_{v1})\ I_{vd}) = S_{v1} \rightarrow O_{v1}|I_p$. Here, determinate value-judgments are objects of Hearth-symbols.

> Formula 3.1 diagrams the defining setting of H2H: a set of stakeholder groups that read signs according to contrary (different) conditions of interpretation. These groups are not necessarily in conflict, unless they are stimulated to value-judgments and action by what outside observers would consider overlapping sets of sign-vehicles.

H-Formula 3.2: Conflicts among H-Symbol-specific Monovalent Interpretants. $[(S_1 \rightarrow (S_{v1} \rightarrow\ —\bullet|I_{v1})\ I_{vd}) = S_{v1} \rightarrow O_{v1}|I_{c1}$, where $O_v\ V \sim O_v)] \wedge [(S_1 \rightarrow (S_{v2} \rightarrow — \bullet|I_{v2})\ I_{vd}) = S_{v2} \rightarrow O_{v2}|I_{c2}$, where $O_v\ V \sim O_v)] \wedge \ldots [(S_1 \rightarrow (S_{vn} \rightarrow\ —\ \bullet|I_{vn})\ I_{vd}) = S_{vn} \rightarrow O_{vn}|I_{cn}$, where $O_v\ V \sim O_v)]$

> Formula 3.2 maps an illustrative conflict among a set of 3+ monovalent rules for reading what observers may identify as a given Symbol, each rule guided by a different communal interpretant. The Formula indicates that members of different stakeholder groups not only interpret but also perceive the Symbol in different ways: doubly contradicting the claims of outside observers. H2H stands or falls on its capacity to address conflicts of this kind. The procedure begins with Symbols that each group happens to read non-monovalently, even if this means beginning with non-value Symbols. Once the H2H team becomes accustomed to debates that allow a modest degree of polyvalence, facilitators introduce additional Symbols: keeping in play those that appear to maintain or strengthen conversation, moving past those that do not. The goal of this stage of H2H is to enable the team to gather a collective vocabulary of Symbols that may be read non-monovalently,

noting each Symbol's semantic-range within the team and encouraging conversation across that range.

Conversations that keep two or more meanings in play for a given Symbol engage team members (often unselfconsciously) in individual acts of non-binary reading/interpretation. These acts could (in some other setting) be diagrammed as S-O-I, that is, $S_1 \to \Sigma\ (O_T|I_c$, such that ~ $(O_T \vee \sim O_T)$: where readers acknowledge that meanings, within a given range, may differ on different occasions or by different team members. Such readers thereby acquire the habit, within this setting, of reading across a semantic range. The Interpretant I_c names this habit. The next procedure is to encourage side conversations among team members from different stakeholder groups who share in this habit of modestly non-monovalent debate. If, as expected, such conversations display a shared Interpretant (I_c), facilitators may identify it as a pragmatic interpretant (I_p):[60] a condition for non-conflictual debate (and difference) across group borders.

The Facilitators' next goal is to maintain and strengthen this I_p through whatever means may most likely succeed among members of this team. Facilitators might, for example, locate other team members who are prepared to join this side-conversation or uncover other symbols that additional team members read in non-monovalent ways. The penultimate goal is to have nurtured an H2H team the majority of whose members are prepared to join such conversation and, thereby, share in the influence of an I_p. This is a reasonable goal only because H2H is addressed to groups that appear to recognize Hearth-Symbols, and such groups are predisposed to make and discuss value-judgments with respect to a pragmatic interpretant. Moreover, H1H discussions should have prepared stakeholder representatives to join non-monovalent discussions in H2H. Whenever H2H teams fail to nurture a plurality of non-monovalent discussants, the representatives (or replacements) must return to the H1H discussion. It is not possible to continue H2H efforts with any stakeholder group whose representatives continually fail to engage in non-monovalent conversation. H2H efforts must continue with the remaining stakeholders. If most stakeholders fail to engage in such conversation, then facilitators should conclude that these groups cannot function as Hearth-groups, in which case H2H efforts should be suspended. H2H is peacebuilding only for Hearth-groups.

---

60. See elsewhere 175, 207 for initial accounts of pragmatic interpretant; in this case it may be diagrammed as $I_p = \Sigma(S_1 \to \bullet |I_{cn})$.

For teams that engage successfully in non-monovalent conversation, the final procedure of H2H is to move conversations increasingly toward the conflicting value-judgments that representatives bring to the table. Best practices for this effort will vary depending on the conflict setting and participants. I assume that the following practice will prove essential in almost any setting:

Nurturing verbal conflict to stimulate the activity of Meta-Interpretant(s). Communal interpretants (I_c) provide conditions for group-specific reading and conversation. Among I_c, pragmatic interpretants (I_p) may emerge to condition non-binarist conversation within a group. In an inter-group setting, a Meta-I may emerge among I_p to condition non-binarist conversation across groups (in this case, across stakeholder differences within an H2H team). I cannot imagine successful H2H peacebuilding without these transformations ($I_c \to I_p$ and $I_p \to$ Meta-I). I can imagine such transformations taking place only among Hearth-Groups.

To increase the probability that a Meta-I will emerge, the H2H team needs to have: (i) stimulated I_p within H1H teams; (ii) nurtured a form of non-monovalent conversation within the H2H team; (iii) introduced Value-Symbols into such conversation; (iv) introduced Value-Symbols and value-judgments that stimulate increasing verbal-conflict within the H2H team. This is the riskiest and most important stage of H2H, since a Meta-I will not emerge without such conflict, but such conflict may also stimulate irreparable binarist tendencies among stakeholder representatives. Facilitator skills face their greatest test at this stage. If successful, facilitators will have nurtured some degree of non-binarist conversation about increasingly contentious values, judgments and, then, on-the-ground issues. If successful, such conversations are made possible by emergent Meta-Interpretants, which alone mediate Hearth-to-Hearth debates. At a final stage, facilitators become negotiators (or host them).

H-Formula 3.3: Repairing Conflicts among Hearth-Specific Non-Monovalent Interpretants.

$H_1 \wedge H_2 \wedge H_n$, where $S_x = \Sigma \, (S_x \to -\bullet|I_{Hx}) \, |Ip?$, and $(S_1 \to - \bullet, S_2 \to - \bullet \ldots S_n \to - \bullet)$, and $m = S_x \to - \bullet | and \, m \wedge \sim m$.

Conflict among H-Symbol Interpretants is more readily repaired if the Interpretants tolerate a degree of non-monovalence. The procedures are roughly the same as in conflicts among H-Symbols (3.2). Such conflict is more readily reparable, because the H2H participants' degree of linguistic flexibility enables facilitators to nurture non-monovalent conversation as noted in 3.2.

H-Formula 3.4: Binarist Conflicts Among Hearth-specific Monovalent Interpretants

$H_1 \wedge H_2 \wedge H_n$, where $S_x = \Sigma \, (S_x \to - \bullet | I_{Hx}) \, | I_p?$, and $(S_1 \to - \bullet, S_2 \to - \bullet \ldots S_n \to - \bullet)$, and $mv = S_x \to - \bullet | and \, mv \, v \sim mv$.

Formula 3.4 maps each H-Group as a collection of H-Symbols whose meanings are monovalent according to the group's communal interpretant. Formula 3.4 diagrams conflict that has the potential for significant tension or violence, because each stakeholder group interprets any inter-group communication in binarist terms and tends, in settings of negotiation, to resist any move toward non-monovalent reading.

Here, the H2H strategies detailed in 3.2 might not succeed, since stakeholders would tend to resist more than one reading of each symbol and scenario introduced in H2H conversation. According to the logic of H2H, facilitators have three options, none of which is highly promising:

(1) *Extensive H1H work*: Facilitators might devote more time to working within individual stakeholder groups, searching for conditions (I_c) that stimulate some degree of non-monovalent conversation. Facilitators would seek to introduce these conditions into the H2H team setting. The closest analogy is SR among readers who display some degree of non-monovalence around the Hearth (Scripture read at home) but strict monovalence in the SR setting. The strategy is to enable group members to experience some bit of at-homeness in the H2H setting, thereby unintentionally signaling some degree of "warmth" (non-monovalence) to representatives of other groups. The hope is that, over time, members of each group allows a degree of non-monovalence in H2H conversation, opening conditions for the procedures of 3.2. At best, this option takes considerable time and effort. Even then, it fails for groups whose linguistic inflexibility is inveterate. Such groups may employ Hearth-like discourse, but in the absence of Interpretants and Value-Symbols that have retained their Hearth-like functions.

(2) If the first option fails, H2H may offer only one additional peacebuilding strategy. Facilitators would seek out stakeholder-group representatives (or replacements) that display greater tendencies to non-monovalence. One or several H2H teams would be formed with selected representatives from each stakeholder. Within each team,

facilitators would foster more intense, longer-term versions of the 3.2 procedures, until pragmatic interpretants emerge, to be reintroduced in settings of negotiation. Such negotiations might integrate H2H and non-H2H (or conventional) strategies.

(3) *Should both options fail, H2H efforts should be suspended.*

CONCLUDING WORDS

Should both options fail, H2H efforts should be suspended. I conclude chapter 6 with a cautionary sentence, because H2H might not succeed in the case in point. For that matter, H2H has only some probability of success in any case of violence, and this holds for SR in any case of tension. Both H2H and SR are built on knowing only enough, which is a kind of unknowing. My overall argument is that, when seeking to do something about tension and conflict among value-centered groups, peacebuilders should avoid conventional ways of knowing and act only on the basis of unknowing, as we have introduced it. This does not mean avoiding science. It means avoiding sciences whose positivist or either-or instruments of measurement fail to recognize the non-binary patterns of behavior that characterize religious and other value-centered groups. It means getting acquainted with sciences whose multivalued and probabilistic instruments may enable peacebuilders to observe and enter into constructive relation with what they cannot know: these stakeholder groups whose values and discourses, memories and motives for action are not theirs; these conflicts whose reasons they cannot fathom and whose consequences they cannot foresee. The argument of this book is that this kind of peacebuilding begins only when peacebuilders relinquish the desire to know and come, instead, to act through the kind of unknowing that each stakeholder ultimately shares with its opponents. And what kind is that? I don't yet know enough about SR to offer any answer other than the chapters of this book, the words of other scriptural reasoners, their experience in SR, the awful killing among so many groups, and the weakness of international and intra-state efforts to repair it.

For readers who may prefer a more practical conclusion, this book suggests that there are better ways to pursue peacebuilding among religious and value-centered stakeholder groups. One way is to:

- Address the religious behavior you see (or the value-centered group discourse and action) as a species of knowing enough (as characterized in chapter 5).

- Join a team that is prepared to reform its practices of peacebuilding so that they become actions undertaken out of knowing enough. Such a team may choose to:
- Pursue training in SR (or in some other practice consistent with SRL) in order to learn how to reform its peace-related efforts. If the team's goal is to help reduce inter-group tension short of violence, the team may find that this is training enough. If the training was helpful and the team's goal is to address violence among religious or value-centered groups, then the team might pursue further training in H2H (or in some other practice consistent with the logic of H2H as displayed in this chapter).

The next steps are on the ground, regional, and local. Your team may want to:

- Acquire group partners, where each partner shares in some of your goals and all partners, collectively, contribute what is needed to gain appropriate funding and political support, security, engagement with stakeholder value-discourses, lines of access to stakeholder actors, and networks of international, regional, and local agents of some part of a multi-leveled peace process. Depending on the conditions and geography of tension or conflict, these networks may include sources of political authorization (regional and group-specific), socioeconomic capital, value-centered trust and mediation, and/or enforcement plus protection (peacekeeping or military or intra- and inter-group policing).

Bibliography

A Common Word Between Us, Summary and Abridgment. https://www.acommonword.com/the-acw-document.
Adams, Nicholas. "Making Deep Reasonings Public." In *The Promise of Scriptural Reasoning*, edited by David F. Ford and C. C. Pecknold, 41–58. Oxford: Blackwell, 2006.
———. "Reparative Reasoning." *Modern Theology* 24.3 (July 2008) 447–57.
Appleby, R. Scott. *The Ambivalence of the Sacred: Religion, Violence, and Reconciliation.* Lanham, MD: Rowman and Littlefield, 2000.
Albright, Madeleine. *The Mighty and the Almighty: Reflections on America, God, and World Affairs.* New York: Harper Perennial, 2007.
Augustine. *City of God.* Boston: Wyatt North, 2004.
———. *De doctrina christiana* (*Christian Instruction*). Edited by Kevin Knight. New Advent. http://www.newadvent.org/fathers/1202.htm.
———. *De Trinitate* (*On the Trinity*). Edited by Kevin Knight. New Advent. http://www.newadvent.org/fathers/1301.htm.
———. *Confessionum libri* (*The Confessions*). Edited by Kevin Knight. New Advent. http://www.newadvent.org/fathers/1101.htm.
Barer, Deborah. "Law, Ethics, and Hermeneutics: A Literary Approach to Lifnim Mi-Shurat Ha-Din." *Journal of Textual Reasoning* 10.1 (December 2018).
Brooks, David. "Kicking the Secularist Habit: A Six Step Program." In *The Atlantic* (March 2003). https://www.theatlantic.com/magazine/archive/2003/03/kicking-the-secularist-habit/302680/.
Burgess, Paul Matthew. *Play, Metaphor, and Judgment in a World of Signs: A Peircean Semiotic Approach to Christian Worship.* PhD diss., Duke University, 1991.
Cohen, Aryeh. *Justice in the City: An Argument from the Sources of Rabbinic Judaism.* Boston, MA: Academic Studies, 2013.
Cohen, Mark R. *Poverty and Charity in the Jewish Community of Medieval Egypt.* Princeton, NJ: Princeton University Press, 2009.
Colish, Marcia. *The Mirror of Language.* New Haven, CT: Yale University Press, 1968.
Crescas, Hasdai. *Or Adonai.* Charleston, SC: Nabu, 2010.
Davis, Ellen. "Reading the Song Iconographically." In "Healing Words: The Song of Songs and the Path of Love," *Journal of Scriptural Reasoning* 3.2 (August 2003).
Deely, John. *New Beginnings: Early Modern Philosophy and Postmodern Thought.* Toronto: University of Toronto Press, 1994.

Dewey, John. "The Reflex Arc Concept in Psychology." *Psychological Review* 3 (1896) 357–70.
Dreyfus, George. *The Sound of Two Hands Clapping: The Education of a Tibetan Buddhist Monk*. Berkeley, CA: University of California Press, 2003.
Dubois, Heather. "Religion and Peacebuilding." *Journal of Religion, Conflict, and Peace* 1.2 (Spring 2008).
Epstein-Levi, Rebecca. "A Polyvocal Body: Mutually Corrective Discourses in Feminist and Jewish Bodily Ethics." *Journal of Religious Ethics* 43.2 (2015) 244–267.
Faizi, Nauman. "Averroes on the Relationship between Philosophy and Scripture: A Conditional Hierarchy." *Journal of Scriptural Reasoning* 15.1 (March 2016).
Feiler, Bruce. *Abraham: A Journey to the Heart of Three Faiths*. New York: William Morrow, 2005.
Fenton, Miri. "Hasdai Crescas: Grounds for Assertions about God and the Philosophical Use of Scripture." *Journal of Scriptural Reasoning* 15.1 (March 2016).
Figueroa-Ray, Kelly. "'Lady, Give Me A Drink': Reading Scripture, Shaping Community Development." In *Mobilizing for the Common Good: The Lived Theology of John M. Perkins*, 123–29. Jackson, MS: University Press of Mississippi, 2013.
Filler, Emily. "Total Textual Immersion: Considering Biblical Retellings in Exodus and Chronicles." *Journal of Textual Reasoning* 9:1 (December 2016).
Fish, Stanley. *Doing What Comes Naturally: Change, Rhetoric and the Practice of Theory in Literary and Legal Studies*. Durham, NC: Duke University Press, 1989.
Fishbane, Michael. *Biblical Interpretation in Ancient Israel*. Oxford: Oxford University Press, 1985.
Ford, David F. *Christian Wisdom: Desiring God and Learning in Love*. Cambridge: Cambridge University Press, 2007.
———. "Communicating God's Abundance: A Singing Self." In *Self and Salvation: Being Transformed*, 107–36. Cambridge: Cambridge University Press, 1998.
———. "'He is our Peace': The Letter to the Ephesians and the Theology of Fulfillment." "Mysticism and Scriptural Reasoning: Messianism and Fulfillment." *Journal of Scriptural Reasoning* 1.1 (August 2001).
Ford, David F., and C. C. Pecknold, eds. *The Promise of Scriptural Reasoning*. Oxford: Blackwell, 2006.
Ford, Deborah Hardy, David F. Ford, and Ian Randall, eds. *A Kind of Upside-downness: Learning Disabilities and Transformational Community*. London: Jessica Kingsley, 2019.
Fraade, Steven. *From Tradition to Commentary: Torah and its Interpretation in the Midrash Sifre to Deuteronomy*. Albany, NY: SUNY Press, 1991.
———. "Response to Azzan Yadin-Israel on Rabbinic Polysemy: Do They 'Preach' What They Practice?" *The Journal of the Association for Jewish Studies* 38.2 (November 2014) 339–61.
Frei, Hans. "The 'Literal Reading' of Biblical Narrative in the Christian Tradition: Does it Stretch or Will it Break?" In *The Bible and the Narrative Tradition*, edited by Frank McConnell, 36–77. New York: Oxford University Press, 1986.
Fuller, Millard. *The Theology of the Hammer*. Macon, GA: Smyth & Helwys, 1994.
Gibbs, Robert. "Reading with Others: Levinas' Ethics and Scriptural Reasoning." In *The Promise of Scriptural Reasoning*, edited by David F. Ford and C. C. Pecknold, 171–84. Oxford: Blackwell, 2006.

Goodson, Jacob. "Kant and the Nature of Doctrine: A Rule-Theory Approach to Theological Reasoning." *Journal of Scriptural Reasoning* 16.1 (June 2017).

———. *Narrative Theology and the Hermeneutical Virtues*. Minneapolis: Lexington, 2015.

Goodson, Jacob, ed. "Special Issue Honoring the Work of Stanley Hauerwas and His Friends." *Journal of Scriptural Reasoning* 16.2 (November 2017).

Gopin, Marc. "Religion and International Relations at the Crossroads." *International Studies Review* 3.3 (Fall 2001) 157–60.

Greggs, Tom. *Barth, Origen, and Universal Salvation: Restoring Particularity*. Oxford: Oxford University Press, 2009.

Halivni, David Weiss. *Peshat and Derash: Plain and Applied Meaning in Rabbinic Exegesis*. Oxford: Oxford University Press, 1990.

———. *Revelation Restored: Divine Writ and Critical Responses*. Boulder, CO: Westview, 1997.

Hardy, Daniel, et al. *Wording a Radiance: Parting Conversations on God and the Church*. London: SCM, 2010.

Harris, Robert. "Improving the Quality of Our Disagreements." *Journal of Scriptural Reasoning* 15.2 (November 2016).

Hashkes, Hannah. *Rabbinic Discourse as a System of Knowledge*. Leiden, NL: Brill, 2015.

Higton, Mike. "For Its Own Sake; For God's Sake: Wisdom and Delight in the University." In *The Vocation of Theology Today: A Festschrift for David Ford*, edited by Tom Greggs et al., 289–302. Eugene, OR: Cascade, 2013.

Higton, Mike, and Rachel Muers. *The Text in Play: Experiments in Reading Scripture*. Eugene, OR: Cascade, 2012.

Hoover, Dennis, and Douglas Johnston. "Religion and the Global Agenda: from the Margins to the Mainstream?" In *Religion and Foreign Affairs: Essential Readings*, edited by Dennis R. Hoover and Douglas M. Johnston, 1–10. Waco, TX: Baylor University Press, 2012.

Horgan, Maurya P. *Pesharim: Qumran Interpretations of Biblical Books*. CBQMS 8. Washington, DC: Catholic Biblical Association of America, 1979.

Hovil, Lucy, and Joanna Quinn, *Working Paper 17, Peace First, Justice Later: Traditional Justice in Northern Uganda*, 24, 34. Kampala: Refugee Law Project, 2005. https://www.refugeelawproject.org/resources/working-papers/73-peace-first,-justice-later-traditional-justice-in-northern-uganda/.

Hughes, Kevin. "Deep Reasonings: Sources Chretiennes, Ressourcement, And The Logic Of Scripture In The Years Before—And After—Vatican II." *Modern Theology* 29.4 (October 2013) 32–45.

Human Security Index Version 1.0. http://www.humansecurityindex.org/?m=200911.

Iqbal, Muhammed. *Reconstruction of Religious Thought in Islam*. Stanford, CA: Stanford University Press, 2012.

James, Mark Randall. "Scriptural Reasoning as Communal Thinking." *Journal of Scriptural Reasoning* 16.1 (June 2017).

———. "'Pairs' and Other Patterns in Hegel's Logic." *Journal of Scriptural Reasoning* 14.2 (December 2015).

James, William. *The Principles of Psychology I*. New York: Dover, 1950 [1890].

Jenson, Robert. *Canon and Creed*. Louisville, KY: Westminster John Knox, 2010.

Journal of Scriptural Reasoning (JSR). http://jsr.shanti.virginia.edu/.

Journal of Textual Reasoning (JTR) (New Series). https://jtr.shanti.virginia.edu/.

Johnston, Douglas, and Cynthia Sampson, eds. *Religion, The Missing Dimension of Statecraft*. Oxford: Oxford University Press, 1994.

Kadushin, Max. *A Conceptual Approach to the Mekilta*. New York: Jewish Theological Seminary, 1969.

———. *The Rabbinic Mind*. New York: Bloch, 1973.

———. *Worship and Ethics*. New York: Bloch, 1996 [1964].

Kaye, Miriam Feldmann. *Jewish Theology for a Postmodern Age*. Jerusalem: Littman Library of Jewish Civilization, 2019.

Kepnes, Steven. A Handbook for Scriptural Reasoning. *Modern Theology* 22:3 (July 2006) 367–83. See also http://jsrforum.lib.virginia.edu/writings/KepHand.html.

———. *Liturgical Reasoning*. Oxford: Oxford University Press, 2007.

Kepnes, Steven, ed. Why Textual Reasoning. *Journal of Textual Reasoning* 1.1 (2002).

Koshul, Basit Bilal. "Muhammad Iqbal's Reconstruction of the Philosophical Argument for the Existence of God." *Iqbal Review* (October 2008). http://www.allamaiqbal.com/publications/journals/review/oct08/8.html.

Leigh, Robert. "The Energetics of Attraction: Daniel Hardy's Theological Imagination, Sociopoiesis, and the Measurement of Scriptural Reasoning." *Journal of Scriptural Reasoning* 17.1 (August 2018).

Levinas, Emmanuel. "The Temptation of Temptation." In *Nine Talmudic Readings*, translated by Annette Aronowicz, 42–72. Bloomington, IN: Indiana University Press, 1990.

Lindbeck, George. *The Church in a Postliberal Age*. Edited by James Buckley. Grand Rapids, MI: Wm. B. Eerdmans, 2003.

Luttwak, Edward. "The Missing Dimension." In *Religion, the Missing Dimension of Statecraft*, edited by Douglas Johnston and Cynthia Sampson, 8–19. Oxford: Oxford University, 1994.

Markus, Robert A. "St. Augustine on Signs." In *Augustine*, edited by Robert A. Markus, 61–91. Garden City, NY: Anchor, 1972.

McGann, Jerome J. *Social Values and Poetic Acts: The Historical Judgment of Literary Works*. Cambridge, MA: Harvard University Press, 1988.

Mekilta de Rabbi Ishmael II Tractate Beshalach. See Jacob Z. Lauterbach, *Mekilta de-Rabbi Ishmael: A Critical Edition on the Basis of the Manuscripts and Early Editions with an English Translation, Introduction, and Notes*. Philadelphia: Jewish Publication Society, 1961 [1933]. Reprinted in *A Conceptual Approach to the Mekilta*, by Max Kadushin. New York: Jewish Theological Seminary, 1969.

Mermer, Yamina. "Mysticism and Scriptural Reasoning: Messianism and Fulfillment." *Journal of Scriptural Reasoning* 1.1 (August 2001).

———. "Principles of Qur'anic Hermeneutics." "Islam and Scriptural Reasoning," *Journal of Scriptural Reasoning* 5.1 (April 2005).

Nayed, Aref Ali. Vatican Engagements: A Muslim Theologian's Journey in Muslim-Catholic Dialogue. Dubai: KRM, 2016.

Nelkin, Dov. "Editor's Introduction to the Articles." "Healing Words: The Song of Songs and the Path of Love," *Journal of Scriptural Reasoning* 3.2 (August 2003).

Nelkin, Dov, et al. "Healing Words: The Song of Songs and the Path of Love," *Journal of Scriptural Reasoning* 3.2 (August 2003).

Ochs, Peter. "A Relational (non-binary) Semeiotic for Scriptural Reasoning." In *Proceedings of the 20e Congrès de l'Association Internationale de Littérature Comparée*, Paris 2013.

———. "Behind the Mechitsa: Reflections on The Rules of Textual Reasoning." "Why Textual Reasoning?," *Journal of Textual Reasoning* (New Series) 1.1 (2002) 2–47.

———. "Jewish and other Abrahamic Philosophic Arguments for Abrahamic Studies." In *The Oxford Handbook of Abrahamic Religions*, edited by Adam Silverstein and Guy G. Stroumsa, 559–79. London: Oxford University Press, 2015.

———. "Meantime and Endtime Theologies of the Return to Zion." In *Returning to Zion, Christian and Jewish Perspectives*, edited by Robert Jenson and Eugene Korn, 135–63. Jerusalem: The Center for Jewish-Christian Understanding and Cooperation, 2015.

———. "Multivalued Semiotic Models of Inter-Abrahamic Scriptural Reasoning." Appendix to "Beyond Two-Valued Logics: A Jewish Philosopher's Take on Recent Trends in Christian Philosophy." In *Christian Philosophy? Conceptions, Continuations, and Challenges*, edited by J. Aaron Simmons, 260–85. Oxford: Oxford University Press, 2019.

———. *Peirce, Pragmatism, and the Logic of Scripture*. Cambridge: Cambridge University Press, 1998.

———. "Reparative Reasoning: From Peirce's Pragmatism to Augustine's Scriptural Semiotic." *Modern Theology* 25.2 (April 2009) 187–215.

Ochs, Peter, ed. *Understanding the Rabbinic Mind: Essays on the Hermeneutic of Max Kadushin*. Atlanta: Scholar's, 1990.

Ochs, Peter, and Nancy Levine, eds. *Textual Reasonings: Jewish Philosophy and Text Study at the end of the Twentieth Century*. London: SCM, 2002; Grand Rapids: Eerdmans, 2003.

Ochs, Peter, Jonathan Teubner, Nauman Faizi, and Zain Moulvi. "Value Predicate Analysis: A Language-Based Tool for Diagnosing Behavioral Tendencies of Religious or Value-Based Groups in Regions of Conflict." *Journal for the Scientific Study of Religion* 58.1 (2019) 93–113

Ochs, Vanessa. "The Jewish Sensibilities." *Journal of Textual Reasoning* 4.3 (May 2006).

———. "Ten Jewish Sensibilities." *Sh'ma: A Journal of Jewish Ideas* (December 1, 2003). http://shma.com/2003/12/ten-jewish-sensibilities/.

O'Hara, David. "The Sentiment that Invites Us to Pray: The Religious Aspect of Charles Peirce's Philosophy." *Journal of Scriptural Reasoning* 16.1 (June 2017).

Pecknold, Chad. *Transforming Postliberal Theology: George Lindbeck, Pragmatism and Scripture*. London: Bloomsbury T&T Clark, 2005.

Peirce, Charles. *Collected Papers of Charles Sanders Peirce*. Edited by Charles Hartshorne and Paul Weiss. Cambridge, MA: Harvard University, 1934–35. References to this collection will be to CP followed by volume, paragraph number, and date of original essay.

———. "Sixty Lectures on Logic." In *Writings of Charles S. Peirce: A Chronological Edition*, volume 4, 467–89. Bloomington, IN: Indiana University Press, 1989.

Pew Research. "Key findings about growing religious hostilities around the world." http://www.pewresearch.org/fact-tank/2014/01/17/key-findings-about-growing-religious-hostilities- around-the-world/.

Powers, Gerard F. "Religion and Peacebuilding." In *Strategies of Peace*, edited by Daniel Philpott and Gerard Powers, 317–52. Oxford: Oxford University Press, 2010.

Quash, Ben. *Fond Theology: History, Imagination, and the Holy Spirit*. London: T&T Clark, 2014.

———. "Heavenly Semantics: Some Literary-Critical Approaches to Scriptural Reasoning." In *The Promise of Scriptural Reasoning*, edited by David F. Ford and C. C. Pecknold, 59–76. Oxford: Blackwell, 2006.

Rashkover, Randi. "Adams, Hegel, and Transcendental Reflection upon the Word." *Journal of Scriptural Reasoning* 14.2 (December 2015).

———. "Scriptural Reasoning: From Text Study to Inquiry." *Journal of Scriptural Reasoning* 16.1 (June 2017).

Ricoeur, Paul. *The Symbolism of Evil*. Translated by Emerson Buchanan. New York: Harper and Row, 1967.

Roberts, Don. "An Introduction to Peirce's Proofs of Pragmatism." *Transactions of the Charles S. Peirce Society* 14.2 (Spring 1978) 120–31.

Roht-Arriaza, Naomi. "Human Rights and Strategies of Peacebuilding: The Roles of Local, National, and International Actors." In *Strategies of Peace: Transforming Conflict in a Violent World*, edited by Daniel Philpott and Gerard Powers, 231–47. Oxford: Oxford University Press, 2010.

Rosenzweig, Franz. *The Star of Redemption*. Translated by William Hallo. Notre Dame: University of Notre Dame, 1971.

Safi, Omid. "On the 'Path of Love' Towards the Divine: A Journey with Muslim Mystics." In "Healing Words: The Song of Songs and the Path of Love," *Journal of Scriptural Reasoning* 3.2 (August 2003).

Schiffman, Nadav Berman. "Pragmatism and Jewish Thought: Eliezer Berkovits's Philosophy of Halakhic Fallibility." *Journal of Jewish Thought & Philosophy* 27.1 (2019) 86–135

Sifre Devarim Ha' azinu, pis. 306, to Deuteronomy 32:1, citing Louis Finkelstein, ed., *Sifre on Deuteronomy*, 308–35. New York: Jewish Theological Seminary, 1969.

Smith, John E. *Purpose and Thought: The Meaning of Pragmatism*. New Haven, CT: Yale University Press, 1984.

Smith, Wilfred Cantwell. *What Is Scripture? A Comparative Approach*. Minneapolis: Fortress, 1994.

Soulen, Kendall. *The Divine Names and the Holy Trinity*. Louisville, KY: Westminster John Knox, 2011.

Starr, Chloë. *Chinese Theology: Text and Context*. New Haven, CT: Yale University Press, 2016.

Teubner, Jonathan. *Prayer After Augustine: A Study in the Development of the Latin Tradition*. Oxford: Oxford University Press, 2018.

Ticciati, Susannah. *A New Apophaticism: Augustine and the Redemption of Signs*. Leiden: Brill, 2013.

———. "Scriptural Reasoning and the Formation of Identity." In *The Promise of Scriptural Reasoning*, edited by David F. Ford and C. C. Pecknold, 77–94. Oxford: Blackwell, 2006.

UCDP/PRIO Armed Conflict Dataset. https://www.prio.org/Data/Armed-Conflict/UCDP-PRIO/.

Ward, Roger. *Conversion in American Philosophy: Exploring the Practice of Transformation*. New York: Fordham University Press, 2004.

———. *Peirce and Religion: Knowledge, Transformation, and the Reality of God*. London: Lexington, 2018.

Weiss, Daniel. *Paradox and the Prophets: Hermann Cohen and the Indirect Communication of Religion*. Oxford: Oxford University Press, 2012.

———. "Scriptural Reasoning and the Academy: The Uses and Disadvantages of Expertise and Impartiality." *Journal of Scriptural Reasoning* 16.1 (June 2017).
West, Cornel. *The American Evasion of Philosophy, A Genealogy of Pragmatism*. Madison, WI: University of Wisconsin Press, 1989.
World Bank. Human Security Report Project, 2008. *Miniatlas of Human Security*. Brighton, UK: Myriad Editions, 2008. https://openknowledge.worldbank.org/handle/10986/23995.
Yang, Huilin. *China, Christianity, and the Question of Culture*. Waco, TX: Baylor University Press, 2014.
———. "'Scriptural Reasoning' and the 'Hermeneutical Circle.'" *Literature and Theology* 28.2 (June 2014) 151–63. https://doi.org/10.1093/litthe/fru027.
Yazicioglu, Isra. "Redefining the miraculous: Ghazali, Ibn Rushd, and Said Nursi on Qur'anic Miracle Stories." *Journal of Qur'anic Studies* 13.2 (October 2011) 86–108.
You, Bin. "Literacy, Canon and Social Reality: Socio-Cultural Dimensions of the Reception of the Bible among Ethnic Groups in Southwest China." *Ching Feng: A Journal on Christianity and Chinese Religions and Culture* 6.2 (2005) 179–92.
———. "To Be Harmonious with the Heaven, the Others and the Self: Late-Ming Christian Literati Li Jiugong's Meditation and His Comparative Scriptural Interpretation." *The Polish Journal of Aesthetics* 32 (1/2014) 155–73.
Young, Willie. "The Hope-Fulness of Scriptural Reasoning." In "Healing Words: The Song of Songs and the Path of Love," *Journal of Scriptural Reasoning* 3.2 (August 2003).
———. "The Song of Songs: From Affliction to Healing through the Text." In "Healing Words: The Song of Songs and the Path of Love," *Journal of Scriptural Reasoning* 3.2 (August 2003).
Zahl, Simeon. "Tradition and its 'Use': The Ethics of Theological Retrieval." *Scottish Journal of Theology* 71.3 (2018) 308–23.
Zoloth, Laurie. *Health Care and the Ethics of Encounter: A Jewish Discussion of Social Justice*. Chapel Hill, NC: The University of North Carolina Press, 1999.

Index of Ancient Documents

TANAKH/HEBREW BIBLE

Genesis
1.1–4	178–79
1.1–2.4	90–91
2–4	142

Exodus
13:19	175
20	85n1
24:7	2, 140

Leviticus
19:18	144
24	7

Numbers
11:16	49
13:32	197n57

Deuteronomy
6:5	144
11:12	197n57
32:1	51, 169
32:7	48–52, 168–69, 172–73
32:17	197n57
33:2	174

2 Kings
2:12	49

Isaiah
1:16–18	73
26:4	91

Habakuk
2:2	173
2:8b	174n34

Proverbs
10:8	175

Psalms
8:5	92
19:13–14	75
42:8	24
42:7	27
62:121	87
80:8	73
138:4	174.36

Ecclesiastes
12:11	86n4

DEAD SEA SCROLLS

1QpHab
7.1–5	173

1QpHab
9.3–12	174n34

NEW TESTAMENT

Matthew
7:16	43n20

Ephesians
1:22–23	33
2:14	32
3:18–20	34n15
4:15	33, 142
4:2	34, 142
5.505	

Colossians
1:19	34
2:19	34
3:14–21	34

QUR'AN
2:2	85n1
3:58	91
6:95	7
73:8	144
112:1–2	144

RABBINIC WRITINGS

b. Šabb.
88a	2

b. Ḥag
3b	86n4

B, Sanh.
34a.	87n5

Mekilta
176	175

Sifre Devarim
306	51, 169, 174
310	49–52, 168–69, 172–73

Genesis Rabbah
2:2	178

AUGUSTINE

Conf.,
	70–71, 73
1.5	75
1.6	75
3.19	73
4.10	74, 78
6.4–5	76–77
7.18	76–77
10:38	75n23
10:43	76–77
12.3.5	74

Doctr. chr.,
	70–71
1:2	73
1:34	76–77
2:1	73

Civ.
11:26	75
12:18	117

Trin.,
	70–71, 73
4.4.5	121
4	75–76
4:2	75
12:14	75, 75n21
15.2.2	118, 140

HADITH

Sahih Muslim
	172

RASHI

Gen. 1.1–4
	178

HASDAI CRESCAS

Or Adonai
15	119

Index of Subjects

Abrahamic, x, 1, 3, 5–6, 9, 18, 26, 28, 30–31, 38, 81, 84–85, 88–89, 96–98, 101–3, 106n24, 117, 144, 147, 162n10, 171
academy, university, ix, xi, xiii, 1–7, 10–14, 27, 29, 37–42, 54, 57–59, 62, 78–79, 82, 92–96, 101, 107, 110–14, 125–29, 143–44, 150, 156, 162, 166, 171
Acholi, 15, 16n25
al-Qaeda, 12n14
Africa/n, x, 8–9, 13n17, 20, 103, 156, 192
Appleby, Scott, 15–18, 20, 114
argument, 15–17, 21, 31n7, 32, 39, 61n4, 62, 65, 69, 79, 103, 119, 120n10, 129–30, 130n23, 133–38, 133n31,32, 134n34,26, 147n69, 150, 152–53, 155, 157, 203
Aristotle, 73, 107, 113, 119, 127, 129
Augustine, 66, 69–78, 107–8, 117–21, 130, 140
Austin, J. L., 38, 48n33, 168n18
A Thousand Cities, 11n11

Bakhtin, Mikhail, 48, 86n2, 168n18
behavior, 8, 16, 18, 20, 23, 56, 57, 102-103, 126-133, 143-144, 149-154, 157-166, 173-203
Berger, Peter, 153
Bible, 3, 28, 36, 41, 70, 71n13, 73, 73n18, 81
  TaNaKh, 1, 3, 25, 28, 144, 173

New Testament, Gospels, 1, 3, 28, 34, 43n20, 78, 135n4, 136–38, 138n48
Bohr, Nils, 64

Cambridge University, 4, 9
Cambridge Interfaith Program (CIP), 4, 101
Catholic Church, xii, 15, 26, 36, 81, 160, 164n13
China, ix-x, 13n17, 81n30,31, 82, 82n33,34, 100
  Minzu University, 81
  Renmin University, 81
Christ, 13, 33–34, 34n15, 76–77, 136, 144, 152, 183n46
  Jesus, 34, 43n20, 62, 69, 76–77, 138
Christianity (Christian), ix, xii, xv, 3, 7, 9–11n11, 12n11, 13n17, 14, 25–26, 28–29, 28n4, 32–36, 35n15, 45, 62, 70, 76, 81n29,31, 82n33,34, 85–88, 96n13, 117–18, 120n11, 136, 144, 192n53
commentary, xii, 1, 35–36, 44, 46, 48–52, 88–89, 91, 93, 133, 145n66, 168, 168n19, 169, 169n25, 170, 180, 191–92
community, x, xii, 6, 9, 11n10, 15, 17–18, 21, 27–30, 32–34, 35n15, 37–38, 41, 46, 48, 51, 59, 64, 66, 70n11, 71, 73, 79, 85, 87, 92–94, 96n14, 96–98, 100, 102, 109, 110n32, 121, 124, 127, 142, 144n63, 145, 147, 154, 164, 170, 173, 176, 179–82, 193, 195

216 INDEX OF SUBJECTS

concept, xii, 20, 32, 47, 55, 55n1, 56, 77, 82, 92, 97, 104–5, 109n30, 110n32, 115, 123, 132, 135–36, 157–58, 175n39
   universal, 26–27, 44, 92, 134, 146
conflict, ix-xi, xiii, 2, 11, 12, 12n15,16, 13n18, 17, 19, 30, 37–38, 40n17, 41, 54, 83, 97, 100–103, 129–32, 143, 143n60, 146, 148–52, 151n2,3, 152n4, 154–59, 167, 181–82,182n44,183–88, 190–93, 195–98, 198n58, 199–204
   violent, violence, 12–13, 17, 20, 30, 54, 83, 97, 103, 150–51, 151n2,3, 152n4, 154–55, 157–58, 165, 165n15, 166–67, 174n34, 185–86, 187n50, 190, 193, 195–96, 198, 202–4
conversion, 70n11, 73–74, 77
Confucianism, 36, 81
Crescas, Hasdai, 119, 119n9

Davis, Ellen, 45–47
Deely, John, 69, 107
Dewey, John, 57, 68n7, 126
denomination, 17, 35–36, 81, 84, 96, 116, 146n68, 152–53, 182
Derrida, Jacques, 107
Descartes, René, 62, 75, 77, 106, 107, 134
   Cartesian, 60–62, 66, 68–69, 75, 77–79, 108, 122, 129–30, 132n25
Deuteronomy, 48–49, 51, 51n40, 168, 168n19, 172n29, 177, 197n57
diagram, graph 33, 40n17, 60, 67–68, 70, 107, 122, 127–28, 130–31, 134–36, 138, 138n47, 145–48, 150, 164, 164n12,13, 165, 165n14, 167, 171, 175, 177–78, 185, 187, 191, 193–94, 199, 200, 200n60, 202
   Existential Graph, 134, 138n47, 145–46
difference, x, xii, 5–6, 8, 10, 16, 22, 26, 35, 37–38, 40–41, 40n17, 43, 47, 59, 76n26, 81, 82n34, 84, 90–93, 100–101, 105, 114, 116, 124, 143, 147n69, 148, 151n2, 157, 161, 167, 170–71, 182, 184–85, 189–90, 192, 194, 198n58,59, 200–201
disagreement, x, xi, 40n17, 182, 184, 197–98
doubt, 60, 75, 78, 85n1, 117, 125, 131n24
education, x, xii, 11, 94, 100n1, 101, 107, 154, 161
   classroom, 2, 4, 6, 26, 44, 84, 89, 97, 99, 110–12, 115–16, 143, 143n58, 150
   learning, 2–6, 31, 37, 89, 96–97, 99, 101, 106, 116, 143n60, 144n62, 154, 156, 191
   teaching, ix, 1–2, 5–6, 15, 29, 31, 36, 80, 84, 89–91, 97, 100, 106n24, 110–11, 114, 143, 144n62, 152–53, 159, 161–62, 176, 187
   Socialization as, socialization, 4, 144, 159, 187, 191, 196

Enlightenment, 13, 13n18, 26, 107
Ephesians, 32–34, 34n15, 142
ethnography, anthropology (see science, social)
Exodus, 2, 7, 85

faith, x-xi, xiii, 11n11, 12n11, 14, 34, 41, 62–66, 69n8, 76, 85, 96–98, 101, 105, 121–22, 137, 140, 145
fellowship, 1, 4, 6, 7, 8, 9, 11, 25, 26, 30, 31–32, 42, 52, 88, 91, 93, 95, 97, 100, 103–5, 107
foreign affairs, 13, 13n18, 14–15, 100–102, 154, 158
forgiveness, 75–76
Ford, David ix-xiii, xv, 32–34, 55n2, 81, 101, 142
flesh, 32, 46, 55–56, 75–77, 126–27
foreign affairs, international relations (IR), xi, 13–15, 101–3, 154–58
Fraade, Steven, 48–52, 48n33, 49n34, 49n35, 50n36, 50n37, 50n38, 51n39, 51n40, 52n42, 86, 168–69, 168n18, 168n19, 169n20, 169n21, 169n22, 169n23,

INDEX OF SUBJECTS 217

169n24, 169n26, 173–74,
173n31, 174n34, 174n35, 177
Frei, Hans, 25–26, 107

Gibbs, Robert, xv, 28n3, 43n21
God (the name appears on too many pages to list; here are some samples:)
  The Lord (YHWH) God, 7, 16, 73, 78, 85n1, 91, 92, 118, 144, 174, 201n46
  Allah, 7, 26, 85n1, 91–92, 98, 183n46
  Christ, Jesus (see Christ)
  Creator, 30, 53, 76–79, 90, 98, 116–18, 126, 135–38, 178–79, 183n46
  God in Ephesians, 32–34;
    in SR study, 44–47;
    in rabbinic study and TR, 47–52;
    in the "unknowing" of SR, 116–22;
    in Peirce's pragmatism, 132–39;
    in a Muslim interreligious statement, 144–45
Golomb, Rabbi Paul, 11n10

Halivni, David Weiss, 86–87, 86n2
Hardy, Daniel, xv, 88
habit, 4, 8, 13n18, 20, 25–26, 34, 39, 56, 60, 62, 65, 68, 68n7, 94, 96, 109n30, 116, 121, 125–31, 135, 146, 153, 159–60, 168, 175, 177, 183, 192, 200
  habit-change, 4, 68, 72, 168
Habitat for Humanity, 6, 96–97
heart, 19, 29, 35n15, 46, 53–54, 58, 75n23, 141n54, 144, 155, 167, 175
hearth, x, 18–20, 22–23, 82, 101–2, 114, 139, 142, 147–48, 150, 158, 182n44, 186, 186n48, 187, 187n50, 188–89, 191–202
  Hearth-to-Hearth Peacebuilding (H2H), 20, 82, 102–3, 142, 147–51, 158–63, 165–67, 179n41, 186–88, 190–95, 197–204
  religious hearth, 20, 139
Heisenberg, Werner, 64, 107

history, historiography, xi, 13, 15–16, 24, 32–33, 38–39, 41, 69, 83, 85, 93, 99, 106, 124, 142, 172, 174, 180
  Text-historical, 38, 42
humanities, xi, 5, 112–13, 144n62
human rights, 16n25, 17
humor, laughter, joy, xi, 10, 39, 40, 42, 47, 53, 88, 171

India, ix-x
individuality, individual, ix, xiii, 3–5, 7–8, 11, 13n17, 14, 17, 19, 22–23, 26, 28–29, 36–41, 49, 53, 55–57, 61, 71, 81, 86–87, 89, 92, 94, 96, 105, 108, 109, 109n30, 112, 116, 120–21, 123–29, 132, 135–36, 140–41, 144n62, 149, 152–53, 158, 161, 167–68, 172, 175, 183, 183n46, 184, 189, 191, 193, 195, 197, 200, 202
infinity, infinite, 34n15, 98, 116–19, 141n55, 183n46
inquiry, research, 2, 15, 36, 38–39, 42, 57–59, 64, 67, 69–72, 103, 108, 112–15, 124–25, 125n18, 126–30, 133–34, 138, 141–44, 146, 146n67, 68, 147, 152, 156, 159, 166n17, 186–88, 191, 195–96
  genealogical, 60, 62, 78
  pragmatic, reparative, 17–18, 25n1, 27, 30–34, 38, 43, 43n19, 45, 52–54, 57–59, 61–62, 64, 66–71, 71n12,13, 72, 72n15, 78–79, 81, 84, 96–97, 100n2, 102, 104, 108, 110, 110n32, 113–14, 125–26, 125n18, 126n19, 127–28, 128n20, 129–30, 130n23, 131, 131n24, 132, 134, 135n37, 136–39, 142–46, 146n68, 147, 149, 159, 162, 168, 169n25, 175–77, 179–81, 183–84, 186–87, 194, 194n54, 195–97, 199–200, 200n60, 201
  scientific, 14, 39, 59, 62, 64, 66, 68, 75, 77–78, 104, 108, 113, 127–28, 130, 133–34, 137–38, 146n68, 153, 157

218   INDEX OF SUBJECTS

inquiry, research *(continued)*
  Trinitarian, 66, 70, 72, 78
intellect, intelligence, cognition, 4, 13n18, 14, 16, 24, 39, 43, 55–57, 61–62, 66, 75, 79, 82n34, 112, 114, 120, 124, 125n17, 134 153, 159
interreligious, interfaith, x-xi, 1–2, 6, 12, 15, 17, 19, 27, 29–30, 36, 43, 54, 80–83, 91–92, 95, 101, 143–44, 147, 150–51, 155, 184
Iqbal, Muhammad, 107, 119
Islam (Muslim), ix, xv, 3, 7, 9–15, 26–29, 35–36, 45, 57, 66, 84–89, 110, 107, 117–88, 143–45n65, 153, 156–57, 160, 192
Islamic State, 12n14,16, 160, 164
Israel
  People Israel, 174, 49
  Israeli State, x, 9, 12, 14, 101, 103, 175, 197n57

James, William, 57, 64, 68n7
Jews, 9, 13, 26, 29, 32–34, 110, 176
Johnston, Douglas, 13–15
Journal of Scriptural Reasoning, 11, 32, 44, 47, 88–89, 168, 170
Journal of Textual Reasoning, 28, 87–88
Judaism, jewish, xv, 2–3, 6–7, 9–10, 11n11, 12n12, 14, 26, 28, 31, 33, 36, 38–39, 45–46, 51, 54, 57, 84–89, 96, 98, 117–19, 143, 152, 160, 173, 175–77, 192
judgment, claim 10, 17–18, 21–23, 25, 41, 43n20, 46, 53–55, 59–69, 72, 75, 78, 93, 102, 107–10, 113–26, 132, 134, 137–41, 144, 151, 152n4, 154, 157, 159n7, 162–63, 161, 176, 177–79n41, 182–84, 187, 189, 191, 193–99
  constative, locutionary 48, 66–68, 120, 126, 177
  conventional, 17, 20–21, 43–44, 67, 70, 113, 120, 141n55, 155, 189, 203
  operational, functional, illocutionary, 18, 21, 36, 114–15, 129, 139, 152–53, 159, 161, 162n10, 166, 179n41, 180n42, 188, 195n56
  value (see value)

Kadushin, Max, 160n8, 174–77, 181
Kant, Immanuel 62, 77, 107–8, 130n23, 134, 159
Karelitz, R. Avraham, 197n57
Kaye, Miriam Feldmann, 12n11
Kepnes, Steven, xv, 30n6
knowing, knowledge, xi, xii, xiii, 1, 4–5, 13n17, 20–24, 46, 62, 63, 76, 112–25, 138n49–142, 149, 170, 180, 20–204
  knowing enough, unknowing 46, 112–49, 170, 203
  knowledge by participation 76, 90, 120–23, 140–41
Kook, R. Avraham, 197n57
Koshul, Basit Bilal, xv, 119, 119n6

Levinas, Emmanuel, 2, 2n5, 53
Language, linguistic, 18, 23–24, 34, 39, 43–45, 56–57, 66–68, 74, 77, 82n33, 83, 86, 92, 94, 100, 102, 104, 115–16, 120, 124, 134, 141n54, 145, 149, 158–66, 178, 186–92, 196–98n58, 202
  flexibility/inflexibility 188–92, 196–98 160–65, 188–92, 202
  spoken, speech, 10, 19, 34, 56, 73, 78, 85, 87–88, 98, 102, 105, 118, 139, 147–48, 152, 159–63, 167, 175, 187–90
  written, writing 11, 25, 30, 43, 56, 76, 86n4, 102, 106, 162, 163, 171, 187
Lindbeck, George, xii, 26n2, 107
love, 10, 31–35.n15, 44–47, 53, 72, 79, 104, 135–38, 142–45, 152, 170–71
liturgy (see prayer)
logic, xiii, 2, 5, 32–43,59–66, 69–78, 82–83, 94, 107–8, 113, 122–25, 128–49, 167–202
  abduction, 134–38, 175, 194
  argument (see argument)

INDEX OF SUBJECTS 219

binary, binarism, 50–52, 122, 128–30, 136–39, 143–45, 146n68, 149, 171, 182, 186, 197n57, 198, 200, 203
contradiction, contradictory, either-or, zero-sum, 3, 7, 17, 27, 29, 37–41, 44, 61–65, 79, 98, 114, 119, 181–85, 199, 203
contrariety, contrary, 38–41, 64, 183–85, 199
deduction vs. induction, 134–36
multi-valued, 107, 113–14, 132n25, 203
of faith, 62–66, 69n8, 76, 122, 137, 145
of pragmatism, of repair, 34, 34n15, 126–28, 146–51, 167–203
of relations, 23, 122–24, 135, 136, 145, 149, 163
of science, 59–66, 78, 122, 145
of scripture, of SR 62, 66, 69–83, 145–51, 167–203
of propositions, two-valued, 62–64, 112–14, 132, 178
Stoic 69–76, 78, 107

Markus, Robert, 69, 69n8, 72, 72n14, 73n17, 74n20
Maimonides, 119
mathematics, 59, 105, 107, 125n18, 128
 probability 55, 61, 63–64, 103–6, 113, 122, 201
 quantum, 64, 104–7, 113, 132n25
meaning, reading, interpretation
 monovalence, 22, 23, 36, 143, 173, 179, 182–83, 183n46, 184–88, 192–202
 polyvalence, polysemy, multivocal multivalent, 16–17, 21–23, 31, 45, 51, 87, 116, 143, 169–70, 174, 180, 183n46, 185–88, 193–202
 semantic, 25, 39, 41, 54, 87, 102–3, 159, 187–90, 192, 196, 197, 200
 pragmatic, performative, 25, 31–42, 54-56, 85–87, 113, 116, 134
 vague, vagueness, ambiguity, 17, 20–22, 34, 34n15, 49–52, 95, 107, 113, 123, 132–33, 137–38, 143n58, 169, 175, 180–81, 195
 plain sense (*peshat, zahir, sensus literalis*) 38–41
 interpreted sense (*derash, batin*), xiii, 10, 28, 31–42, 45–56, 70n11, 80–94, 100, 105–10, 141n55, 145–46, 152, 168–88, 195, 199, 200
conventional, unconventional, 17, 20–21, 43, 67, 70, 113, 120, 141n55, 155, 189
medieval 17, 28, 38, 66, 70n11, 77, 178
Micronesia 19, 102, 192–93
midrash (see also meaning), 10, 33, 48, 51–52, 85–89, 168–81
Mill, John Stuart, 62, 134
Modernity, modernism (see West)
Moses 2, 49, 174–76, 181n43

Nayed, Ali Aref, 156
Newman, John Henry Cardinal, 16
Newton, Isaac, Newtonian 105, 113, 171

Ochs, Vanessa, 9, 10, 160n8

Palestine, Palestinian, 9, 101, 103
Pascal, 62, 115
peace, peacebuilding, peacekeeping, ix, xiii, xv, 1, 11–17, 20, 32, 34, 38, 41–42, 54, 75n23, 83, 97, 100–104, 143n60, 147, 150–203
Peirce, Charles, 20–21, 32n9, 32–35, 38, 43, 57–72, 75–79, 104, 107–8, 120, 120n10 122, 125–41, 125n18, 126n19, 130n21, 130n23, 131n24, 132n26, 132n27, 133n31, 133n32, 133n33, 134n34, 134n36, 135n37, 136n39, 137n41, 137n42, 137n43, 137n44, 137n45, 138n46, 138n47, 140n50, 144–48, 147n69, 195
Pfister, Olivier, 104–5

INDEX OF SUBJECTS

philosophy, 6, 39, 58–62, 68, 78–79, 120, 125, 127–30, 134–35, 137n43, 138, 143
Philpott, Daniel, 15
Plank, Max, 64
Plato, 70, 107, 117
poetry, poetics, 20, 38, 102
politics, political, 10, 12–13n17, 13n18, 14–15, 17, 20, 84, 86, 101–3, 124, 128, 155–58, 189, 204
practice, ix-xiii, xv, 1–11, 15–24, 29–32, 35, 39–45, 48–49, 53–61, 67–70, 77–83, 85–115, 124–34, 137–52, 155–61, 166–68, 171–73, 179–80, 184–85, 191, 194–204
problem, trouble, burden, maculation, ix-x, 13, 17, 27–33, 35n15, 40, 42, 45–46, 52, 55, 57–59, 62, 82, 86–87, 100, 109–10, 110n32, 125, 131, 142, 146, 152n4, 156, 176–77, 183, 194
pragmatism, pragmatic, xiii, 17–18, 24–84, 96–97, 100n2, 102, 104, 108, 110, 110n32, 113–14, 125–49, 153, 158–63, 167–69, 171–201
 imperative, 126, 128–29, 130n23, 131–32, 136–38, 144–45, 173
 maxim, 132, 145, 159, 164
 pragmaticism, 62, 130–31, 131n24, 135
 proof of, 65, 125–49
prayer, worship, xi, 34n15, 35, 75–77, 105, 112, 115, 121–22, 127, 160n8

Quantum, Quantum Theory, 64, 104–7, 113, 132n25
Qur'an, 1, 3, 7, 10, 26, 28, 45, 85n1, 89, 91–92, 98, 110, 116, 119, 144, 147
 hadith, 10, 26, 145n65
 Sunna, 26, 28

Rabbinic Judaism, rabbinics, midrash, 2, 1025–32, 37–41, 47–52, 69, 85–91, 118–21, 186–87, 121, 147, 160, 168–83
Rashi, 178, 196
Rashkover, Randi, xv, 28n3, 43n19, 146n67
reasoning (excluding the names Scriptural Reasoning or Textual Reasoning), 4–6, 25–27, 31–32, 36–37, 42, 52–83, 89–91, 104–10, 119–24, 128–30, 133–42, 191
 A-reasoning, 130–32
 B-reasoning, 130–32
 critical revelatory, 147–49
 deep, 24–32, 38, 42–46, 52–54, 60, 67, 78, 86–89, 95–96, 132, 142–49
 diagrammatic 130, 131, 136, 138, 145, 146
 narrative, 99–101
 probabilistic, 62, 115, 134–36
 reparative, pragmatic, 30–32, 43, 52–83, 131, 139–49
 relational, relations, x-xi, 2, 4, 9, 20–23, 25–26, 28–30, 34, 36–37, 40, 42–43, 45, 48, 50, 53–55, 55n2, 57, 59, 63, 65–66, 68, 92–93, 96, 100–107, 109, 109n30, 112–13, 115, 119, 122–24, 126, 132n25, 135–38, 141–42, 144–45, 149, 163, 165n16, 168–69, 172, 176–77, 182, 193–94, 198n59
religion, religious, ix-xiii, 1, 4–24, 30, 35–36, 38, 40, 43–44, 54, 58, 62, 65, 69n8, 70n11, 78 81–82, 84–85, 86n2, 89, 91–99, 100, 100n1, 101–3, 112–17, 120, 124, 127, 132, 134, 136–39, 142, 145, 146n68, 148, 150–59, 160n9, 161–63, 165–68, 179–86, 191, 194, 195n56, 197n57, 198n58, 203–4
 experience, 15–16, 22–23, 32, 34, 36, 65, 85–86, 93, 109, 119, 133,139–41, 144–45, 152–54, 158, 183n46, 202

INDEX OF SUBJECTS 221

groups, 13n17, 15–19, 21–23,
  92–93, 95, 102, 148, 152, 154,
  157–58, 159n7, 161–63, 166, 186
values, 139, 152, 161–62, 191
violence, conflict, 2, 54, 101, 184
revelation, 86, 98, 104, 136–37,
  147–48, 168n19
dibbur, 118, 147, 175
Ricci, Matteo, 81
ritual, 24, 37–38, 89, 94, 102, 109n30,
  112, 158, 162, 192n53
Rorty, Richard, 128n20

sacred, holy, 15, 18, 20, 28, 144, 153,
  175, 183, 197
science, xi, 5–6, 13, 38, 42, 59, 61–62,
  64–66, 78, 105, 112–13, 124,
  127–28, 132–33, 137–38, 171,
  203
  experimental, 61–62, 64–66, 78,
    137, 171
  natural, 65, 68, 104, 107, 115,
    125n17, 127, 189
  social, 15, 34, 38, 84, 103, 107, 112–
    13, 127, 152n4
Scripture, scriptural canon (the terms
  appears on too many pages to
  list)
  logic of (see under logic)
Scriptural Reasoning (SR) (the term
  appears on too many pages to
  list)
  Asian, 1, 5, 57, 162n10
secular, ix, xi, 10, 13, 13n19, 14, 17,
  142n55, 153, 155, 176
  secularism, 10, 13, 13n19, 14,
    142n55
  secularization, 13, 13n19, 14, 17,
    153
Searle, John, 48n33, 168n18
Seidel, Kevin, 11n11
semiotics, 26–29, 30n5, 34, 50–51,
  55, 67–74, 78, 107, 110n32, 113,
  120n11, 128, 148, 159, 175
service, 6, 9, 17, 62, 66, 89, 96,
  127–31, 143
  service institutions, 127–29, 143
Sifre Deuteronomy 48–52, 168–69

sign, signifier, 26–27, 30, 34, 34n15,
  35, 50–51, 55, 67–74, 78, 109,
  122–24, 126–27, 132, 134–35,
  142–46, 171–202
  Icon, iconic, sense 47, 67, 71n13,
    126, 130, 134–35, 145–46,
    172–85, 192–202
  index, reference, 36, 67, 72–74, 126,
    134, 172–85, 192–202
  Interpretant, 51, 67–68, 122–23,
    171–85, 192–202
  lekton, 73–74, 173–74
  object 67, 72–74, 122–23, 126, 135,
    171–85, 192–202
  rheme 172–76, 181, 192–93, 196
  symbol 67, 72, 123, 172–85,
    192–202
  vehicle, material sign 123, 146,
    171–72, 185, 192–202
sin, error, 2, 35n15, 57–61, 65, 71–72,
  74–75, 76n26, 78, 79, 121, 125,
  130, 153, 176, 183n46, 194
Smith, John E., 132–36
social, 4, 8, 12, 13n17,18, 15–16, 19,
  26, 28, 31, 48n33, 54, 61–62,
  68, 93, 98, 100n2, 106, 109n30,
  110n32, 112–13, 120, 124,
  125n17, 126–27, 128n20, 132,
  137, 141–44, 147n69, 149, 151–
  53, 155, 157–59, 164n13, 168,
  180, 187–89, 191, 193, 195–96
Socrates, 107, 116
Song of Songs, 45–47
South Africa, x, 8–9, 103
  Cape Town, 8–9, 11, 100, 143
stakeholder, 54, 99, 149–50, 152,
  186–88, 191, 193–204
state, nation, 12–15, 101, 154–57, 203,
  204n
Stoics (see Logic)
story, narrative, 6, 27, 50, 59, 66, 85,
  91, 99–100, 104, 165, 170
study 1–3, 11, 15, 25, 112–14, 128
  of religion, 11–16, 93–94, 152,
    156–68, 170–203
  reparative, 30–32, 96–104, 128,
    142–44, 170–203
study *(continued)*

222 INDEX OF SUBJECTS

scriptural, SR, ix-xi, 1–13, 18–30, 36, 39–50, 69–82, 88–116, 141n55, 143–44, 148, 166–67, 168–70, 184–203
   textual 35–52, 80–90, 115–16, 142, 167–68, 181–83
   literary 81–82, 85–87
suffering, affliction, 27, 30–32, 35n15, 45–47, 58–59, 71, 79, 98, 110, 121, 126, 143, 144, 170–71, 176

Talmud (see rabbinics)
terrorism, 12n14, 165, 166
Teubner, Jonathan, 76, 121
texts, textuality, Textual Reasoning (the terms appear on too many pages to list)
theology 6, 15, 32, 38, 77, 80, 99, 120, 127, 137n40
theory, xii, xiii, 1–2, 13, 22, 29, 38, 41,43, 58, 61, 64, 67, 81–82, 99, 104–11,135, 147,150–204
Torah (see also Tanakh), 25, 51,86n4, 147, 153, 174
Tradition [throughout] (the name appears on too many pages to list; here are some samples and some representative sections of the book:)
triadic, 50, 69n8, 70, 73, 78, 109, 122–24, 138
truth, truth-function, truth or falsity, 21–22, 33,37–41, 59, 62–63, 74, 76, 112–14, 122, 125n18, 130, 132n25, 139, 142, 178, 183n46, 187, 196

United Kingdom, UK, x, xv, 11, 12, 101
University of Virginia 4–6, 87n6, 88n8, 89–90, 96–99,101–6, 186
United Nations, UN, 154–55
U.S. Department of State (DOS), 101–2, 155, 156

vagueness (see Meaning)

value, values, 15, 18, 37, 46, 82, 102, 114, 139, 148, 152–53, 157–61, 166–70, 174, 183, 188–202
   deep, x, 8, 18–21, 29–31,43–44, 54, 67, 87–91, 102,148–53, 158, 167–70,191, 194
   indigenous, 41, 101,152, 160–62,187, 191, 199
   judgments, 102, 131n25, 138, 149, 152, 161–63, 165n16, 176–77, 187–201
value-centered groups 148–49, 159, 159n7, 161–62, 186, 193, 195–98, 203–4
Value Predicate Analysis (VPA), 160–66, 186n47
   Semantic Range Analysis (SRA), 187–88, 196
   Linguistic Flexibility Analysis (LFA), 188–92, 196–98
   linguistic sensitivity, 188–89, 196
   interpretive license, 188–89, 196
   Action Recommendations (ARN), 190–91, 195
Vatican II xii, 145n66

Weber, Max, 153
West, Western, modern West, xi, xiii, 4–6, 10, 13–15, 17, 20, 26, 28,35, 54, 58–62, 66, 68, 77–82, 92, 102, 104, 106–7, 125, 128–29, 132n25, 134, 139, 144, 153–58, 171,192n53
White, Jerry, 101, 155–57
world, nature, environment, x, 5, 16–23, 26, 30–31, 40, 64–65, 68, 70–77, 86n4,104–5, 107,114–15, 117–20, 124–27, 133–38,159–62, 176, 181, 183, 189, 191–93
Wilken, Robert, 89
Wittgenstein, 38, 107

Yang, Huilin, 81–82
You, Bin, 81

Zoloth, Laurie, xv

Index of Authors

Adams, Nicholas, x, 42, 43, 43n19
Albright, Madeleine, 155, 155n6
Appleby, Scott, 15–18, 15n24, 16n26, 16n27, 17n28
Augustine, 75, 75n21, 75n22, 75n23, 117–21, 117n3, 118n4, 118n5, 121n12, 140n52

Barer, Deborah, 87n6
Bakhtin, Mikhail, 48, 48n33, 86n2, 168n18
Brooks, David, 14, 14n21, 14n22, 14n23
Burgess, Paul Matthew, 69n8

Cohen, Aryeh, 28n3, 96n13
Cohen, Mark R., 98, 98n18
Colish, Marcia, 77, 77n27, 78
Crescas, Hasdai, 119, 119n9

Davis, Ellen, 47, 47n30
Deely, John, 107n25
Dewey, John, 68n7

Epstein-Levy, Rebecca, 96n13
Faizi, Nauman, 119n8, 166n17
Feiler, Bruce, 9n9
Fenton, Miri, 119n9
Figueroa-Ray, Kelly, 97, 97n16
Filler, Emily, 90n10
Fish, Stanley, 48n33, 168n18
Fishbane, Michael, 90n11
Fodor, Jim, 28n3
Ford, David F., ix, 28n4, 32–34, 32n8, 34n15, 96n13, 142

Fraade, Steven, 48–52, 48n33, 49n34, 49n35, 50n36, 50n37, 50n38, 51n39, 51n40, 52n42, 86, 168–69, 168n18, 168n19, 169n20, 169n21, 169n22, 169n23, 169n24, 169n26, 173–74, 173n31, 174n34, 174n35, 177
Frei, Hans, 25, 26n2
Fuller, Millard, 99, 99n9

Gibbs, Robert, 28n3, 43n21
Goodson, Jacob, xvn1, 11n11, 88n8, 104n23, 130n23
Gopin, Marc, 15, 17n29
Goshen-Gottstein, Alon, 45, 47, 170
Greggs. Tom, 120n11

Halivni, David Weiss, 86, 86n3, 87
Hardy, Daniel, 88n7
Hashkes, Hannah, 175n39
Higton, Mike, 28n4, 43n22
Hoover, Dennis, 13, 14n20
Horgan, Maurya P., 173

Iqbal, Muhammad, 107, 119, 119n7
James, Mark Randall, xvn1, 43n19, 87n6, 93n12
James, William, 57, 64, 68n7
Johnston, Douglas, 13, 14n20, 15

Kadushin, Max, 160n8, 174–77, 175n37, 175n39, 177n40, 181
Kaye, Miriam Feldmann, 12n11
Kepnes, Steven, 3n6, 28n3, 30n6
Koshul, Basit Bilal, 119, 119n6

Lederach, John Paul, 15
Levinas, Emmanuel, 2, 2n5, 53
Levine, Nancy, 28n3
Lindbeck, George, xii, 26n2
Luttwak, Edward, 13, 13n18

Magid, Shaul, 28n3
Markus, Robert, 69, 69n8, 72, 72n14, 73n17, 74n20
Mermer, Yamina, 98n17
Moulvi, Zain, 166n17
Muers, Rachel, 43n22

Nayed, Ali Aref, 145n66
Nelkin, Dov, 44n23, 45, 45n24
Novick, Daniel, 100n2

Ochs, Peter, 28n3, 31n7, 32n10, 33, 33n11, 33n12, 33n13, 35n15, 61n3, 66n6, 71n12, 71n13, 160n8, 166n17, 186n47, 197n57
Ochs, Vanessa, 160n8
O'Hara, David, 115n2

Peirce, Charles, 32n9, 43, 43n20, 57–72, 72n16, 75–79, 120, 120n10, 122, 125–41, 125n18, 126n19, 130n21, 130n23, 131n24, 132n26, 132n27, 133n31, 133n32, 133n33, 134n34, 134n36, 135n37, 136n39, 137n41, 137n42, 137n43, 137n44, 137n45, 138n46, 138n47, 140n50, 144–48, 147n69, 195
Pecknold, Chad, 73n18
Powers, Gerard F., 15, 16n25
Quash, Ben, 42n18, 137n40

Rashkover, Randi, 28n3, 43n19, 146n67
Ricoeur, Paul, 123n15
Roberts, Don, 130n21
Roht-Arriaza, Naomi, 15, 16n25
Rosenzweig, Franz, 46, 46n29

Safi, Omid, 45, 45n25, 47, 170
Schiffman, Nadav Berman, 175n39

Shank, Reuben, 109n27, 110n32
Smith, John E., 132–36, 132n28, 133n29, 133n30, 133n33, 134n35, 136n38
Smith, Wilfred Cantwell, 107

Teubner, Jonathan, 76n24, 76n25, 76n26, 121, 121n13, 166n17
Ticciati, Susannah, 30n5, 69n9, 120n11

Ward, Roger, 69n8, 70n11
Weiss, Daniel, 63n5
West, Cornel, 79, 79n28

Yang, Huilin, 81–82, 81n31, 82n32, 82n33, 82n34
Yazicioglu, Isra, 137n8
You, Bin, 81, 81n29, 81n30
Young, Willie, 45–47, 45n26, 46n27, 46n28, 47n31, 47n32, 170, 171, 171n28

Zahl, Simeon, 88n8
Zoloth, Laurie, 96n13

www.ingramcontent.com/pod-product-compliance
Lightning Source LLC
Chambersburg PA
CBHW020407230426
43664CB00009B/1221